THE SKILLS DEVELOPMENT
MANAG

THE SKILLS DEVELOPMENT HANDBOOK FOR BUSY MANAGERS

Pat O'Reilly

McGRAW-HILL BOOK COMPANY

London • New York • St Louis • San Francisco • Auckland • Bogotá • Caracas • Lisbon • Madrid • Mexico • Milan • Montreal • New Delhi • Panama • Paris • San Juan • São Paulo • Singapore • Sydney • Tokyo • Toronto

Published by
McGRAW-HILL Book Company Europe
Shoppenhangers Road, Maidenhead, Berkshire, SL6 2QL, England
Telephone 0628 23432
Fax 0628 770224

British Library Cataloguing in Publication Data
O'Reilly, Pat
   Skills Development Handbook for Busy Managers
   I. Title
   658.4

ISBN 0-07-707682-6

Library of Congress Cataloging-in-Publication Data
O'Reilly, Pat, 1943-
   The skills development handbook for busy managers / by Pat O'Reilly.
     p. cm.
   Includes bibliographical references and index.
   ISBN 0-07-707682-6
   1. Executive ability–Handbooks, manuals, etc. 2. Executives–Training of–Handbooks,
   manuals, etc. I. Title.
   HD38.2.073 1993
   658.4'09–dc20
                                           92-45730
                                            CIP

12345 CL 96543

Typeset by TecSet Ltd, Havelock House, Blenheim Gardens, Wallington, Surrey,
and printed in Great Britain by Clays Ltd, St Ives plc

CONTENTS

In today's business climate, managers are often expected to achieve increased results with decreasing resources. They have to keep pace with changing technology and systems, new legislation, the drive for higher productivity; and, at the same time, they face demands to operate in a more enlightened management style. With all these pressures it is no wonder that busy managers find themselves in need of guidance that will quickly, yet comprehensively, help them perform to the best of their abilities.

The Skills Development Handbook for Busy Managers provides this guidance in an easily digested form. It covers the essential knowledge and skills which every manager needs in order to be successful at work.

This book is written in the straightforward style I've come to expect of Pat O'Reilly. He covers each topic in a no-nonsense way, illustrating concepts with practical examples and summarizing them in easily understood check-lists to guide the user.

I find these check-lists particularly useful. They help you to do things in the right way and, where you need it, they can also provide valuable evidence of your skills as a manager.

I know this book really works. The contents have been developed and proved over many years in both large and small organizations. Each chapter provides an essential part of a management self-development framework. The structure and practical approach will assist you in establishing your competence, and this in turn can help you to become qualified under the national competence framework for management qualifications.

Pat O'Reilly is an excellent management tutor. He communicates his subject with authority, enthusiasm and exceptional clarity. He is an established author, and this book is a fine example of his craft.

The Skills Development Handbook for Busy Managers has proved successful for employees in my organization. I recommend it to you wholeheartedly.

Greg Whitear
Personnel Development Manager
Siemens Plessey Systems

PREFACE

YOUR MANAGEMENT CAREER — ACCIDENT OR DESIGN?

Results are the building bricks of a rewarding career. But to get results as a manager you need worthwhile objectives *and* the skills, determination and time to achieve them. This book will help you set those objectives and develop the management skills for success in industry, commerce or public service. And, as you work through your skills development programme, you will be able to measure the improvements in your performance—a great morale booster to fuel your determination further.

But what about time? You could surely do with more. Then why not start by freeing up the time you need to make and manage a personal development plan? This book starts by showing how you can do this, but not with lists of *things to take into account* and no suggestion of how to do so—twelve years in management training have taught me that people don't need my lists of things to worry about. They've already got plenty of their own. No, the system proposed here is unsophisticated but practical and, like everything else in the book, illustrated by worked examples. You could even substitute your own information and be up and running with a basic plan in half an hour.

Would you study a 200 page guide to writing effective reports? And then another weighty tome on interviewing, and yet more such works on the many other subjects essential to your career? Many busy managers tell me they simply can't spare the time, so in this book I've broken down each subject into about ten topics, and then summarized each one on a single page.

Learning by example

Remember the first time you tried to use a personal computer? When you needed to format a floppy disk, the instruction manual said something like:

> *To format a disk use the command Format DRIVE:[option[option]], using option /S for a system disk, and /V to add a volume label. (Other options denote track and sector requirements.)*

Gobbledygook! But then, turning the page you found the magic words:

> *FOR EXAMPLE, to format a document disk for your word processor, insert a blank disk in drive B, type* FORMAT B: *and then press the* ENTER *key.*

Suddenly, you could do it. You felt good. That's why I thought you would like each topic in this book to have a worked example on the facing page—a guide to get you started.

Competence is the key

Once *in* a job, what you *do* is far more important than what you *know*. The key to success is competence. Professional management qualifications are moving this way too. In the UK, for example, the Management Charter Initiative places overriding emphasis on the competences necessary to achieve objectives and continuously improve performance. Qualifications are awarded on evidence of competence demonstrated at work, rather than on an ability to answer examination questions.

Check-lists that work for you

And that brings us to the matter of check-lists. If they are simple, well-designed and properly tested, they can save you time. The check-lists in this book have been used and improved over many years. They really do work. Each chapter has one or two—some for information gathering, others for recording decisions in a form people can understand. If you are registered on a competence-based management development programme, keep completed copies of the check-lists as part of your portfolio of evidence. (The pages carry a copyright waiver.) In any case they will help you check the effectiveness of your meetings, interviews and so on. Use them, and see how quickly your results improve.

What do the old stagers think?

Ask a group of mid-career managers whether they think career planning and skills development programmes work, and you're likely to get a mixed response:

1 **The cynic:** 'Listen pal, business is a string of accidents looking for fall-guys. Keep a low profile when the muck hits the fan, and you get to replace those who can't duck fast enough. It's survival of the fittest in the management jungle.'
2 **The regretful drifter:** 'The trouble is, until you've had a career you don't really know what sort of career you *do* want. Or how to plan it. If I had my time again I wouldn't get lumbered with this Management Albatross. It's a trap. You get further out of touch with the real work until you're fit for nothing *but* management.'
3 **The happy go lucky drifter:** 'Just do your best and keep smiling, I say. Anyway, I've not done too badly, considering... and, there's more to life than work. As long as my people are contented they should be able to do what's needed to keep the place running smoothly. And you can't ask a lot more, can you?'
4 **The achiever:** 'Yes, definitely! But you must measure results and take action to stay on target. Mind you, I wish I'd started with a boss who took skills development seriously; it could have saved me a lot of time. That's one reason I go out of my way to help develop my staff. The other reason's a selfish one: these days I get judged mainly on the results of my team.'

Whichever type of manager you have, this book can be the basis of your self-development programme. I hope it will give you ideas and encouragement to improve your management skills.

Pat O'Reilly

ACKNOWLEDGEMENTS

Some of the ideas in *The Skills Development Handbook for Busy Managers* are my own; the majority, however, are not. Any work with so wide a scope must draw upon the pioneering of such intellectual giants as Belbin, Berne, Kepner and Tregoe, Hertzberg, Jung, Maslow, McGreggor, Peters and Waterman, and others. Their inspiration is respectfully acknowledged. However, a great deal of my material has also come from discussions with the many thousands of managers who have attended my courses and seminars over the past 15 years. For their enthusiastic participation, and for all they have taught me about the real world of management, I am most grateful.

Organizing the information for a book such as this is no small undertaking, and I have been fortunate in receiving invaluable assistance from friends in industry, commerce and public service. Without their help the project would certainly have foundered at the outset. The plan for this book owes much to my discussions with Mike Coker of Roke Manor Research Ltd, Tony Collins of Siemens, Jenny Cridland of GEC, Dave Downer of Siemens, Tony Edwards of Lansing-Linde, Bob Elward and Brian Johnson of British Gas, Steve Gould of The Hannell Partnership, Pam Guiles of Flight Refuelling Ltd, John Harper and Neil McDonald of The Welsh Development Agency, Mike Shadwell of Ashotron, Mike Skelt of Olympus Keymed Ltd, and Richard Wallwork of A E Piston Products. Many other managers have commented on individual chapters. For all these valued suggestions I offer a sincere thank you; but for any errors or omissions I alone am responsible.

I must also express a special thank you to Greg Whitear of Siemens Plessey Systems. Greg has painstakingly read several drafts of most of this book and provided much valued guidance throughout its preparation. His wealth of personnel development experience proved invaluable when, over a period of six years, I worked with him to devise the set of simple but effective management development check-lists now incorporated into this book.

The following software trademarks are acknowledged:

Adobe Illustrator	Adobe Systems Inc.
Ami Pro	Lotus Development Corp.
Auto CAD	Autodesk
CA-SuperProject	Computer Associates International Inc.
Corel Draw!	Corel Systems Corp.
IBM	International Business Machines Corp.
Lotus Organizer	Lotus Development Corp.
PC Paintbrush	ZSoft Corp.
PostScript	Adobe Systems Inc.
Ventura Publisher	Ventura Software Inc.
Windows	Microsoft Corp.

FICO is a **FI**ctitious **CO**mpany. So are its employees. Their roles in this book are to show by example how you can put management skills into practice. Any resemblance to a real company and real people is purely coincidental—although I expect you will recognize awkward situations and difficult behaviour you have met before.

The organization

FICO Inc was founded in Boston Mass. in 1983. In 1992 FICO took over Autojector Ltd, a British manufacturer of overhead projectors (OHPs). The group now employs 540 people, of whom 400 work at the Boston headquarters and the remainder in the UK subsidiary. FICO's vice president, Europe, is also chairman and chief executive of FICO UK.

Fig 1

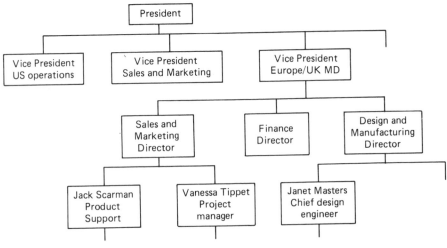

The products

FICO Inc. manufactures, sells and leases a range of visual aids products from marker boards to slide projectors. The parent company supplies products via FICO UK as well as through a worldwide dealer network. FICO UK has two divisions, one manufacturing OHPs and the other providing design consultancy and refurbishment services for conference centres, hotel groups and educational establishments world wide.

The Autojector

FICO has just brought out an OHP capable of automatically focusing and sizing a screen image so it is centred and exactly fills the screen regardless of the distance from projector to screen. Currently under development is a 35 mm slide projector offering similar facilities.

Fig 2

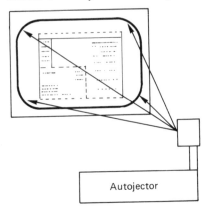

Dedicated to the many colleagues and clients who have helped me develop my management skills.

CHAPTER 1

HOW TO MANAGE YOURSELF
AND FIND TIME TO MANAGE YOUR CAREER

Would you like to become a better manager? You can, you know. Of course, *wanting* to improve isn't enough—you will have to *do* the right things. And skilfully.

Your skills development plan should be a key part of your career development plan. And you do have a plan, don't you?

Not as such? Then maybe this is a good time to take the initiative.

The challenge

To take control of your management career you will need to:

- Understand what makes you tick and know what you want from your career.
- Free up time from your present schedule so you can think carefully about your future, make plans and spend time acquiring and practising new skills.
- Know how to create and manage a career development plan.

In some organizations, career counselling *is* taken seriously. Employees can get help from a personnel development manager who will guide them through target setting, planning and managing a career development plan. Some of the career planning systems used by large organizations are quite complex, but, in my experience, most of them are good. If this sort of help is available in your organization I urge you to use it.

If, on the other hand, you are among the majority of managers who have to plan and manage their own careers with little or no help from their employers, then you should find the simple career management system in this chapter easy to use.

The benefits

When you have worked through Chapter 1, you will have a career development plan of your own, and you should know in what order to tackle later chapters. The order won't be the same for every reader; that's why each of the chapters which follows is self-contained.

YOUR UNIQUE TALENTS

You are unique. There is nobody on earth with the same talents, skills and knowledge as you. Surely, then, you owe it to yourself to have a successful career and to enjoy your life to the full. And look what you've got going for you:

- Your intelligence.
- Your technical skills and experience.
- Your inter-personal skills.
- Your determination to improve.

And now you've got this book, too!

Points of view

You know what you think, what you see and how you feel; other people only know you by how you behave—what you say and do. But your behaviour doesn't just depend on *who* you are. The situation at the time, and your experience—in particular your recent experience—all play a part. For example, suppose a normally confident and enthusiastic person makes a mess of three tasks in succession. Asked to take on another similar job, that person might well feel reluctant—resentful, even—at being chosen. In contrast, there is nothing like a run of successes to boost the confidence of a normally insecure person. And yet all that has changed is experience.

Your strengths

Discover what your natural talents are, so you can develop them, through the right sort of experience, into major strengths. Building upon these potential strengths is, I suggest, the key to career success and fulfilment.

Your weaknesses

There may be things you are naturally poor at; few of us are all-rounders. You may not have the eye for detail necessary for a good administrator. Or you might not be the most imaginative thinker, the most eloquent orator or the most receptive listener. Be aware of your weaknesses, whatever they may be, so you can make use of others who have strengths in these areas.

I'm not suggesting you shouldn't try to develop in these areas: you won't always be able to fall back on others. But if you try to build a career by concentrating most of your development effort on your weak points, don't be too surprised if you only reach the lower echelons of mediocrity. Put *most* effort into developing your natural talents; then by all means do *something* to shore up those weak spots.

Your prejudices

Most of us get on best with people who are like ourselves, or like the person we wish we were. So do you tend to undervalue people who are different from you in terms of their racial, social or religious background, their gender or their intelligence? In business you need the wholehearted contributions of people of various abilities, not all of which are intellectual.

You may not like all types of people, but you should learn to value them.

WHAT MAKES YOU TICK?

Suppose you arrived back at work after a trip to find someone else sitting at your desk.

> *'You've been moved to C Block, haven't you heard?'*

What would your first reaction be? How about:

1   Great! My promotion must have come through.
2   Why *me*? I knew I shouldn't have taken leave with all these changes in the air. If I'd been here maybe they would have picked on somebody else.
3   But what's happening to Pete and Sylvia; will we still be working together?
4   I wonder what new challenge is lined up for me.

In pressure situations you may tend to polarize towards one of these attitudes, behaving naturally, unable to 'put on an act' for appearance sake. That's when your behaviour can indicate which *psychological need* you feel most strongly.

Fig 1.1

1 Status matters most to me

I am confident of my value and expect others to show respect for my position. I know what I am capable of, and set myself tough targets. I don't rely heavily on other people and I expect others to be equally self-reliant.

I am decisive and don't shrink from making unpopular decisions when I know I am doing what's right for the business.

I have no time for ditherers and people who look for compromise solutions.

4 Achievement matters most to me

I believe good teamwork is essential to making real progress. Individual success needn't be at the expense of other team members.

Some decisions I make alone, others I delegate. And sometimes I need contributions from several of my team members.

Although I prefer to be with confident, enthusiastic people, I have learned to value contributions from all types of people. I can learn from them and help them improve their performance, too.

2 Security matters most to me

I am careful and thorough, unfortunately not everyone is so conscientious, and my good work sometimes gets spoilt by other people's lack of attention to detail.

I like to have all the facts so I can work through decisions quietly alone. I like to be certain before telling others what I've decided.

I'm happy to work on my own. I don't feel confident in meetings where people are judged by how they talk, rather than what they achieve.

3 Relationships matter most to me

I know my limitations and wish everyone else would show more humility. I work hard towards the success of our team, and benefit from involving others.

I like to consult widely to obtain team decisions, as I believe best results come from decisions which have the commitment of all concerned in carrying them out.

I have most difficulty with self-centred autocrats who try to impose their solutions against the wishes of others.

How do others see you?

When the going gets tough your behaviour reflects these needs. Then how do your colleagues see you?

1   **Aggressive:** If I had my way I'd nail the person responsible for this mess.

2   **Resentful:** It's not my fault: I warned them but they wouldn't listen.

3   **Acquiescent:** These things happen; there's no point in getting too upset about it.

4   **Assertive:** Our top priority must be to put it right and prevent it happening again.

IT'S GOOD THAT WE'RE DIFFERENT

The world might be a better place if everyone wanted to achieve and to help others succeed, too. But business wouldn't work if we were all the same. People see the same situation differently because they look from different viewpoints. They arrive at different answers when trading off security versus excitement; status versus popularity.

Matching courses to horses

Psychologists suggest your personality traits are partly inherited and partly moulded by your upbringing. Once you grow up your personality changes little. Experience enables you to cope with more responsibility, so you appear more confident and assertive because you don't feel pressured; but the psychological needs which determine what gives you satisfaction are within you for life. This would suggest that the old idea of defining a job in terms of what needs doing and how it should be done, and then looking for someone best qualified for the job, is ill-founded. Instead, how about helping each person find a job, and a way of doing it, which gives them *real* job satisfaction?

Fig 1.2

1 Don't some tough jobs need an autocratic leader?

A fire-fighter who calls his staff together for consultation meetings in the middle of an emergency is nothing short of a liability!

When time is of the essence, what's needed is a good crisis manager, not a coach.

4 Are you truly assertive?

Do you consider others while being determined to achieve? Are you willing to take the blame when things go wrong, and yet to share the credit for successes?

Do you ask for help, without bluffing or being embarrassed when you are unsure? Then you are indeed an assertive person: a rare breed.

2 Who needs an optimistic security guard?

`I shouldn't think there'll be trouble tonight; to hell with checking windows!'

You'd be better off with this fellow: `I know my luck! If I don't check all the windows, some joker will break in and my neck will be on the block. I'm playing safe and checking the lot!'

3 What job satisfaction can there be for a waiter?

You only have to carry the food to the tables without spilling it; what could be simpler?

But hold on! Haven't you noticed how top class waiters have the people skills to make their clients want to come back again? They are the marketing department of the restaurant.

Situational managers

If you are naturally assertive, many will envy you. The rest of us have to learn to behave assertively in difficult situations. But even assertive (Quadrant 4) behaviour should be rationed; it is certainly not the key to success at all times and in all jobs. Skilled managers learn to behave autocratically (Quadrant 1), when short-term crises demand it. They take on supportive (Quadrant 3) roles to encourage others to take responsibility. And occasionally withdrawing from a difficult situation (Quadrant 2) is the best thing to do. 'Situational' managers who can switch their style convincingly between quadrants are rare, however.

You will be more convincing when your behaviour under pressure is just that needed for success. You won't have to put on an act. So, get to know what makes you tick, and then manage your career so you can be yourself most of the time.

1.2 WHERE DOES YOUR TIME GO?

Do you want to know *why* you're so short of time to do the things you really would like? A simple time log kept over a few days could be a real eye opener.

Date & time	Activity		Who is getting good value from this time?			
	Description	Category	My employer	Our customers	My career	Nobody gains

Note each task you tackle through the day. There will be interruptions, so add these to your list too. Mark the *Category* column with the most appropriate of the following:

- Thinking—planning and problem solving.
- Self-development—reading and attending training sessions.
- Staff development—formal training/counselling and informal briefings.
- Writing.
- Technical work.
- Meetings and interviews—scheduled and unscheduled.
- Phone calls—outgoing and incoming.
- Being interrupted.
- Travelling—driving and as a passenger.
- Administrative work.
- Breaks—coffee, lunch etc.
- Other activities.

You could extend this list to include activities outside work. This would show the balance between work and recreation, solo and social activities, and intellectual and physical exercise.

Are you getting a fair deal?

If you ticked *My employer* and *Our customers* more often than *My career*, ask yourself:

- Which categories are most important to success in my present job?
- Are our customers getting good value from my time being used this way?
- Am I getting a fair deal, or are my career needs being brushed aside too often?
- Am I spending time on low pay-off tasks? What would happen if I ignored them?
- What should I spend more time on in future?
- What should I spend less time on or delegate to someone else?

What should the scores be?

You will never reach the Utopian ideal of ticks in each of the *Employer, Customer* and *Career* columns and no entries under *Nobody gains*. Some routine administrative tasks are essential, and interruptions can't always be avoided. And remember, what to you is a low priority reactive task can be someone else's *raison d'être*. So if you get at least 60 per cent in each of the first three columns and no more than, say, 5 per cent in the *Nobody gains* column, you're doing well.

EXAMPLE Jack Scarman is Sales Support Manager at FICO Systems. Most days he arrives at work forty minutes before the official start, brings sandwiches so he can catch up on paperwork during lunch break, and rarely leaves work before 7 p.m. Even so, Jack finds it necessary to take work home most weekends. A colleague advises him to log his time:

Monday 18 Feb Time	Activity		Who is getting good value from this time?			
	Description	Category	My employer	Our customers	My career	Nobody gains
7:45	Write liaison meeting minutes	Writing	*			
8:25	Jim calls in: chat	Interruption				*
8:35	Write liaison meeting minutes	Writing	*			
8:50	EM Lab phones	Telephone-in	*	*		
9:05	Plan EM project	Thinking	*	*	*	
9:15	Complete production meeting minutes	Writing	*	*		
9:20	Copy minutes	Administration	*			
9:25	Meet Liz: chat	Interruption	.			*
9:35	Plan EM project	Thinking	*	*	*	

The analysis

After four days Jack sorts all 423 activities into categories. He highlights the activities that contribute to job success and career development, and the proportion of time he has devoted to each. The results come as a shock. He realizes each year's experience will contribute little to his development as a manager if he continues using his time—and letting others abuse it—in this way.

Target setting

Jack adds an extra column to his table, setting what he feels are acceptable targets for the main categories.

	Task category	Actual		Target
		Hours	%	%
1	**Thinking**	9	**3**	20
2	**Self-development**	3	**1**	5
3	**Staff development**	6	**2**	10
4	**Writing**	45	**15**	10
5	**Meetings**	84	**28**	25
6	Technical work	12	4	
7	Telephone calls	27	9	
8	Interruptions	18	6	
9	Travelling as part of work	6	2	
10	**Administrative work**	63	**31**	10
11	Breaks	3	1	
12	Other activities	21	7	
	Totals:	297	100	

He would like to spend 70 per cent of his time on work where *he* can take the initiative, and no more than 10 per cent on administrative tasks.

1.3 QUALITY—THE KEY TO PRIORITY

If a job's worth doing, it's worth doing well.

This much-quoted maxim is often interpreted as: *'Do your best in all you do'*. Adopt this philosophy and you will always be busy. But will you be effective? In most management jobs there's not enough time to do everything well, and those who try simply fail to meet their deadlines. This perfectionist philosophy is a recipe for mediocrity and career failure, and the cause of much stress-related illness.

So what quality should you aim for, and how do you decide which jobs get priority?

A matter of urgency

Urgency has an inevitable influence on the decision what to do next. When is it needed, and how long will it take? If a six-hour job must be finished by the end of the day, you had better start it early. Unless, of course, it can be turned into a two-hour job. Or delegated to someone else. Or left undone. So ask yourself:

- Does it really have to be done at all?
- How long will it take me?
- When must I start it if I am to meet the deadline?

Look for the pay-off

A more significant decision factor is *importance*. What are the costs of not doing the task well, or the benefits in doing a first-class job? Ask yourself:

- Does it help me to achieve what I'm being paid for?
- How well does it need to be done?
- Am I going to enjoy this or gain useful experience?
- Do I really have to do this myself?
- Is there something more useful I could do to satisfy the requirement?

The priority map

The tasks which give the highest pay-off are in Categories 1 and 4 on this map (Fig. 1.3). Yet reacting to urgency is second nature to most people, so Category 2, low pay-off tasks, often gets priority over longer term tasks such as planning and career development.

Fig 1.3

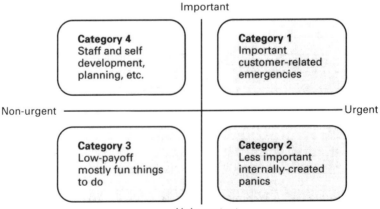

Category 1 work, those rush jobs on which so much seems to depend, has to take top priority and be done as well as possible in the time available. But how many of these panics could be avoided with a little more planning? Maybe there would be time to do the job really well if it was started sooner, while it was still a Category 4 task.

No wonder Jack Scarman is feeling the pressure! In a typical day he spends most of his time reacting to urgent problems, except when a real emergency arises, when he has to concentrate on that, pulling out all the stops. Then only a screaming crisis will divert him.

The crisis manager

Jack is a crisis manager. Here is a priority map of a typical day in his life:

Fig 1.4

- Started planning staff appraisals. Asked Personnel for last year's records.
Total: 15 minutes

- Tried out new computer graphics program and made Christmas cards to send over e-mail system.

- Saw Eddie Stanton. He had a lot of moans about the new expense claim procedures.
Total: 2 hours 15 minutes

- Mary off sick. Arranged deputy for customer meeting.

- Boss needs capital expenditure budget for next year — required by 4pm. Called urgent staff meeting to discuss. Nobody had any useful views.

- Budget meeting at 4pm. Criticized for being late. Not fair! Photocopier out of order so I had to use sales dept's.
Total: 3 hours 20 minutes

- Called to urgent meeting to discuss Christmas party; agreed to make catering arrangements.

- Phoned caterer three times. Manager not available.

- Pete asked for a hand to shift his furniture around.

- Site Services asked for list of all damaged desks and tables. Immediately typed them a three page report.
Total: 2 hours 15 minutes

But Jack isn't the only one feeling the pressure. His staff remember how much happier they were when Carol was running the department. There didn't seem to be so many panics. There was time to discuss plans, to get things organized before they became urgent. They worked less overtime, yet the work still got done on schedule.

Important matters like staff appraisals don't get the attention they deserve. Perhaps that's one reason Jack's staff turnover is so high. The consequent recruitment and re-training are only *part* of the cost: the people who left were the most able.

Control is easily lost

More than two-thirds of Jack's time goes on reactive tasks over whose timing he has no control. Some of these are what he is there for: responding to customer enquiries, for example. But many more are internally generated activities, some necessary to keep the business running smoothly, others merely time wasters.

Jack *could* control more of his time if he would only:

- Think about next year's budget *before* his boss asks for the figures.
- Phone the caterer just *once*, leaving a message asking the manager to phone him back at a specific time.
- Set up a deputization plan for when people are off sick.
- Be more assertive when Pete and Eddie want time he can't spare.

1.4 INFLUENCING THE PAY-OFF

In reality, tasks don't fall into tidy compartments of *Important* or *Unimportant*. Jobs carry a range of costs and benefits from trivial to life-threateningly serious.

Why not see if you can chop a few low pay-off tasks down in size? And how about trying to shift some of the non-urgent tasks between categories?

Dealing with trivia

What can you do about the many unimportant tasks—interruptions to your more important work—which demand immediate attention? They aren't worth much time, but even a small interruption can be disruptive if you are writing a difficult report.

Fig 1.5

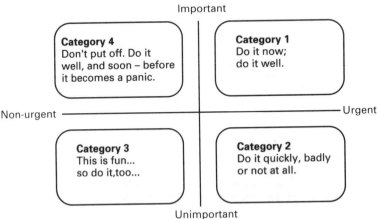

Here are three ideas for reducing the amount of time you spend on Category 2 trivia:

- Delegate it back to the original owner, explaining why you can't spare the time.
- Ignore it and see if it goes away. (This is OK if you're sure it *is* unimportant!)
- Do it so badly that you never get asked again. (This can backfire on you, of course, if the original owner of the task is a perfectionist.)

Have fun...But shift the pay-off first

Unimportant, non-urgent Category 3 jobs steal valuable time from those in Category 4—long-range planning, staff development, finding improved working methods and the like. So should you be doing this Category 3 stuff? *Yes, you should!* Because you enjoy it, and because you do it well. But before you do much Category 3 work, get your customer and your company to value it and to want you to do it. Then it becomes a Category 4 high pay-off task. Speaking up about what you want to do is often all that's necessary; but you must do so *before* the work is dished out.

> 'Next time there's a trade fair, I'm keen to help plan it and to man our stand.'

If necessary, make room in your schedule for the things you want to do by delegating some other Category 4 work to your staff, your other colleagues or back to your boss. You make it easier for them to say yes when you give them plenty of notice.

Delight your customer

Having set your priorities as suggested here, *quality* is now driving your time management:

- If both you and the customer value it, *exceed* your customer's quality expectations.
- If it's needed to keep the organization running smoothly, do it adequately.
- If it's of little value, waste little or no time on it.

EXAMPLE

Now that Jack Scarman sets his priorities on a quality basis, he no longer types up reports on the state of furniture in his department. Such jobs get what they deserve—a brief handwritten memo. He is brief and to the point on the telephone, too, and he has asked frequent callers to use the low tariff period after lunch. When anyone asks for his number, Jack's standard reply is:

> *'You can usually get me on this number between 1:30 and 2:30.'*

And that's exactly what most people write in their telephone books, often not realizing that Jack is on that number throughout the day.

In the time he has saved, Jack is able to keep up with his reading, to spend time coaching his successor, and to think about his future. But his life seems less exciting now that there are fewer crises.

Taking the initiative

Jack needs to take the initiative and do more things he feels would be fun. Top of Jack's list is the International Customer Care Conference. For the past two years he has booked up and then, because of work pressure, had to let someone else go in his place. Now, when he has the time, the budget has been cut and his company won't be able to fund either his time or his expenses. He could always pay for himself, of course. After all, it's an investment in *his* career. But there's a better way!

Here's how Jack *gets paid* for attending the conference:

- **September:** Reads up on new developments in customer care and homes in on the exciting new subject of Custogenics. Contacts Professor Wellesley at the university and arranges to visit him one evening after work.

- **October:** Arranges for Professor Wellesley to talk to the local branch of the Institute of Managers. Makes contact with several others working in this new field.

- **November:** Writes to the editor of *Customer Care Today*, urging her to include the new subject of Custogenics in next year's ICC Conference programme.

- **December:** *Exhibition And Conference International* phone Jack asking him if he knows who they could contact to present papers on Custogenics at next year's ICC Conference. Jack says Yes, he does know!

- **January:** Receives an official invitation to chair the session on Custogenics, all expenses paid plus a daily fee.

- **February:** Jack officially invites Professor Wellesley and four other experts to present papers at the ICC Conference in May. They are most grateful to Jack for the opportunity to publicize their work.

- **May:** The ICC Conference session on Custogenics is a great success. The organizers ask Jack if they can book him as session chairman for next year's event, to be held in Vienna.

Looking ahead

Jack is well pleased with himself. He has turned a cost into a profit, gained kudos for himself and his company, and made influential new friends. And next year he intends getting one or two of his most valued customers to present papers at the ICC Conference, saying how much they have benefited from the Custogenics approach provided by Jack's company, FICO. That really *would* be good for business!

1.5 PLANNING YOUR TIME

Here is a method of planning your work for the short to medium term, say up to a year or so. (Longer term career planning is covered later in this chapter.)

Medium-term plan

Some of your goals for the year ahead will be set by the organization you work for. Don't plan these in detail, as things could change between now and then. Just pencil in time allocations and target dates for each objective; you can fill in the detail nearer the time.

A year-at-a-glance planner is useful for showing fixed activities, such as holidays, training courses, conferences and regular meetings. For other tasks, where *you* decide on the timing, try to schedule the activities so that you have a mixture of short and long projects throughout the year. That way there should be some worthwhile achievement every few weeks to help you maintain motivation.

Once happy with your plan, transfer target completion dates to your diary. Mark the *must start by* dates, so you don't turn over a page and find you've got just a few hours to do something which will take four days.

Short-term tactical plan

A daily or weekly plan will help you sort your priorities, cope with routine administrative work and meet deadlines on your important tasks. It will also tell you when to delegate more down to your staff, across to colleagues around you or upwards to your boss. Here is how you can make such a plan:

- List all tasks you know have got to be started this week, noting when they need to be finished.
- Prioritize them as High, Medium, or Low, according to how important it is that they are done well.
- Estimate how long each will take you to meet the required quality level.
- Add all durations to see how many hours planned work you have.
- Allow a break for lunch, and time to check your mail each day.
- Allow 30 minutes each day for planning and problem-solving.
- From your experience add an allowance for essential interruptions and extra tasks delegated to you from elsewhere.
- If the total time required exceeds your normal working week by more than a couple of hours, look through the task list and decide which you can delegate.
- If there is still an overload, re-negotiate completion dates on low-priority tasks.
- Schedule the work through the week leaving time each day for the unplanned work which may arise and have to be fitted in.

At the end of each day, update the task list, crossing off those completed, adding any new tasks and re-scheduling if necessary. Re-negotiate low-priority deadlines if necessary—although you may find some of these jobs simply go away; it's amazing how much non-work there is in most organizations!

All this is a lot easier with a computer-based Personal Information Manager, such as *Lotus Organizer*, which runs under *Windows* on portable, desktop or networked personal computers.

Jack Scarman is determined not to let people needlessly interrupt his planning and writing tasks; and he now realizes how much of his time is dominated by routine administrative work. Most of all, Jack feels guilty for giving up more time to people who phone or call in for social chats than he does for briefing, training and delegating to his staff.

All that is going to change! Jack invests in a copy of *Lotus Organizer*, which he runs under *Windows* on his desktop computer. (See also Chapter 9: How to manage information.) The first step is to prepare a To Do list at the start of a week:

Fig 1.6

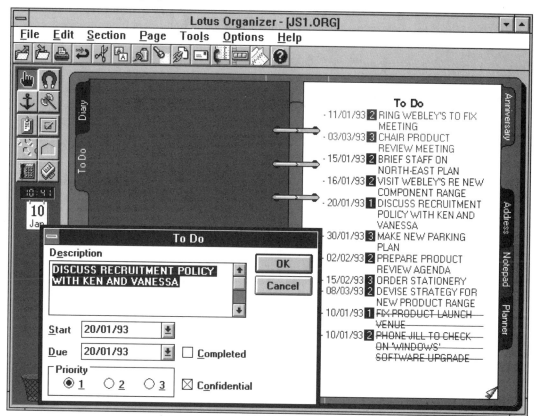

Next, Jack makes a schedule of work in his diary. He leaves at least two hours clear each day; this is the time he needs to think, to revise his work plans as new opportunities or problems arise, and to deal with any tasks which cannot wait. Checking the morning mail and taking proper breaks for lunch are features he can plan across every working day; it only takes a single command to copy these repeating items throughout the year.

When he has scheduled in all high-priority tasks, and those essential medium and low ones he cannot delegate, Jack can see whether he needs help. He might even be able to take on something extra his boss might need a hand with.

Coping with changes

Finally, Jack has the option of printing out a hard copy of his diary on standard six-ring organizer stationery. This is particularly useful for a manager who isn't confined to one location, but moves between departments or off-site altogether. And, if he has to re-schedule tasks later in the week, it's a simple matter to reprint the changed section of the diary.

1.6 TAKING CONTROL OF YOUR TIME

Could you do some of those difficult jobs better or more quickly if you could get on with them uninterrupted? Then you now need to control how your time is used.

The dreaded open door policy

Good managers make themselves accessible to their staff... but not at all times. Let your colleagues and your boss know when you need to think without disturbance—times when you should only be interrupted in a real emergency. Many of us are at our best in the first hour or so each day, while in the hour right after lunch we may have most difficulty concentrating. Not everyone is the same: some people come alive in the evenings. Discover your prime time. Are you a lark or an owl?

Managing interruptions

Some interruptions are *what you are there for*, and you have to respond immediately. But your colleagues have a vested interest in your efficiency and may be prepared to see you later. Ask just enough to be able to prepare, and suggest a time that suits you.

If anyone makes a habit of calling just for a social chat, you could suggest an after work meeting: quite likely they will be too busy to spare the time!

Managing the telephone

Telephone calls tend to get instant priority. Here are some ideas for reducing their effects:

- Let others know when you prefer to receive non-urgent calls; phone tariffs are lower after lunch, so your callers will benefit, too.
- Use call screening to divert incoming calls to a secretary or colleague when you are working on a difficult task, holding a meeting or interviewing someone.
- If you must receive an incoming call during a meeting, keep your reply brief, and if possible arrange a time to call back.
- Plan several calls and make them in a time block.
- Open your calls with *'Can you spare me about two minutes of your time.'* Most calls can be completed within a two minute time slot.

Coping with the paperwork

When you are busy it is easy to lose things, particularly under a pile of papers. Then all the other tiresome features of your work environment can conspire to cause frustration and stress. Here are some tips for avoiding a paperwork mountain:

- Have things you use frequently close to hand.
- Focus on one task at a time by keeping other work off your desk until you need it.
- Tidy your work space after finishing each task.
- Intersperse routine tasks with the more exciting; sedentary work with more active.
- Deal with the daily influx of paper when it arrives. Answer urgent letters right away, discard junk mail, and relegate less important reading until after lunch.
- Cut interesting articles from trade magazines to skim after lunch, and bin the rest of the magazine.
- Get rid of your pending tray; often it is no more than an excuse for procrastination.
- File only what you will need again, or are legally obliged to retain.

CHECK-LIST: TIME MANAGEMENT

Use this check-list to see how effectively you are prioritizing tasks, planning your work schedule and managing your time.

Time management review for period		to		
Mark your assessment using 4 = Excellent: very little scope for improvement 3 = Good: scope for minor improvements 2 = Fair: considerable improvement possible 1 = Weak: major improvement essential	4	3	2	1
Prioritising your tasks				
How clearly did you summarize your objectives?				
Did each objective have a pay-off related priority?				
Did you influence the pay-off for things you like doing?				
Did you allocate time according to quality needs?				
Did you allow enough time for thinking and heading off crises?				
Did you allow yourself time for reading and self-development?				
Planning your work schedule				
Did you prepare usable medium and short-term plans?				
Did your plan reflect the priorities you placed on tasks?				
How realistic were your estimates for important tasks?				
Did you schedule blank time slots for essential interruptions?				
Did you schedule prime time for thinking and planning?				
Did you avoid planning regular overtime/weekend working?				
Did you plan a complete break at lunch times?				
Managing your time				
Did you refer to your plan and keep it up to date?				
Did you monitor and control the time given to each task?				
How well did you deal with time-wasting interruptions?				
Did you deal with important mail promptly?				
Did you delegate enough to your staff and your manager?				
Did you make use of colleagues to minimize interruptions?				
How well did you manage incoming telephone calls?				
Total score				

Improvement targets:	

If you scored 70 or more you're doing fine; less than 50 and you are still not managing your time well. Why not set yourself targets for improvement in the next three months? Put highest priority on items where your scores were 1 or 2.

'The Skills Development Handbook for Busy Managers' by Pat O'Reilly, ©1993 McGraw-Hill International (UK) Ltd. This page may be photocopied for personal use only.

1.7 THE BUSINESS OF CAREER MANAGEMENT

Imagine a time three or four years from now. What would you like your life to be like? You may want a more senior management job, or to run your own business. But holding on to what you have got, or easing up a little as retirement approaches, are equally commendable goals. Then make a plan for getting what you want.

A business-like approach

If you were running a business you would consider past performance and present position, and what you intend doing in future. The Profit & Loss Account would show what had happened during the past trading period: how money had come into the business from selling goods and services or gaining from investments, and how you spent money. It would also show whether there was any profit left over at the end of the year.

The Balance Sheet would show what the business was worth and, by comparison with a year ago, whether it had increased or decreased in value. It would also show the assets and liabilities of the company: the financial strengths and weaknesses.

With this information, and knowing what external resources (for example bank loans) you could draw upon, you would then set targets for the year ahead and make a Business Development Plan for meeting those targets.

You can manage your career in much the same way, by preparing:

- A Personal Profit & Loss Account showing what you did to get where you are.
- A Personal Balance Sheet, showing where you are right now.
- A Personal Development Plan showing where you would like to be, what you intend doing to get there and what other resources you need.

The analogy with planning and managing a business is useful, but shouldn't be pushed too far. In business, money flows into and out of the business. If a business needs extra money to achieve its targets it can borrow. If the business loses money one year there is a chance to recover it the next. But the primary commodity in career management is time. You can only use your own. And only once! Effective career management can help maximize the amount of time you spend doing things you like. Time invested setting up an opportunity is repaid with interest as time spent enjoying the benefits—rather like financial investment and return analysis of a business venture.

The importance of monitoring

It would be foolish to leave your business running uncontrolled for a whole year, of course, so you monitor progress towards the targets. The frequency of monitoring will vary according to how volatile the economic and market environments are and how quickly your intervention can bring you back on course.

When you make a career plan, you will have to monitor more often than once a year, particularly in the early stages of your career when you are learning what you can and cannot do (and learning what you enjoy doing!). Once you have a Career Development Plan up and running, you monitor progress by comparing achievements with targets. So the starting point has to be setting targets for your first year. Initially these targets may not be quite right, but in time you will get better at estimating what is achievable, and better at achieving what you want.

EXAMPLE: A PERSONAL PROFIT & LOSS ACCOUNT

Jack Scarman has decided to set up a Career Management System. He begins by looking back over successes and failures over the previous 12 months. Here is Jack's Profit & Loss Account for the year to 31 March 1994:

Personal P & L account of:		J P Scarman	**Review period:**	1/4/93 to 31/3/94
Main responsibilities during review period:		First year in new job as sales support manager. Plan and manage all customer support activities, with five staff.		
Activities undertaken	Start date	Finish date	Experience gained	Skills/knowledge/ qualifications acquired
Planned initiatives				
None				
(But watch me next year!)				
Opportunities I seized as they arose				
Organized MSP launch	7/4/93	6/5/93	First overseas trip	No new skills/ knowledge
Attended basic finance course for non-financial managers	5/8/93	6/8/93	Basic management accounting	Attendance certificate only
Tasks delegated to me				
Delegated for marketing director at the MSP launch	16/5/93	17/5/93	Made presentation to 350 potential clients	Improved presentation skills during rehearsals
Graduate recruitment interviews	16/1/94	12/2/94	Useful interviewing experience plus a chance to keep in touch with my old university	Had to read up on interview techniques and hold two practice interviews before visiting the universities

On reflection

Jack had seized and benefited from two opportunities which arose during the year. The rest of his P&L Account assesses the value of the work he was given by his manager, as well as any major reactive tasks he found necessary to keep his part of the business running.

On balance, though he enjoyed the experience, his two-day trip to Hamburg had taught him nothing new. This was because he spoke no German, and the deal had been negotiated in the customer's first language.

A resolution

Jack's biggest disappointment was realizing that he had behaved almost entirely in reactive mode. He had planned no initiatives at the beginning of the year, and hadn't stopped to assess whether his career was progressing the way he wanted it to. So he promised himself that in the year ahead things would be different. Instead of waiting for things to happen, he would make things happen the way *he* wanted.

EXAMPLE: A PERSONAL BALANCE SHEET

The next step was for Jack to draw up a Personal Balance Sheet, showing what he had to offer compared with what was needed for success in his present job and in his next career step.

Personal balance sheet of:		*J P Scarman*		**Prepared on:**	31/3/94

Mark levels of skill, knowledge & experience, and development priority using:
4 = Excellent: continue doing this well; no development action proposed.
3 = Good: scope for minor improvements; development action low priority.
2 = Fair: considerable improvement possible; development action medium priority.
1 = Weak: major improvement essential; development action high priority.

Skill/knowledge/ experience	Current level	Required for present job	Required for your next job	Development required	
				Action	Priority
Management skills and experience:					
Time management	3	3	4	Continue system	High
Listening	2	3	4	Self-development	High
Assertiveness	3	3	4	Self-development	Medium
Presentations	2	3	4	Training course and on-the-job coaching	High
Writing	3	3	3	None	Nil
Managing meetings	3	3	3	None	Nil
Commercial awareness	3	3	3	None	Nil
Financial awareness	2	2	3	Training course and on-the-job coaching	Medium
Project management	3	3	3	None	Nil
Team management	3	3	4	Self-development	Medium
Others:				None	Nil
Academic and professional qualifications:					
Management charter initiative—Diploma in management	Adequate, but much room for improvement	The skills would be more useful than the qualification	The diploma would strengthen my application	Register with local university on industry-based scheme commencing October 1994	
Technical expertise:					
Conversational German	1	No, but useful	Essential	Evening classes	High

Jack felt sure his future lay in the sales field: would he make a good Area Sales Manager? The P & L account highlighted those areas where he needed to concentrate his efforts. Some could be tackled via a self-development programme of study and practice. Others would require outside help, preferably in the form of an initial training course followed by on-the-job coaching. For this, Jack needed to seek the support of his manager.

EXAMPLE: A PERSONAL DEVELOPMENT PLAN

Jack's Personal Balance Sheet has highlighted his strengths and weaknesses in relation to the job he has now and to the job he would like to have in three or four years' time. It covers:

- Personal organization.
- Management skills and experience.
- Academic and professional qualifications.
- Technical skills (languages, computer literacy etc.).

The final step is to decide on career goals and to define specific objectives by which these goals can be met. Here is part of Jack Scarman's Personal Development Plan, which summarises all this:

Personal development plan of:		*J P Scarman*		Plan period:	1/4/93 to 31/3/94
Investment required				**Benefits expected**	
Goals and corresponding objectives planned	Target start date	Target finish date	Help & other resources needed	Experience to be gained	Skill/knowledge/ qualifications sought
Career goal No. 1	To be solely responsible for organizing the company's sales exhibitions and product launches worldwide within two years.				
Specific objectives:					
1 Learn to speak German	1/5/94	31/3/95	£50 for books/ audio tapes	—	Working ability in technical German
2 Attend commercial awareness course		31/10/94	Finance from training budget	—	Understanding of contract terms
3 Organize stand at Expo 95		7/11/95	Need to convince boss!	Major exhibitions	—
Career goal No. 2	To gain promotion to area sales manager (Europe or Middle East for preference) within four years.				
Specific objectives:					
1 Improve my French	1/5/94	31/3/96	£20 fees for evening class	Could make useful contacts	Good ability spoken/ written
2 Obtain Diploma in Management by distance learning	15/4/94	20/6/97	£1500 in fees, £120 for books	Discipline of self-development	DIM and improve management competence
3 Make my senior management aware of my ambitions (tell them!)	10/4/94	30/4/94	Practice being assertive!	—	—
Sporting/hobby goal	Improve general fitness, as anyone in a sedentary but stressful job like mine really should.				
Specific objectives:					
1 Arrange squash session with Pete once a week		10/4/94	Get a new racquet	Chance to get Pete's views	—
Family/social goal	Have a proper holiday this year, instead of going in to work two or three times a week to see if all is well (it never is!).				
Specific objectives:					
1 Book a holiday touring Germany		30/4/94	The family deserves it!	Relax and have fun	Chance to practice German

On reflection

Jack realizes that his goals must be flexible, however. If personal circumstances change, some targets may no longer be realistic. Or unforeseen opportunities might arise which allow him to bring forward his plans. Then he may need to re-think what route to take.

CHECK-LIST: YOUR SELF-PERCEPTION SUMMARY

Before preparing your own career development plan, take ten minutes to summarize what *you* think you are like. You may learn things from later chapters which cause you to change your views, so be prepared to return to this check-list and update your self-perception summary.

Self-perception inventory of:		
Date:		
Me as a thinker	Strength	Weakness
I have imaginative ideas and often find new approaches to problems		
I can usually work out logically what is the best of several alternatives		
Me as a leader		
I tend to take a somewhat autocratic approach when leading a team		
My natural reaction is to involve my team in all important decisions		
Me as a follower		
I am a loyal team member, and get very committed to meeting team goals		
My thoroughness prevents the team failing through poor attention to detail		
My ability to relate to others		
I enjoy meeting strangers, quickly getting on well with most people I meet		
I take time to get to know people; then I can usually sense their feelings		

Activities I enjoy	In my work	Outside work

Activities I dislike	In my work	Outside work

Activities I would like to try	In my work	Outside work

Skills I want to develop	In my work	Outside work

The prejudices I would most like to rid myself of:

'The Skills Development Handbook for Busy Managers' by Pat O'Reilly, ©1993 McGraw-Hill International (UK) Ltd. This page may be photocopied for personal use only.

CHECK-LIST: YOUR PERSONAL PROFIT & LOSS ACCOUNT

Complete this check-list for the past 12 months. If this is your first attempt at a career plan, you could extend the period, or use a separate sheet for the period up to a year ago.

Personal P & L account of:			Review period:	
Main responsibilities during review period				
Activities undertaken	Start date	Finish date	Experienced gained	Skills/knowledge/ qualifications acquired
Planned initiatives				
Opportunities I seized as they arose				
Major tasks delegated to me				

CHECK-LIST: YOUR PERSONAL BALANCE SHEET

Complete this audit of your skills, experience and personal qualities, to help you decide what aspects to develop in the year ahead. Update your audit when a new career opportunity arises or if you change your long-term goals. (Use extra sheets if necessary.)

Personal balance sheet of:			Prepared (date):		
Mark levels of skill, knowledge & experience, and development priority using: 4 = Excellent: continue doing it well; no development action proposed. 3 = Good: scope for minor improvements; development action low priority. 2 = Fair: considerable improvement possible; development action medium priority. 1 = Weak: major improvement essential; development action high priority.					
Skill/ knowledge/experience/ personal quality	Your current level	The level required for present job	The level required for your next job	Development required Action	Priority
Management skills and experience:					
Time management					
Listening and reading					
Assertiveness					
Presentations					
Writing					
Managing meetings					
Commercial awareness					
Financial awareness					
Project management					
Team management					
Team management					
Others:					
Academic and professional qualifications:					
Technical expertise:					

'The Skills Development Handbook for Busy Managers' by Pat O'Reilly, ©1993 McGraw-Hill International (UK) Ltd. This page may be photocopied for personal use only.

CHECK-LIST: YOUR PERSONAL DEVELOPMENT PLAN

List the initiatives you intend taking during the year ahead to help you achieve your goals. State for each initiative what experience, skill and knowledge you expect to get and any qualifications or awards you could obtain. (Use extra sheets if necessary.)

Personal development plan of:				Plan period:	
Investment required				**Benefits expected**	
Goals and corresponding objectives planned	Target start date	Target finish date	Help & other resources needed	Experience to be gained	Skill/knowledge /qualifications sought
Career goal No. 1					
Specific objectives:					
1					
2					
3					
4					
Career goal No. 2					
Specific objectives:					
1					
2					
3					
4					
Career goal No. 1					
Specific objectives:					
1					
2					
3					
4					
Sporting/hobby goal					
Specific objectives:					
1					
2					
3					
Family/social goal:					
Specific objectives:					
1					
2					
3					

IMPROVE YOUR LISTENING SKILLS
THE ART OF ADVANCED COMMUNICATION

Most of us begin talking before we are two years old. Soon we are using sentences and gestures to make our demands known. Decades later it can still be the devil's own job to get us to listen, to take in what's being said and to think about it. The majority of us remain better talkers than listeners throughout our lives. We may hear perfectly well; but hearing just happens. Listening is more active.

The challenge

Without spoken words, it would be difficult to share knowledge and feelings with other people. Difficult, but not necessarily impossible:

> *A girl holds up a mouse cupped in her hand, smiles and makes a soft humming noise in her throat. Her friend shies away, arms drawn tight across her chest, making a hissing sound as she breathes in sharply through her teeth. Neither has said a word, but you can tell who does and who doesn't like mice.*

The vocal and visual parts of a message usually carry more impact than the verbal part. So you need to listen with your ears *and with your eyes*, and think about what you hear and see.

The benefits

Much of this book is about getting other people to do what you want. You need to know when they don't understand, or are not convinced. Understand the listening process and you should be able to talk to others in a way they find easy to follow.

However well you speak, you won't always get your message across right first time. Research shows that around 50 per cent initial understanding is typical, and only part of this is remembered for more than a few hours. Fortunately, there are ways of detecting and correcting these communication errors. Complex electronic telephone systems have spare capacity built in because the designers know messages will get scrambled and distorted. These extra circuits check and put right errors as they occur. You can learn to do that, too, by comparing what is said against how it sounds and what you see.

THE TUNING-IN PROCESS

When you talk to someone, you don't start with fully formed sentences, but with a jumble of emotions and ideas which you turn into words in your head. The way you express your ideas—the emphasis you put on certain words, and the gestures and facial expressions which the listener can see as you talk—are unique to you. If the other person were to express the same ideas he or she might do so in a similar way, or in a quite different way, depending upon personality, experiences, culture and prejudices, as well on as the characteristics of his or her voice. If you make a point with which another person would agree, and you do so in much the same way as that person would, then the listener has no difficulty understanding you. (There is also no need for you to make that point!)

What happens if you and your listener are quite different in all these respects? Maybe what's good for you he sees as bad for him. Not only does he have problems with *what* you are saying, but he doesn't much like *the way* you are saying it. He might find some of your words confusing or offensive; your tone of voice aggressive, arrogant or whining; your speech painfully slow or much too fast. And he might not like what he sees either: threatening gestures (it's only your enthusiasm, of course) or a sinister sneer (but you *always* smile like that!). The greater the differences between you, the more you may need to communicate. And the harder it is to do so!

Fig 2.1

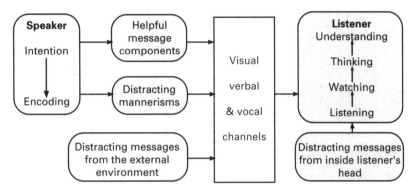

Abstract ideas need words, while emotions are expressed mainly in visual and vocal (non-verbal) messages. The best way to stir the emotions of others is to show genuine emotion yourself, visually and vocally. Friendly greetings are voiced softly and accompanied with a smile; without the smile you would appear insincere. Threats are voiced harshly and accompanied by a scowl; when threatening words and sounds are accompanied by a smile, the effect can be sinister. Other non-verbal signals are often more fleeting—a facial expression of surprise or disgust may last only a fraction of a second, but this is still difficult to conceal from an attentive listener.

Using feedback to tune in

As you get to know someone better, so communicating becomes easier. You will tune in more quickly if you go more than half way to make listening easy for the other person. Note their turn of phrase so you can use their words when asking for clarification. Then check by paraphrasing in your own words what the other person has said. Do this well and you will get a reputation for being good at creating *rapport*.

2.1 BARRIERS TO EFFECTIVE LISTENING

Background noises, or activities which catch your eye, prevent you concentrating. Other distractions come from within you: a more interesting conversation going on in your head. As these competing messages win your attention, you absorb less of what the speaker is trying to put across. Occasionally your attention is recaptured by an accentuated word or phrase, and when the speaker has finished you try to make sense of these fragments. It might be more or less what was intended. Or it might not...

> 'Morning Jean, how was the great metropolis?'
> 'I got fined, Roger.'
> 'Great! Well, let's get started, there's a lot to do...'
> 'Huh! Just wait until you get a parking fine. See how you like it!'

Roger wasn't concentrating. He expected to hear 'Fine' or perhaps 'It was awful', so his inattentive mind inserted the option closest to what he heard. Had he been watching Jean's face, or listening carefully to her tone of voice, their communication might have been more successful.

Here are nine more common reasons for not listening attentively:

Reason for not listening	My problem? (Y/N)
I don't need to hear what you've got to say; I know already	
I don't want to hear what you've got to say; it might embarrass me	
I don't care what you say, so I'm thinking about my reply	
I don't want to listen to you because I don't like you	
I'm getting bored because you're taking too long to make a simple point	
I'm getting confused because you're going too fast for me	
I've got more important things on my mind right now	
I'm more interested in what is going on over there	
I'm in a hurry, and if I show interest you might keep me here longer	

The barrier of brilliance

English is spoken at typically 150 words per minute, but most people can understand speech at two or three times this speed. Intuitive people often speak quickly. When listening to slow speech, their active minds look for something else to think about and fill the gaps. Soon these thoughts (conversations in the head) are running at 500 to 1000 words per minute, and the speaker's message channel is disconnected.

Of course, if the speaker is talking loud enough they will know when the speaker shuts up: the background buzz will stop. Then they may try to cover up their inattentiveness with a 'Hmm... I see.'

The secret of successful listening is to give the mind a bigger challenge: analysing the verbal, vocal and visual information coming in from the speaker. This is *active* listening.

EXAMPLES

Here are nine ideas to help you break down common barriers to listening:

I don't need to hear what you've got to say; I know it already

Imagine how you will feel if you are wrong—if there is important information available and you ignore it. Can you work out how the speaker *feels* about what he is telling you?

I don't want to hear what you've got to say; it might embarrass me

Pretending the problem doesn't exist won't make it go away. Maybe if you listen you will hear the subject from a fresh angle, and get some new ideas which could help you feel more comfortable whenever you have to think about it.

I don't care what you say, so I'm thinking about my reply

If you can't be bothered to listen to others, why should they make the effort to listen to you? You don't have to agree with what is said, but at least show you have thought about it before deciding on your reply. If you have a strong case, it will be all the stronger for taking account of both sides of the argument.

I don't want to listen to you because I don't like you

Should you reject the message because you don't like something the messenger has said or done in the past? Information is for the future; it cannot change the past.

I'm getting bored because you're taking too long to make your point

Some people trip over words whenever they try to speak quickly; so do try to consider their feelings before showing your impatience. Use the long gaps to sort what you hear into a logical structure, especially if the speaker tends to go back over old ground.

I'm getting confused because you're going too fast for me

This is serious! If you really need this information, you had better do something. Raise your hand and ask for clarification. If the problem persists, ask the speaker to slow down. Do this early on, rather than getting frustrated or depressed.

Formal presentations pose a more difficult problem. You could try to catch the speaker's eye and signal your confusion. Skilled speakers pick up such messages from facial expressions, and respond by back-tracking or including an example.

I've got more important things on my mind right now

If you're upset about something, perhaps you could use this opportunity to forget your worries for a while. You never know, you might even hear something to cheer you up.

I'm more interested in what is going on over there

Look at the speaker. Does her posture suggest how she feels about what she is saying? Focus on the eyes to see what they are trying to tell you. Now those other visual distractions have become invisible.

I'm in a hurry, and if I show interest you might keep me here longer

Only if you listen will you learn whether what is being said needs a response right now. If it is important but less urgent than your other engagement, say that you are interested and arrange to meet and discuss the subject when you have dealt with the more urgent matter.

THE SKILLS OF ACTIVE LISTENING

Skilled radio operators can understand Morse code signals much quieter than the background noise. They do this by concentrating on what matters to them. You too can listen for the main ideas behind the detail. Separate the facts from the opinions and mull over any emphasized points that don't fit your views of what is important.

Motivate yourself to listen

The most important requirement for active listening is that you should *want* to listen. Convince yourself that you really need to understand the message and how the speaker feels about what he is saying, and you will have less difficulty coping with distractions around you. Even if the speaker has the most unusual voice or mannerisms, it's no trouble listening if you are really interested.

If you view the discussion or presentation as worthwhile, then try to prepare for it. Read any background material and think how you could benefit from listening. A little prior knowledge helps you remain interested and attentive. Everything *can* be interesting if you try, but if you tell yourself it's going to be boring you *will* get bored.

Motivate the speaker

Show you are interested by looking at the speaker. This will encourage her to look at you more. Nod your head to show you agree; interject the occasional 'I see' or 'Uh-huh', at the ends of important sentences; make the occasional comment of reflection, or paraphrase what you have heard to check on important points.

Put questions in a positive way. Rather than asking the speaker to repeat a point, focus a question on its meaning, or ask for more details, saying why you would like the extra information. Positive questions motivate a speaker; negative ones are discouraging.

The concentration curve

It is easy to concentrate on the beginning of a message, because it is something new and you are busy tuning in to the speaker. After a while your concentration may fall away; that's when distractions can take over. Then, as you realize the speaker is about to finish, your attention is heightened and you strive to make sense of what you can remember of the message.

Even within these concentration regions your attention will tend to fluctuate as subconsciously you make value judgements about individual phrases. Your mind is geared to concentrating on the beginnings of sentences and, to a lesser extent, on their endings. So, if the speaker puts important points in the middles of long sentences, you will need to make a special effort or you may miss them.

Avoid interrupting

When you're pretty sure you know what's coming next there is a temptation to butt in. If you are a fast-talking, enthusiastic person you may have this annoying habit of hijacking other people's sentences and finishing them off, not always in the way intended. Do this and you can upset people by breaking their train of thought, particularly when conversing with those who speak slowly and carefully. Being aware of this problem is the first step towards solving it; active listening will improve this aspect of your self-control.

EXAMPLES

The power of positive questioning

When Bill, from Company Centre, pays a visit, the regional office manager, Jean, is in an uncooperative mood:

> Bill: '...and so each area will order its general stationery and consumables via Central Purchasing. Is that clear, Jean?'
>
> Jean: 'No, it's far from clear. What about the problem of customer specials? Going through central purchasing would cause quite unacceptable delays.'
>
> Bill: 'Listen, Jean. I'm not asking you; I'm telling you. We set the rules. It's your job to follow them!'

Not a good start! Jean used negative language and Bill took this as a personal criticism. Here is a positive approach to the same situation:

> Jean: 'Thanks, Bill. I'm clear about the general stationery, letterheads and so on. Now I'd like your ideas on how we can get our logo and customer details put quickly onto special presentation items. You know, proposal binders and the like. We often need these in a hurry, so we use local suppliers.'
>
> Bill: 'Hmm... Sounds as if we'd better carry on as we always have. There's nothing to be gained by centralizing the purchase of small quantity specials.'

You talk like I think

Jim is a quiet, thoughtful chap, and very sensitive to atmosphere. Once he gets to know someone, he can usually sense how they are feeling. He listens carefully to their tone of voice and can detect the slightest hesitation—something most of us wouldn't notice.

Pete is a more extrovert character. He says he dreams in colour, and he has the most amazing ability to find his way about cities he has only visited once before.

Fortunately, both Pete and Jim are skilled communicators. When they get together, each uses language and non-verbal cues matched to the other's style of thinking:

> Jim: 'I visited McWhittles last week. They've moved to Orchard Court. You know, that bright blue monstrosity of a building—a giant grain silo with windows.'
>
> Pete: 'Good! I'm anxious that we keep in touch with young Nancy McWhittle. I've a feeling she's likely to become their next chief executive.'

And now, meet Mr 'I Know'

Have you ever tried holding a conversation with this fellow:

> 'Hi, Joe. Guess what? I saw Danny Klauninger yesterday. We were talking about the plans for this year's Summer Camp, and he told me...'
>
> 'Yes, I know, it's being moved to Spenton Falls. I heard last week.'
>
> 'No, not the venue, Joe. The age limit. They've introduced a new rule for...'
>
> 'Oh yes, I know. Under twelves get an extra discount. I heard that, too. Good idea... encourage the youngsters!'
>
> 'No. Not the kids. The teachers. It seems they can't get insurance for the over 50s. So I'm afraid you won't be eligible. Sorry! We'll send you a postcard, of course... er... unless you've seen them all before.'

2.3 USING THE VOCAL (NON-VERBAL) AND VISUAL CHANNELS

There is a lot more information in your voice than that in the words alone. And the visual messages you transmit when talking are often crucial to effective communication.

Voice tone

You enter a room, and someone says: *'You're back'*. How do you feel? Does it mean *'Welcome home'*, or *'Oh no, not you again?'* It all depends, of course, on *how* they say it. Voice tone says a great deal. So, when communicating gets difficult, open up more channels. Listen not only to the words, but also to the way they are expressed.

Body language—the risks and benefits

Use your eyes to learn about the person talking to you. Body language can give clues to personality, confidence and honesty. But there are risks, particularly when you don't know the other person well. Someone shifting constantly on her seat could be worried about what she is saying. Or she might just have a stiff back after a long journey!

Gestures

Visual messages go two ways. You may nod agreement as someone explains complex equipment. But, if he is busy operating the controls, he may not realize you are happy with the explanation. If he doesn't make eye contact with you, the visual channel is a one-way link; so, give verbal reassurances. Throw in the occasional *'Ok'* and *'Got it!'*.

Gestures, particularly hand movements, help emphasize key points. But beware: gestures can be misinterpreted, particularly when people of different cultures first meet.

Appearance

Most people vary the way they dress and how well they groom themselves, depending on what they are going to do and who they expect to meet. But can you infer if a particular individual views you with respect by how they appear when visiting you? Much depends on the circumstances:

- Did they know in advance who they were likely to meet?
- Have they had any opportunity to prepare?
- Do they feel appearances are important?

Position and posture

It seems that people, like other animals, feel the need for their own bit of territory, or personal space. When travelling in a crowded train you tolerate others sitting or standing right next to you, but if the train is almost empty, there is an unwritten rule that you don't sit next to someone else unless you know them and get on well with them.

If someone stands closer to you than you would like, you feel uncomfortable. Unless you realize the cause of this discomfort, you might later recall the conversation and feel uncomfortable about *what* was said. Indeed, if someone grasps your arm in their enthusiasm to make a point, you may miss the verbal message completely and be unreceptive to what follows as you brood over the incursion into your personal space.

As you begin a conversation and tune in to the other person, watch for signs that a closer spacing would be welcomed. They can range from a direct *'Come and sit here, where we can hear each other more easily'* to a subtle leaning forward whenever you speak. But remember: being poor of hearing or having a bad back cause the same effect.

Stressing one word, by saying it more slowly and with a slight pause before it, can change the whole meaning of a sentence:

> I *didn't say you stole my pen.*
> I *didn't say* **you** *stole my pen.*
> I *didn't say you* **stole** *my pen.*
> I *didn't say you stole* **my** *pen.*

People who rant, as if their every word is of crucial importance, achieve no more emphasis that those who drone on in a monotone. Only when used sparingly do changes in pitch, loudness, pace and tone carry non-verbal signals of emphasis.

Our minds are drawn back to full attention by marked vocal changes only if they are introduced sensibly. Incorrect use of emphasis causes confusion:

> I **didn't** *say you* **stole** *my* **pen.**

Not all gestures are universal

Extrovert people tend to show their feelings by energetic, expansive gestures, while shy people make fewer gestures and do so in a more subdued and contained way.

Fig 2.2

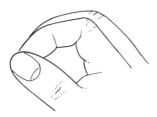

This gesture means *perfect* in many Western countries, but in Japan it means *worthless*. Part of the tuning in process is to learn the body language of the other person.

Are you poker-faced?

Some people can control their facial muscles to the point where it's all but impossible to sense their emotions. But few can avoid making those fleeting eye movements which, to the careful observer, betray interest, suspicion, concern and so on.

> Jim: *'Dave. Have you seen my camera; I think it might have been stolen?'*
> Dave's eyes flicker downwards momentarily. *'No, sorry, I haven't.'*
> Jim is far from convinced.

Had Dave's eyes moved upwards, suggesting he was trying to recall what the camera looked like or where he had last seen it, maybe Jim's suspicions would not have been alerted. (Of course, a piece of grit *might* have been making Dave's eye feel uncomfortable all day!)

Visual and vocal channels carry clues to the interpretation of verbal messages, and to the motivation behind them. Making full use of these non-verbal channels is an essential part of active listening. On their own they can be misleading, but combined with the verbal channel they either provide a coherent message or prompt you to ask for clarification.

2.4 PARAPHRASING—CLOSING THE FEEDBACK LOOP

The world would be an even more confusing place if everyone relied on perfect verbal communication. But we don't. The simple one-way model of encoding, sending, receiving and decoding messages is incomplete. Even using verbal, vocal and visual channels, the messages don't always make sense. Sometimes a sentence is incomplete:

> 'Pass the whatsit...'

At other times the words themselves are quite clear, but maybe the voice wavers, or the posture is defensive, giving an impression of uncertainty or nervousness:

> Jean: 'It's OK. We're not lost. I recognize that clump of trees over there.'
> Phil: 'Are you sure?'

In the first example the words don't make sense to the listener. In the second, it's the feelings behind the words that matter more.

A message can also seem confusing if you lose concentration and miss a key point.

You don't have to live with these uncertainties. There is a feedback loop for checking your understanding of what was said: simply let the speaker know what you have got from the point she has made. You can do this using various styles of paraphrasing.

Fig 2.3

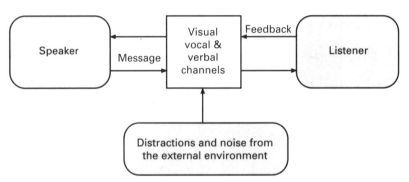

Correcting or completing information

Sometimes you feel sure the speaker has made a mistake, or you realize your attention drifted and you missed part of the message. Rather than asking for a complete repetition, outline the areas you understand and ask for clarification.

Checking the facts

When checking back to make sure you have got facts and figures right, use the speaker's words, picking out just the key phrases. This type of summarizing is useful when confirming steps in a task, route directions and the like.

Reflecting aloud on the meaning

When you understand what you have been told, you may want to let the speaker know how you see the implications. This would apply where the speaker has tried to persuade you into a new belief or course of action.

Testing for the feelings behind the words

Here you have caught what was said, and you realize its implications, but you want the speaker to know why you think he made the point this way. You can use this type of feedback to find out why someone disagrees with you. It may not solve the problem entirely, but recognizing you have different viewpoints is a good start.

EXAMPLES   Let's see how these feedback techniques can help.

- Filling in the missing words

When faced with:

> 'Pass the whatsit...'

You could respond with:

> 'Pass the what?'

Or, being a cooperative soul, you might take a guess and reply:

> 'Is this what you want?'

- Filling in where your concentration wandered

Instead of a vague 'Pardon?', ask for just the information you need:

> 'Thanks, Ursula. I'm clear on the travel and accommodation arrangements, but could you run through the insurance scheme again? I'm particularly concerned about what happens if personal property gets lost or damaged. I mean, what about cameras and the like; are they covered?'

- Reconciling verbal and vocal messages

> Ruth: 'It's OK. We're not lost. I recognize that clump of trees over there.'
> Phil: 'You don't sound too sure.'
> Ruth: 'Yes, I'm quite certain. But it's so cold my teeth are chattering.'

- Checking the facts

> Driver: 'Can you tell me the way to Newtown, please?'
> Local: 'Certainly! Carry straight on across the next two roundabouts. At the third roundabout, turn left, take the right fork at a Y junction about a mile from there. Newtown's another two miles along that road.'
> Driver: 'So... third roundabout. Turn left. Right fork at the Y junction. Yes?'

- Reflecting aloud on the meaning

Here you use a different style of paraphrasing, often beginning with a phrase of the form:

> 'I see. So this means we will have to...'

And, when you finish paraphrasing, you look to the speaker for confirmation that this is the meaning intended.

- Checking the feelings behind the words

> Ursula: 'It might not be a good idea to pin our hopes on the Durnley job.'
> Pete: 'From the way you put it, I get the impression you don't see this project as having much potential, whereas I think it's the biggest opportunity we've had in years. Am I right?'
> Ursula: 'It's not so much that, Pete. In fact whoever gets phase two should do very well out of it. It's just that I'm not convinced we are in a strong position to win the contract.'

TEST YOUR LISTENING SKILLS

Leave a tape recorder running while you listen to a five minute news summary on your radio. Fifteen minutes later, complete the questionnaire below. Replay the recording of the news broadcast and check your score—one point for each correct answer. (If a question is not applicable, award yourself a point if you answered N/A.)

Complete another questionnaire a day later. After replaying the bulletin compare the two scores. Surprisingly, many people score *fewer* points the second time.

News bulletin listening test		
Test of:	**Date:**	
Question	**Your answer**	**Score**
What was the lead story about?		
Which person was mentioned by name in the second item?		
List three locations which were mentioned by name.		
How many items were headlined in the bulletin?		
Which event occurred nearest to your home?		
Which international organization was mentioned?		
Which country was mentioned by name the most times?		
Which foreign political leader was mentioned the most times?		
What was the largest sum of money mentioned?		
Summarize in between 15 and 25 words the third item covered in the news bulletin.		
	Your total score (Maximum = 10):	

This procedure is best carried out each day over a period of a week. Average your scores for the seven tests. Then, if you are not satisfied with your results, work on putting into practice the ideas in this chapter.

Why not repeat the exercise three months later to see how your listening skills are improving?

TEST YOUR OBSERVATION SKILLS

Arrange for two colleagues to discuss a problem at work while a video camera observes their discussions. Start the recording and leave the room while they get on with their meeting. Replay the video film with the sound turned off, and see how well you can read the visual clues which indicate how the meeting is going. Pause the recording whenever you want to make a note. (Logging the counter reading each time will ensure you can quickly return to the same position.)

Once you have made ten entries, rewind the tape and replay the meeting with the sound turned on. Award +1 for each correct interpretation and –1 for each incorrect entry.

Typical entries are shown below.

Visual clues observation test					
Counter reading	Contributor	Visual clue	Interpretation of visual clue	Correct interpretation	Score
0023	Janet	Frowning	Confused	Annoyed	-1
0039	Peter	Leaning forward, frowning	Threatening	Interested in what Janet is saying, and trying to understand her	-1
0050	Peter	Smiling and nodding	Agreeing with Janet's proposal	Agreeing with Janet's proposal	+1
0064	Janet	Shaking her head and frowning	Disagreeing with what Peter is saying	Disagreeing with what Peter is saying	+1
0072	Janet	Looking down while talking	Unhappy about what she is saying	Admitting she made a mistake	+1
0080	Peter	Shaking head and smiling	Condescending	Admitting he was partly to blame	-1
0088	Janet	Smiling, throwing back head	Enthusiastic about Peter's proposal	Agreeing to support Peter	+1
0095	Peter	Leaning forward, listening	Checking understanding	Checking understanding	+1
0106	Peter	Folding arms and leaning back	Not receptive to Janet's proposal	Not receptive	+1
0112	Janet	Palm of hands open	Asking what has upset Peter	Stating she can do no more to help	-1
				Your score	+2

By repeating this exercise with later parts of the meeting your score should steadily increase as you get to know the participants better. And, by training yourself to be more observant, you will become more skilled at interpreting body language and gestures, so that you more rapidly 'tune in' to the visual messages of others.

CHAPTER 3

MANAGEMENT BY INFORMAL COMMUNICATION
THE EVERYDAY SKILLS OF MANAGING PEOPLE

Managers must communicate. That is why you need to be able to get your message across effectively using a range of media—presentations, written reports, meetings, interviews and so on.

But are you making full use of a communication technique you've been developing since before you could walk: the art of conversation? You really should, because you're almost certainly better at informal communication than you can ever hope to be using any of the more formal communication processes.

The challenge

As a manager, your success will depend largely on your ability to motivate other people. And it is during chats in the corridor, over lunch or a drink after work, as well as periodic walkabouts to see the people working for you, that you get to know what are the real barriers to achievement. Armed with this inside information you are in a better position to do something about breaking down those barriers and getting things done.

The benefits

Do people make you promises and then let you down? Informal communication channels are the best way of finding out how committed others are to the targets you have agreed with them.

Are you frequently disappointed to learn, through formal reports, about problems which, had you been informed of them earlier, you could have resolved easily? Learn to cultivate informal communication channels and you will be more in touch with the action.

Does the grapevine undermine your attempts to motivate your staff by team briefing and other formal systems for keeping them informed? Learn how to use the grapevine to your advantage.

EVERYONE IS DIFFERENT

Treat everyone the same and you will get average results: mediocrity. Excellence comes from able, motivated people working together effectively towards a common goal, and communication is essential to direction and motivation.

This doesn't mean you should display favouritism. What it does mean is that you need to get to know each of your people as individuals, each with personal hopes, fears and personality traits. Only with this understanding can you treat each person in a way which they find motivating.

Predicting individual behaviour

Psychologists have tried for years to produce a model of personality which would provide a reasonable prediction of behaviour. What is clear is that people respond differently according to:

- The situation, and in particular how exciting or threatening they perceive it to be.
- Their personality.
- The behaviour of others around them.
- Their experiences of similar situations. In particular, recent experience seems to carry more weight than those of long ago.

You may be the architect of the difficult situation: asking a team member to take on a new and more demanding role, for example. And if you are the only other person present, you should be in control of your behaviour. But you will only acquire an insight into your team member's personality and be aware of his or her recent experiences if you keep in close touch with them. This is where frequent informal communication is an advantage.

It's the way you tell 'em

When you have information for a colleague, you will want to pass it on in a form they will appreciate. Choose your language to suit their vocabulary and avoid jargon words if they aren't as familiar as you are with the work.

Each of us has preferred styles of communication. We may find it easiest to understand a message if it is presented in one or more of the following forms.

- **Vocal skills**. These people like to hear at first hand. They need you to talk to them.
- **Visual skills**. Pictures are more useful than words to some people. Let them study the illustrations; then point out details by reference to features they can see.
- **Numerical skills**. Use numbers and spreadsheets or tables so these people can more easily see values and the relationships between items.
- **Literal skills**. Give these people written summaries of important messages.
- **Practical skills**. Hands-on demonstrations are the best way of getting a message across to some people. They may need to handle something before they will believe in it fully.

Tune your transmissions to the receiver

Get to know how each of your staff prefers to receive information, and use that style. Visual images influence most people, but when talking with a group of people it's wise to back up the visual message with one or more of the other forms mentioned above.

3.1 MANAGEMENT BY WALKING THE JOB

As your career progresses, informal one-to-one communication may take up an increasing amount of your time. This is fine as long as most of it is productive.

Benefits of one-to-one communication

By meeting face-to-face with your peers, subordinates or superiors in the organization, you get to know how they feel about your ideas and proposals before you float them officially in memos, reports or formal meetings. Often these informal channels are your best means of winning the support of those whose approval you need. But don't undervalue the benefit of winning over those who will have to carry out your plans once they are approved; their commitment could be essential to your success.

Often these informal consultations help you to prepare a better proposal. On other occasions they may be your means of deciding *how* best to present your case. You could even repeat their words in your proposal, explaining how they will be affected and showing you have considered the implications from more angles than just your own.

Most of the time you will walk the job to listen to other people, rather than to talk. Ask how they are getting on and you will learn a lot more than ever you get from official reports.

How often?

You can't spend all your time listening to other people, so it's a good idea to have a plan. A lot depends on what sort of job you have, but as a starting point consider this:

- At least once a day see all who report to you.
- At least once a week see all who contribute directly to your objectives.
- At least once a month see all who make indirect contributions to your objectives.

Choose your time

Interruptions aren't always welcome, so think before barging in on others. The start of the day, just after lunch and the last few minutes before normal finishing time are often more acceptable than mid-morning or mid-afternoon.

Counselling and consulting, not spying

If this style of management is new to you, then at first people might think you're simply checking up on them. Dispel that concern by taking an interest in them as *individuals*. Spend a minute or two listening to their personal concerns, even if they're nothing to do with work. If you want people to care about the work they do for you, show concern for their welfare, as well as for the work they are doing. You could make a note to see someone more often if they are going through a difficult patch. Don't pontificate on what you would do if you were them. You're not! Instead, be a friendly listener, helping them get things clearer in their own minds. Most people appreciate a little counselling when times are hard, and they will remember if you have been a caring and helpful confidante.

Accept the bad news

When the news is bad it's easy to get cross with the messenger, especially if they are responsible for much of the problem. Bite your tongue and count to ten. Keep calm as you ask for more information. If you don't, the supply of information is likely to dry up rapidly, and this will ensure you get to hear less bad news in future... at least until it's too late to do much about putting things right!

EXAMPLES   ## SUPPORTING THE TEAM

Janet Masters, chief design engineer at FICO UK, spends the first hour of every Monday visiting each of the staff of her development laboratory:

> Janet: 'Hello Peter. How did the rehearsal go last night?'
> Peter: 'Well, at least everyone turned up. Stage lighting was a disaster, though, but we eventually found the fault and it should be all right on the night.'
> Janet: 'Next Wednesday, isn't it? I'm hoping to be there and I'll have my fingers crossed for you.'

Then she calls on Tim Hurst, one of her best electronics engineers.

> Janet: 'Hi, Tim. Everything OK?'
> Tim: 'Yes, not too bad. Er... Well, actually, no. Not OK really. I mean... it's not your problem, I know, but Purchasing are holding up my orders far too long. I seem to be spending half my time chasing components. Purchasing just don't seem to realize how much pressure we're under on this project.'

Janet can't afford to ignore this problem. She sits down with Tim and asks for more details. After a couple of minutes she comes up with a proposal.

> Janet: 'Well look, Tim. I'll be over in Admin. shortly. How would it be if I gave a list of priority items to Larry Winslow himself. He owes me a favour, and I'm sure he'll pull out the stops for us once he realizes how important this job is.'
> Tim: 'Would you, Janet? That'd be great. Thanks a lot.'

Four months later Janet calls in on Larry Winslow.

> Janet: 'Hello Larry. Remember the rush job you did for me some weeks ago? Housings and components for the new Autojector. Well, we've got the first prototype working now. I thought you and your people might like to come across to the lab and see it working.'
> Larry: 'That's really thoughtful of you, Janet. You know, my people hardly ever get to see the results of all their hard work. I'm sure they would all like to come.'
> Janet: 'Well, how about ten to five? I'll ask Tim to set the system up with some colour slides. He's very proud of the new baby, and dead keen to show you how clever it is.'

On reflection

With Larry on her side Janet is unlikely to encounter many problems due to bottlenecks in Purchasing. And Larry and his team gain too: they get to know more about the business they are trying to serve, and they feel their contribution is valued.

Service areas like Purchasing and Finance receive far more brickbats than bouquets. A few minutes spent once in a while to get them involved and committed to the objectives of the business pay disproportionately large benefits. Janet realizes this and makes a point of periodically visiting every department. It's not written anywhere in her job description, but without walking the job like this she would not be able to give her direct staff the support they need.

3.2 THE GRAPEVINE

The unofficial communication network—the lunchtime eating place or a nearby bar—passes organization news around quickly, but not always accurately. It is particularly good at sideways and downwards communication through the organizational structure.

Good news, bad news

Psychology professor Frederick Herzberg describes aspects of working conditions such as an organization's official communication system, as 'hygiene factors'. When they are bad, hygiene factors—like bad drains—will demotivate people; when good, they usually get taken for granted. So, when an organization suffers a major set-back, and the news is bad, people often feel that the organization's communication system is bad. That's when the grapevine takes over.

The grapevine is especially quick in spreading bad news, but you can use it for spreading good news, too. And you can also use the grapevine to head off some of the misunderstandings which otherwise cause people to huddle in groups in the corridors adding conjecture to sparse facts about impending events which may affect them.

Using the grapevine

The more senior you become the more difficult it is to see all you depend on as often as you might wish. Your seniority can deter people from speaking their minds, and so you can find it difficult to judge what support you have when proposing a change.

Fortunately, you can overcome many of these problems by skilful use of the grapevine, for which you need a network of contacts. Some of these are people who talk too much. Their idea of a secret is *something you tell to one person at a time*. Anything confidential you discuss with corridor whisperers will be broadcast through the grapevine in no time.

The most valuable 'corridor whisperers' are people well respected by their colleagues. When you share your ideas with them they pass them on in a way most likely to gain support. Steer clear of the 'Oh Gawd ain't it awful' types who only pass on the negative aspects of proposals.

The grapevine can also be an important source of information: a way of finding out in advance how your proposals might be seen by people at various levels in the organization. Having leaked a proposal you need to listen to your 'moles'. Moles are often people who try to ingratiate themselves with managers by 'telling tales on others'. It's often best to be seen to seek informal views from many sources, otherwise your moles may feel too exposed. Most of these will, of course, simply give you their own opinion, but your moles will tell you what the feeling is across a section of workers.

Lies and spies?

All this may seem rather underhand, but I'm not suggesting you should use the grapevine to spread untruths. Sometimes these unofficial channels are the only practical way of testing ideas whose success depends on their acceptance by people at many levels in the organization. Often the feedback via the grapevine will help you modify a proposal, or perhaps alter the way you introduce it, and so avoid creating disruption and demotivation in some other aspect which you hadn't considered. The grapevine can be an effective means of achieving worker participation in management.

EXAMPLES

Advance warning

Jack Scarman, product support manager at FICO UK, would like to reorganize the way spares are defined during the design stage of new products. To get his idea accepted he needs the approval of the design department, where Janet Masters has recently joined the organization as Chief Engineer. So, when Jack meets design engineer Tim Hurst, in the staff restaurant, he brings the conversation round to changes in the organization.

> Jack: *'Your new chief engineer seems like a breath of fresh air, Tim. I find her attitude to new ideas very positive. Old Sandy was all right, but I guess he'd been in the same job long enough. He needed a change, and so did we. I'm looking forward to meeting Janet... she sounds very interesting.'*
>
> Tim: *'Yes, She's quite a good boss to work for. Mind you, she expects a lot.'*
>
> Jack: *'I was hoping you'd say that. It's what we need right now. In fact I was thinking of asking her for help in getting an improved spares system approved, but perhaps she's snowed under with her own problems right now.'*

Two days later, when Jack calls on Janet, he finds her most receptive to his ideas: Tim, his grapevine whisperer, has done a good job.

The Russian front strategy

Before the takeover by FICO Inc., The Autojector Company had got into financial difficulties while developing a new product range: the project had taken almost a year longer than planned. The directors considered their options, which appeared to be:

- Close the manufacturing plant. This would involve large-scale redundancies, as all except pilot production would be subcontracted out.
- Try to obtain a substantial long-term loan. The interest payments would greatly reduce the profitability of the company; so, if sales revenue fell for any reason, the company might be unable to service the debt burden. The penalty for insolvency is receivership and possible bankruptcy.
- Seek a friendly takeover which would provide the financial investment to complete the development of the new product range. The company name might disappear, however, and control might fall into the hands of people less familiar with Autojector's markets.

On balance the directors favoured the takeover option. However, they used the grapevine to ensure rumours of impending collapse associated with options one and two reached every level of the organization. Soon the moles were feeding back information: if management tried to close the manufacturing plant there would be an all-out strike. And although no one could see an alternative to increased financial gearing—taking on a long-term loan—the workers felt decidedly uneasy about their future. Only then did the directors leak the possibility of a third option—rescue by a White Knight in the form of an American corporation currently involved in the audiovisual aids market.

By this time people throughout the organization were, like the soldiers in the Second World War, ready to accept *'anything... but please don't send us to the Russian front'*.

INFORMAL BRIEFING SESSIONS

Managers and their teams need to meet frequently to discuss their futures. Team briefing is one way of achieving this. It is a system of regular communication meetings at which all teams in an organization meet about once per month. The timing is formalized so that all teams meet on the same day, but the briefings are meant to be customized. Each team should hear from their team leader about matters of relevance to their work.

To start the system off, managers at the top of the organization create a *core brief* of business policy, performance and other news. A written summary is passed right down the organization, and at each level team leaders present it from the point of view of people at that level: how it will affect what they do, how they do it, and so on. In addition the team leader also passes on a *local brief*, prepared after discussions with other managers at the same level. The local brief would normally dominate, so that team briefing meetings are relevant and interesting to those attending. And of course, staff can question their leader about the local brief and the core brief. Most questions are easily answered, but occasionally the team leader has to refer upwards questions on the core brief.

That is the theory!

Formalized briefings often fail

In practice, team briefing is rarely done well. Sometimes the briefing sessions demotivate rather than positively motivate large sections of the workforce. Three common reasons for this are:

- The core brief is initially prepared at director level, but after a few months this job is delegated to someone, often in the personnel department, who does not have access to the information necessary to create an up-to-date core brief; so the grapevine gets news to staff more quickly—often with a negative tone.
- Middle managers present the core brief with little or no local emphasis, so staff find team briefing meetings boring.
- Questions about the briefing information—especially the core brief—never get answerered. Middle managers pass questions upwards, but don't pursue answers; senior managers view questions about the core brief as a nuisance; staff soon stop thinking about the briefing information because they feel management doesn't really want them to be involved.

Briefing sessions that work

The secret is to retain the informal briefing environment that good managers have always nurtured. Treat the core brief as a bonus to be exploited during *your* briefing meetings—the meetings at which you present *your* brief to *your* staff.

If you believe in keeping your staff informed, spend time preparing a brief which is useful to them. The key word is *relevance*. Think of the things you know are happening in the company. Think not from your own point of view as a manager, but from the point of view of your staff. Team briefing can be a boring waste of time if it is done in a perfunctory way with no real thought or effort. But done well, it can make people feel valued by the company. And it can reinforce your position as a team leader—a position the grapevine is constantly undermining. Your staff will repay you many times over for the effort you put in to involve them by communicating informally and frequently.

EXAMPLE: # ORGANIZING A BRIEFING

John Harman, site services manager at FICO Ltd, is preparing to brief his team. He has several items to present:

1 A reorganization of office accommodation on site. Although site services staff are not to be relocated, they will have to work overtime during the move. John expects to get more information on this at a team briefing meeting chaired by his team leader, the personnel director.
2 A forthcoming visit by a team from Wellbrook Inc., headed by their president Mr Dave Wellbrook. John has been asked to set up special display facilities for this visit.
3 Mary Stennet leaving after 22 years with FICO. Mary spent four years in site services before becoming secretary to the manufacturing executive. Several of John's staff know her well and will want to contribute to a leaving present.
4 A two-minute run down on business performance. This is something John's team are particularly interested in. Each month he gets information from Sales, Marketing and Finance on important new orders, output and financial results. Then John tries to look ahead to see how this news might affect the work he and his team are likely to be doing in the months ahead.

In allocating time to each topic, John considers:

• How relevant and important it is to his team, and whether any resulting actions will affect their workload.
• What they are likely to know already. John is anxious to avoid boring people by going over too much old ground.
• What questions they are likely to ask. Not only does this help him prepare, but he leaves enough time so that important questions can be answered in enough detail.

The most important guiding factor is relevance. John rarely spends more than five minutes on the core brief, unless it relates closely to the work of his department, whereas he spends three or four times as long on local issues. Experience has taught him it is essential to relate the content of the brief to the needs and interests of his team; otherwise the meeting is a waste of time.

The briefing process

John's meetings are quite informal. People get 24 hours' notice, and John provides a written copy of the core brief for anyone who wants one. He also keeps a file of the notes from which he presents his brief. The file also holds a list of questions answered and the answer given. This file comes in handy when John meets his own manager; he lets his boss know what questions came up, and for any he couldn't answer himself he asks for help. Usually the personnel director can answer, but when he doesn't know either, the question has to be referred upwards.

Knowing his boss has a terrible memory, John follows up with a memo asking the question. A copy of the memo goes into the team briefing file, so it's there to remind him to chase up the answer.

3.4 DEVELOPING YOUR ASSERTIVENESS

It is easy to be pleasant and positive when things are going well and everyone else is being nice. But how do you cope with pressure? Do you strive for what you want without hurting others? Do you become aggressive and self-centred? Do you back down to keep the peace? Or do you give up and try not to get involved?

A model of behaviour

These four extremes of behaviour—assertive, aggressive, acquiescent and apathetic—reflect the personality and motivations of the individual (Fig. 3.1). Aggression seems to arise from a need for respect and esteem from others; acquiescence from the need to be accepted and popular; withdrawal and apathy from a lack of self-respect and the need to escape to a situation of safety. But assertive people value themselves *and others*. They seem determined to achieve fulfilment without interfering with the right of others to do so, too.

Fig 3.1

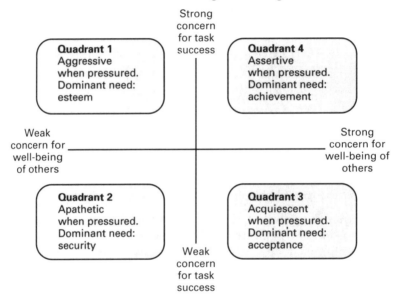

Of course, most of us respond to a combination of these motivators. For example, under strong pressure we may behave somewhere between open aggression and complete apathy, perhaps by showing resentful submission.

But regardless of personality, everyone can learn to cope more effectively with pressure, and so behave more assertively.

Interaction of behaviour

Aggressive behaviour makes other people feel angry and can lead to confrontation. Usually one or other party comes off worse and has to back down, albeit resentfully, for fear of the consequences of continuing the battle.

Apathy is infectious. It can cause others to feel: 'He doesn't seem to want to sort this mess out, so why should I bother?'

Fawning behaviour rarely achieves much in the long term. Familiarity breeds contempt, and such people often end up as the victims of aggression.

The one behaviour which seems to *win* people over is assertiveness. Enthusiasm is infectious, and if you show strong commitment to getting things done, with a concern for the needs and feelings of other people, you should find it easier to win the support you need.

EXAMPLES: DIFFICULT SITUATIONS

Here are some situations with non-assertive or aggressive responses and alternative, assertive responses which are usually more effective.

Situation	Non-assertive or aggressive response	Assertive response
You are making a request for help.	'Jim, I don't suppose there's any chance you could...'	'Jim, please would you...'
You are refusing a request from someone else because you can't spare the time.	'Oh dear. I do hope you don't mind but its not easy for me to fit that in right now...'	'I can't help right now; I've a meeting in five minutes.'
Someone interrupts you with a question before you have had time to complete your explanation.	'I'm sorry...I hope I haven't confused you...'	'I want to explain the whole process. Then I'll be pleased to take questions.'
Someone asks for a lift home and takes out a cigarette with the intention of lighting up.	You open your window wide so they 'get the message'.	'Please don't smoke in the car, Jim.'
You are asked to buy raffle tickets to raise money for an organization for which you have no sympathy.	Buy just one ticket to avoid causing a scene.	Smile politely and say: 'No thank you, Jean. It's not for a cause I want to support.'
You attend a meeting at which the chairperson ignores your attempts to contribute.	Ignore her and get on with something useful, such as drafting a report.	Raise your hand and say: 'Please may I contribute at this point, Andrea?'
Someone makes a sexist remark, calling you 'dearie'	'Listen, dumbo, I'm not your dearie.'	Smile and state firmly: 'I'm Jean. Now how can I help you?'
Your manager doesn't pass on your applications to attend training courses.	'I know the training budget's limited, and maybe there are others with a stronger claim than mine, but I wondered if I might...'	'I want to improve the quality of my written reports, and so I'd like to discuss with you which writing skills course I should attend this year.'
Your manager has withheld news that your project is to be cancelled. Now you have found out via another source.	'You spineless coward! You didn't have the guts to tell me yourself.'	'I am really disappointed that you didn't inform me yourself. I feel you don't value me; is that correct?'
Your manager is angry because you have made a silly mistake through not checking your work carefully.	'Nobody's perfect. Anyway, you make just as many mistakes as I do. Perhaps more!'	'I'm sorry. I was wrong. I will check my work more carefully in future, Kim.'
There is an emergency and you instruct staff to leave the building at once. Jim stops to gather up his personal belongings.	'You explain to Jim that the regulations state that in an emergency all staff must leave without delay.' (This is an assertive response...but is it *right?*)	You grab Jim by the collar and shout: 'Get out, Jim. NOW!' (Yes, this is being aggressive...and so you should be!)

3.5 COPING WITH CRITICISM

Criticism is an essential part of business life. When things go wrong at work the people who have made the mistakes aren't always aware there is a problem. Or they may not realize they are the cause of the problem. They need to know about and accept responsibility for their mistakes, or things will continue to go wrong.

Part of your job as a manager is to provide constructive criticism, but before you can do this you need to know how to accept criticism, too.

Accepting criticism

In the face of criticism, particularly from an angry complainant, it's easy to feel that *you* are being attacked. It is quite natural to feel that you must defend yourself. Here are some guidelines for receiving criticism:

- Try to keep calm; getting angry yourself is unlikely to solve problems, and it could be harder to work with this person after you have had a blazing row.
- Show you appreciate how the other person feels. You don't have to agree with their criticism, but acknowledging that they are upset can help take the heat out of the situation.
- Get them to separate fact from opinion. Try to establish what has happened and how it has caused problems for the other person.
- If the criticism is valid, admit you made a mistake and apologize. Then discuss what you can do to improve the situation.

Criticizing others

It is unfair to criticize people for things they can do nothing about, like their intellect or personality. Focus on the facts and the way people behave: these are things that can be changed in future. Here are some guidelines for giving criticism:

- Decide why you want to criticize. Is it to punish, to shift the blame, or to change future actions?
- State the problem in objective language: the facts and the issues involved. Steer clear of criticizing personalities and opinions. Try to keep cool!
- Discuss what would be an acceptable solution and how you would like the other person to contribute.
- Get their commitment to carrying out the agreed actions.

Coping with unfair criticism

What if you are criticized for something which is not your own fault? Should you just accept it, or should you make sure the blame ends up where it is deserved?

Say, for instance, a member of your department has made a mistake for which you are criticized by an outsider. If you can ensure the mistake doesn't happen again it may not be worth wasting more time explaining that you were not involved; indeed, this sort of 'passing the buck' may only serve to stoke the fires of wrath.

At times you may *need* to refute criticism. Acknowledge that the problem exists and show you appreciate how it has made things awkward for the complainant. State assertively that you were not involved and get the complainant to accept your assurance. Then, if appropriate, offer to help put things right by talking to the person responsible.

EXAMPLE: A CUSTOMER COMPLAINT

Jane Symonds works in the Customer Service department. As part of her job she provides customer support, sometimes dealing with complaints about FICO overhead and 35 mm slide projectors. Not all of these complaints are justified. In many instances, irate customers phone suggesting the product is faulty when they aren't using it correctly. It's not uncommon for Jane to have to explain where the On/Off switch is, even though there is a diagram in the front of the handbook and a clear label on the projector!

One evening just as Jane is about to leave work, she gets a call from a hot and flustered conference organizer, Philip Matthews. Philip leases projector systems from FICO, and this afternoon he has just tested the three projectors in his main conference room. None of them is working, and his conference is due to start shortly.

> *Philip: 'I want an engineer down here right away. If this lot's not up and running by the time the delegates arrive you can take the whole lot back. I'll find myself a supplier of reliable projectors. It's a total shambles.'*
>
> *Jane: 'I appreciate it must be very worrying for you, and I'm anxious to do all I can to help you have a successful conference.'*
>
> *Philip: 'Listen. I didn't ask for your help; I need a service engineer and three new projectors... pronto!'*
>
> *Jane: 'Yes, I do appreciate the urgency. Could you tell me which models you're having trouble with and when the delegates will be entering the conference suite; we'll need to have things sorted out by then.'*

By concentrating on the facts Jane calms down the complainant and gets the information she needs. She agrees to contact her field service engineer and to call the customer back within five minutes. This she does:

> *Jane: 'Mr Matthews? Hello, this is Jane Symonds of FICO. I've spoken with our field service engineer and he will be with you in less than half an hour. He's bringing replacement projectors, but he says the symptoms you describe suggest the Remote/Local switch on the chairman's control console may have been inadvertently left in the Remote position. This would, of course, prevent the presenters operating the projectors themselves.'*

An embarrassed conference organizer checks the control console and finds the diagnosis is correct. He apologizes to Jane.

> *Jane: 'That's no problem, Mr Matthews. Oh, and while he's with you I've asked our engineer to help you check over the system. We want you to get the very best service from our products. After all, our future depends on you. Do call again if there's any way I can help.'*

On reflection

Jane uses 'we' not 'they' when referring to FICO—even when talking about departments other than her own. She is also careful to offer only what she knows she can deliver. In this example it was only after checking with the field service engineer that she made a promise of what help she could provide and how soon it would be available. Once the problem had been cleared Jane didn't raise the issue of whose fault it was, as there was nothing to be gained from doing so.

CHECK-LIST: HOW WELL DO YOU COMMUNICATE?

Use this check-list to audit you own use of informal communication channels.

Self-assessment: use of informal communication channels				
Review date:				
Please mark your assessment here using: 4 = Excellent: continue doing this well 3 = Good: scope for minor improvements 2 = Fair: much improvement is possible 1 = Weak: major improvement is essential	4	3	2	1
Management by walking the job (MBWJ)				
Do I see each of my team members often enough?				
Do I visit often enough the direct contributors to my job goals who work in other departments?				
Do I meet often enough with subcontractors and other indirect contributors to my job goals?				
Do I take enough personal interest in the welfare of my colleagues?				
Do I show enough interest in the achievements of others?				
Do I openly voice my appreciation of the contributions of others?				
Do I support my staff when they are having difficulties?				
Overall: How effective is my MBWJ?				
Use of the grapevine				
Have I cultivated 'corridor whisperers' who are in touch with those I need to communicate with via the grapevine?				
Do I listen to the right 'grapevine moles' so I know what people in various departments are concerned about?				
Am I testing my ideas effectively via the grapevine?				
Am I getting advance warning, via the grapevine, of threats to achievement of my goals?				
Overall: How well is the grapevine serving me?				
Assertiveness in informal communications				
Am I assertive when making requests of or criticizing others?				
Do I receive criticism assertively?				
Overall: How assertive am I when under pressure?				
Informal team briefing sessions				
Do I meet sufficiently with my team for informal briefings?				
Do I make sure the briefings are relevant and interesting?				
Do I obtain answers to questions raised in briefing meetings?				
Overall: How effective are my briefing sessions?				

Improvement targets	

CHECK-LIST: HOW ASSERTIVE ARE YOU WHEN PRESSURED?

Use this check-list to audit your assertiveness at work and to set targets for improvement.

Self-assessment: assertiveness at work	4	3	2	1
Review date:				
Please mark your assessment here using: 4 = Excellent: continue doing this well 3 = Good: scope for minor improvements 2 = Fair: much improvement is possible 1 = Weak: major improvement is essential	4	3	2	1
When dealing with my manager				
Do I state my wants and opinions openly, giving my reasons?				
Do I admit when I am wrong and apologize frankly?				
Do I accept criticism without becoming angry?				
Do I accept responsibility for my failures without trying to shift the blame to my subordinates?				
Do I say no when I cannot provide what I am asked to?				
Do I accept it without sulking when my ideas are overruled?				
Do I criticize my manager when he behaves wrongly?				
Overall: How assertively do I deal with my manager?				
When dealing with my staff				
Do I give praise and credit when it is due?				
Do I give constructive criticism when it is appropriate?				
Do I encourage my staff to voice their wants and opinions?				
Do I make clear requests, with reasons, when I want them to do more than the norm?				
Do I admit it and apologize when I am wrong?				
Overall: How assertively do I deal with my staff?				
When dealing with other people who interrupt me while I am busy				
Do I reject unnecessary or inconvenient interruptions without making the person feel rejected?				
Do I help people to help themselves, rather than taking on part of their work load as well as my own?				
Overall: How assertively do I deal with interruptions?				
When dealing with criticisms from customers or suppliers				
Do I show concern for and appreciation of their problems?				
Do I avoid apologizing when there's nothing to be sorry for?				
Do I offer in a friendly tone help that I know I can deliver?				
Overall: How assertively do I manage these criticisms?				

Improvement targets	

ADD PUNCH TO YOUR PRESENTATIONS
A STRATEGY FOR IMPROVED CAPABILITY AND CONFIDENCE

Making presentations: it seems you either love it, or you hate it. The *'love it'* brigade jump at every opportunity, and some become polished speakers. The *'hate it'* majority use every trick in the book to avoid being put on the spot.

Audiences aren't so lucky. They have to take what's served up to them, and all too often it's an indigestible mess. That's why the ideas in this chapter are mainly to help your audience, but it's you, the presenter, who must take the medicine. Make life enjoyable for your audience, and maybe you will come to enjoy giving presentations. You will certainly have more influence with people.

The challenge

Perhaps you are worried about being nervous or making a fool of yourself. You wouldn't be alone! Just about every speaker has suffered from presentation nerves at some time. Indeed, a little pre-event anxiety can spur you on to greater achievement, provided, of course, all this nervous energy is channelled productively.

Even experienced speakers can get nervous when put upon without notice:

> *'Hi! Sally, spare a minute? I've got Sir Peter in my office. Could you fill him in on our plans for next year's sales campaign. We really need his support.'*

Hardly an enviable situation! But you can apply many of the ideas in this chapter to impromptu presentations. You will find them especially useful in those all-important discussion groups and meetings where decisions affecting your future are made—just when you most need to influence the decision-makers.

The benefits

Do your ideas receive less consideration than they deserve? Maybe you're not putting them across convincingly. See how you can make friends and allies who will support your views, so more decisions go the way you want.

Perhaps you feel you *could* be more convincing if only you had more time to prepare. Well then, you need a really efficient system where little or no effort is wasted. That should help free the extra time you need to do the job properly.

WHAT MAKES A SUCCESSFUL PRESENTATION?

Communication has been described as the art of being understood. For some presentations that may be all you require. More often you will be trying to influence people. Influential speakers don't just change other people's knowledge; they change their attitudes and their beliefs, and so influence future events. Influencing others is your means of getting them to commit themselves to your plans.

To increase the effectiveness of your speaking, you will need to create a rapport with your audience. Do this by responding to their needs. Select the right material, pitch it at the right level, and put it across in a style they appreciate.

Benefits for all

The audience will find your presentations:

- Clearer and more easily understood.
- More relevant and interesting.
- More brief and to the point.

And for you, the speaker, they will be:

- More influential.
- Easier to remember.
- Less time-consuming to prepare.

Steps to success

Break the task down into stages, dealing with each one in turn. After all, is there any point in worrying about preparing the venue if you don't even know why you are giving the talk, who will come, or whether a memo would do the job just as well?

Here is such a structured approach:

Fig 4.1

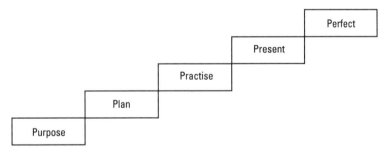

- **Clearly define the purpose**
  Understand the problem before building the solution. The biggest difficulty is often finding out exactly what your audience expect to get from your talk.
- **Plan and prepare the talk**
  Decide what you need to say and what visual aids could help get your message across.
- **Practise and polish the presentation**
  Never omit the rehearsals; they are a mark of professionalism.
- **Present the talk**
  Make the most of both visual and vocal communication by using body language and voice emphasis to reinforce your words.
- **Set improvement targets for next time**
  Collect feedback both on the content and style of your presentation. Then create an action plan so that your next presentation is even more successful.

4.1 SETTING OBJECTIVES AND PRIORITIES

Before preparing your presentation you need to know who will attend and what they expect to get from attending. Only then can you decide whether the presentation could help you achieve *your* aims. (Would it not, for example, be better to write to each person, or to see them individually?)

Is a presentation the right approach?

Talking face-to-face with people is often the best way of winning their support because:

- It is easier to show how strongly you *feel* about a subject, so you need fewer words to put across the same information.
- You have the opportunity to monitor audience reaction; if they aren't listening, don't understand, or don't agree with you, then you can take corrective action.

If you can't benefit from these features of a live presentation, maybe you should play safe and write to your audience, when:

- It is easy to hide your emotions, especially annoyance or anxiety.
- Complicated messages can be edited before they are sent.
- Each of the readers can study the information at their own pace.
- The writer and readers give up time each at their own convenience, and they don't have to gather in one place.
- Questions about the message are usually in writing, giving you time to research your answers.

Find out what your audience want

Try to discover, if necessary by asking a few questions before making your plan:

- What they expect to get out of the presentation.
- Their views on the relative importance of topics.
- How much they know already about the subject.
- How much time they are prepared to give you.
- Their likely responses - who will be supporters and who opponents.

If all of your audience need the same amount of detail and have much the same prior knowledge of the subject, then make just one presentation. Even where each group needs only part of the information, you could still present a common core, with the more specialist material on hand-outs to be studied after the presentation. But if there is no common core, make separate presentations, each tailored to specific needs; otherwise you could bore or confuse people.

Be clear about your own aims and priorities

If you don't first give your audience what *they* want, you will find it hard to win allies to your cause. So, make your presentation audience-centred, at least at the outset. Later, when you have broken through any barriers of indifference, suspicion or outright hostility, you can begin putting across your own views and testing for their acceptance.

If there is one key decision-maker in the audience, plan most of your talk to provide what this person needs, allocating time according to their priorities. You can then weave in other messages directed at those individuals in the group who have influence with the decision-maker.

EXAMPLE

Janet Masters is the manager of FICO's design department. She has to present to senior management her proposal for full development of a new product. The new machine, an automatic, format-sensing laminator, would be capable of encapsulating in clear plastic any flat material, from a business card to a large engineering drawing. Janet wonders whether she could later re-use the presentation to interest customers in the product.

Audience concerns	Priorities—low, medium, high	
	Directors	Customers
What does the new product do?	M	H
How, exactly, does it work?	M	L
Why is it better than existing products?	H	H
When will it be available?	H	H
What production equipment is needed?	H	L
How profitable will it be?	H	?
Who will manage this product?	H	?

There is an obvious conflict of interests: the two groups have different needs and priorities. The directors say they want a half-hour presentation followed by a question and answer session. But Janet knows that few customers can spare more than fifteen minutes, including a hands-on session where they try out the machine. Not only that, but some of the information the directors require Janet would certainly not want her customers to hear about—like how much profit the company will be making on the deal!

Janet decides to go for two separate presentations:

Topic	Directors	Customers
What the product does	3 minutes	1 minute
Why it is better than existing products on the market	10 minutes	3 minutes
Expected cost savings and other benefits to the user	2 minutes	5 minutes
What new production facilities will be needed	5 minutes	Not planned
A schedule of events up to full production	4 minutes	Not planned
How soon the product will be delivered if ordered now	Not planned	1 minute
Investment and return summary showing forecast profit	6 minutes	Not planned
A hands-on demonstration for all who are interested	Not planned	As required
Total time (minutes)	**30 minutes**	**10 minutes +**

The 'Pet subject' trap

As a professional engineer, Janet could easily fall into the trap of spending too much time explaining just how the product works. She must resist this temptation and concentrate on the high-priority items on the audience's needs list. Of course, if some of her customers have a technical background, she might say:

> 'You may be wondering just how the machine knows what size your document is. Well, our engineers solved that problem in quite a novel way—remarkably simple, as all the best inventions are. And it's extremely reliable. If you can spare a few minutes afterwards you might like to see inside the machine. But for now, let's move on to the installation aspects...'

4.2 GATHERING AND STRUCTURING THE INFORMATION

A common method of preparing a presentation is the 'collect and sift' approach. This simply involves gathering everything that might be useful, before sorting it into categories. The hope is that the information itself could spark off useful ideas on how to organize the flow of your talk. This isn't a bad approach if you have plenty of time and things are a bit slack at work. Enough said?

There is a more structured approach. Here you consider various ways to organize the material for your presentation, and then choose the best of these structures. This approach has the advantage of time-efficiency: you only gather the information you need. It requires thought, however, or you could plump for a far from ideal structure.

You could decide on a structure by brainstorming several alternatives, assessing each from the viewpoint of your most important audience group. Which of the options makes for ease of understanding? If more than one meets this criterion then consider other factors—for example, which would be the most entertaining?

The next step is to decide on the topics to include under each heading:

- Allocate time to each main section according to the priorities of the most important audience group.
- Don't allow material required only by secondary audience groups to dilute the impact of your presentation on the key decision-makers.
- Provide specialist information as hand-outs to be studied before or after the presentation. Alternatively, offer a follow-up session to discuss technical details.

Timing

On your lists of points—corresponding to *spoken paragraphs*—make a guess at timing. Allow about one or two points per minute, but remember to add in more time if you are demonstrating equipment or showing slides people will need to study.

Your topic list for a twenty minute presentation could have between twenty and forty subheadings as a first draft. The rehearsal will show whether changes are needed.

Headings that work

Make your headings earn their keep. They should work for the audience *and* for you. Copy them onto your cue cards and speak them loud and clear at the start of a new topic.

Just imagine rounding off a topic and losing track of what comes next. You glance at your cue card to find the single word: **CONCLUSION**.

What a great memory jogger that is! Instead, how about:

WELL, SO MUCH FOR TECHNICALITIES. FINALLY A LOOK AT PROGRESS.

- COSTS—NOW UNDER CONTROL.
- PROGRAMME SLIPPAGE—LARGELY CORRECTED.
- STAFF SHORTAGES—SOLVED BY SUBCONTRACTING ASSEMBLY WORK.

These are user-friendly prompts. With help like this there's every chance you can get back into your stride and complete your presentation in a confident, dynamic style.

EXAMPLES

Convenient vs. helpful structures

Suppose you have to make a presentation about personal computers. How can you structure your talk? There are so many options:

- Early computers/modern electronic computers/future trends.
- Personal computer hardware/operating systems/applications software.
- Glass parts of a personal computer/the metal parts/the plastic parts.
- Choosing a computer/using a computer/what to do if your computer goes wrong.
- How to design a computer/how to build a computer/how to test a computer.

What about the audience? Are they historians, science students, scrap merchants, grocers hoping to automate their accounts, or electronics hobby enthusiasts?

Suppose your audience is senior management, whose approval you need for investing in a desktop publishing system. You may have to choose between keeping your most interesting material until the end, or opting for a structure which is easiest for the audience to follow, even though it leaves rather pedestrian material to last.

Structure 1		Structure 2	
1 The DTP software		**1 Problems with our present method**	
	1.1 What it can do		1.1 Slow response
	1.2 How it is used		1.2 Poor graphics
	1.3 Hardware needs		
2 The hardware		**2 Advantages of proposed DTP system**	
	2.1 The computer		2.1 Speed and flexibility
	2.2 The scanner		2.2 Improved graphics
	2.3 The laser printer	**3 Cost-benefit justification**	
3 The costs			3.1 Cost-benefit analysis
	3.1 Hardware costs		3.2 Return on investment
	3.2 Software costs	**4 Plan for introduction and operation**	

Structure 1 is convenient for collecting the data, but is it suitable for a selling presentation? A better approach—structure 2—is to seek acceptance that there is a problem, before proposing a solution.

A place for humour

For a long presentation—and twenty minutes is a long time to expect people to listen attentively to one speaker—try to introduce changes of tone. Humour, at the right times and in sensible doses, can help people relax. Afterwards, they may listen with renewed interest to more of the serious stuff.

Unless you have the reputation for being a funny person, jokes are not the best way to introduce humour. Obvious understatement, or a throw-away line with a long pause is all you need to help the audience see a difficult problem in perspective:

'Well, the news isn't bad. We're on the short list. But we've really got to win this one, and we know Dempsters will be in there. They beat us on the Norwegian contract, so we'll have to do something pretty smart to turn the tables this time.' (Pauses and smiles) *'Unless you fancy being runner up in a fight to the death.'*

4.3 PREPARING YOURSELF

The presentation plan answers the questions *'Why?'* and *'Who?'*—why are you making the presentation, and who is going to be in the audience? Keep the answers to these questions prominent on your desk while you deal with the next stage, preparing yourself for the event by deciding how you will put your information across in the right order and within your time allocation.

How will you remember it all?

The first step is to put all the facts and figures into your structure. Then you will probably need some system to remind yourself of the sequence of events. For a formal presentation to a large audience—a new product launch, for example—you may need the impact of colour slides, large-screen video and the like. These events need complete scripting and many rehearsals to get the timing right, otherwise they can turn into costly disasters.

Cue cards are much better than a full script when talking to small audiences. You maintain eye contact with your audience and see how they *feel* about what you are saying. Work from brief notes—headings and subheadings with an indication of when to show slides, etc.—all marked in block capitals on index cards. Remember to number the cards. (You will be glad you did if you should drop them during your talk!)

If it helps you feel more confident, write the opening sentence or two in full on your first cue card. Mark key words with a highlighting pen, so as soon as you feel at ease you can stop reading, knowing your cue card is available if you need it.

Decide what is best put across visually and what they need to hear from you. Where you plan to show a slide, decide what, if anything, you need to say to make the message complete. Don't be afraid of silence; it has an important place in presentations.

Can you really say that?

Rehearse what you intend saying, and do so *out loud*, perhaps making a tape recording, as some words and phrases are easier to read to yourself than to say to others.

Try out the timing

Few business presentations keep to schedule; let yours be the exception. It's easier to keep to schedule if your plan is detailed, with time allocations to each section of the talk. You could try setting a large-faced watch to the hour at the beginning of your talk; then minutes past the hour show the elapsed time.

What if?

Few projects go exactly to plan, and presentations are no exception. Make provision for dealing with difficulties by asking yourself, in advance:

- What could they have difficulty understanding?
- What might they find hard to believe?
- What can I do to solve these problems if they arise?

Provide for these eventualities by having available extra examples and case studies, or a practical demonstration. If necessary, you will have to cut later material to keep to your time allocation. Decide in advance what you will sacrifice if you find yourself overrunning.

EXAMPLE: # A CUSTOMER PRESENTATION

Vanessa Tippet is UK sales manager for FICO, a training aids company specializing in audiovisual and multimedia equipment. Her main customers are large organizations who run their own in-house training courses.

FICO recently launched the Autojector, an overhead projector which automatically senses the size of both the slide and the display screen, and centres a perfectly focused, full-screen image. Now Vanessa is finalizing her on-site presentation to potential customers, most of whom attended the official launch at the National Exhibition Centre.

Planning for problems

The product launch went well, except that security radio systems caused interference with the auto-centring circuitry. This caused adverse press comment. The design engineer has now fitted interference suppressors to the Autojector, but Vanessa knows her customers will want assuring the problem has been fixed once and for all.

Should Vanessa raise the problem, or leave it to the customer to do so? She decides to make no big issue of it:

> *'At the product launch you may have noticed, because of interference from the security radios in the hall, we had to use the manual centring and focusing controls. We weren't too happy about that, so we got our engineers to fit extra suppression circuits. But now I'd like to move on to the special warranty terms...'*

Just in case she gets quizzed on the matter of interference suppression, or sees some of her audience looking uncomfortable at this point, Vanessa has a couple of slides available. One gives details of the r.f. interference testing which the final production units undergo—reassurance to any technical experts present. The other is a Certificate of Compliance with international regulations on radio-frequency interference and susceptibility, issued by an independent testing authority.

Vanessa's cue cards not only contain reminders on *what* to say, they also prompt her on *how* to put it across. She has added a column showing where she intends to speed up, slow down or pause for emphasis.

Fig 4.2

SECTION 1: WHY CHOOSE THE AUTOJECTOR?			
REF.	WHAT TO SAY	WHAT TO SHOW	WHAT TO DO
1.4	STRESS BENEFITS OF AUTOSET FACILITY	OHP 2	MOVE QUICKLY TO CENTRE STAGE SPEAK **SLOWLY!**
1.5	REMAIN SILENT	VIDEO TAPE DEMO	**LOOK** FOR AUDIENCE REACTIONS
1.6	SUMMARIZE PERFORMANCE	NO SLIDE	LOOK AND SOUND CONFIDENT SPEAK **MORE QUICKLY!**
1.7	INVITE QUESTIONS ON SECTION 1	NO SLIDE	**MOVE FORWARD** TO AUDIENCE
1.8	THANK QUESTIONERS	NO SLIDE	RETURN TO LECTERN. **SMILE!**

4.4 CHOOSING, PREPARING AND USING VISUAL AIDS

A picture says a thousand words... and that's great, if they're the right words! Every visual aid you use should have just one clear message. Slides should either speak for themselves, in which case you must remain silent while the audience studies them, or they should reinforce (not compete with) what you say. Ideally, decide on the type of image you want and then choose the best medium to project it. In practice, however, you will have to limit yourself to just one or two media. You might use an overhead projector or a 35 mm slide projector for your stills, together with a working model, a piece of cine film or a video when you need to show action.

For small audience presentations—up to 30 people—give preference to visual aids you can use without darkening the room. Dimmed lighting means loss of eye contact. And don't forget, facial expressions are the best visual aid for showing how you feel about what you are saying. Help those at the back of the room by using slightly exaggerated expressions and hold them a little longer than you would in one-to-one conversation.

For OHP slides, keep your diagrams simple. Include only the detail necessary to illustrate your point. Text slides, too, are best kept as brief bullet lists to serve as milestones for you and your audience. If you need more than eight items on a bullet list, gather similar items together into groups and show one group at a time. Text slides soon lose impact if they follow in rapid succession, so try to intersperse them with other graphics.

Selecting visual aid media

This chart could help you decide how to display visual material.

Medium	Practicable group size	Required lighting	Cost to produce	Ease of use	Visual impact
OHP	up to 100	any	moderate	moderate	moderate
Flip chart	up to 30	bright	low	fairly difficult	low
Writing board	up to 30	bright	very low	difficult	very low
35 mm slides	up to 100	darkened	moderate	moderate	high
Video film	up to 30	dimly lit	high	easy	high
Cine film	up to 1000	darkened	very high	easy	very high

Testing your projectors

Here are some points to check if you intend using slide projectors:

- Check that your lens has the correct focal length to fill the screen.
- Clean the lens to get a clear image.
- If your screen is adjustable, tilt it to obtain a rectangular image.
- Make sure that your slides fit onto the OHP without losing details at the edges.
- Find out how to switch in the spare lamp bulb.
- If you intend showing 35 mm slides, run through the sequence checking they are all the right way up and none are back to front.
- Before using a projector with a remote control, find out which buttons control forward and reverse sequencing.

EXAMPLE

Here is a draft OHP slide for use in a talk by John Harman, site services manager of FICO Ltd. John is explaining to senior staff the plans for moving to new office premises.

Fig 4.3

```
DESIGN FACTORS TO BE CONSIDERED
WHEN PLANNING THE NEW OFFICES
We must improve security, especially at night.
The Driveway should be clear for deliveries.
A new computer system will be delivered soon
after the building opens, and that will cause
problems.
There should be a plan showing where each
department will be located.
The existing telephones will be moved to the new
building.
```

It is a poor slide for several reasons:

- The heading is long-winded and repeats the title of the presentation.
- There is no margin around the slide, and this makes reading the characters at the edges difficult.
- Whole sentences make the speaker redundant, rather than focusing attention on what he is saying.
- The slide is over-full; people will read ahead instead of listening to what is being said.

As a result, the slide lacks impact and the impression is of a very amateur job.

In contrast, here is John's improved version.

Fig 4.4

```
            DESIGN FACTORS
            ──────────────

            ● Security
            ● Access for deliveries
            ● Computer facilities
            ● Floor plan
            ● Telephone system


              ( FICO (UK) Ltd )
```

This slide took less time to prepare, and it is better because:

- The heading is attention-grabbing.
- Bullet lines focus interest on key topics, leaving the speaker to put across the message.
- There is plenty of white space: text is kept well away from the edges of the slide.
- The company logo helps convey an impression of professionalism.

Creating picture slides

When he wants to show a floor layout, John retains the same slide format, either using a graphics program to build up an image, or sketching on paper and using a scanner to import pictures onto his slide frame. In either case he uses a prepared blank already containing the heading and company logo.

PREPARING THE VENUE

A comfortable audience is more likely to listen to and think about what you have to say. So, make sure the venue suits the size of audience you expect. The atmosphere will be all wrong if you have ten people in a room suited to 100. Similarly, avoid packing 20 people into a stuffy office with inadequate seating.

Here are some other points to look for when you check out the venue.

Preparing the room

- If the room has a telephone, disconnect it or divert all incoming calls.
- Put a notice outside the room so that other people don't barge in on the presentation.
- Plan the seating so that everyone can see you *and* the projector screen.
- Arrange catering if necessary. A break *is* necessary if your talk runs to more than an hour. Arrange for the tea or coffee to be ready at a prearranged time, but only to be brought in when you give the signal.
- Check the operation of light switches and dimmers, and heating and ventilation controls. Make sure you can see your notes if the main lights are to be dimmed.

Preparing the audiovisual equipment

- You may need a microphone and amplifier for gatherings of 100 or more. Check this out beforehand, and note the volume control setting which allows you to be heard clearly at the back of the room.
- Tape down any mains or control cables where they won't trip people up.
- Don't stand your overhead projector on the presenter's table, where it could block someone's view. Use a low table or stool.
- Make sure you can find the projector On/Off switch. It's amazing how often presentations begin with:

   'I'd like to begin by showing a slide of... Er... sorry, just a minute... Oh blast! Anybody know how to get this thing to work?'

Preparing hand-outs and working demonstrations

- Never leave your hand-outs near the door where people can pick them up on the way in. Have them in labelled sets where you can easily reach them at the end of your talk. That way, people won't be tempted to read them instead of listening.
- If you intend pointing out features on demonstration equipment, or drawing attention to particular points on OHP slides, you will need a pointer. The telescopic ones are convenient for carrying, but beware: many presenters unconsciously fiddle with them as if demonstrating the workings of a bicycle pump. Put the pointer down when you're not using it.
- Test working models thoroughly, and don't be tempted to extend your demonstration into areas not tried in rehearsal. Many working models seem to develop stage fright at the crucial moment!

Final trials

If possible, run through your final rehearsal in the presentation room itself. This way you can iron out any problems and get used to the layout before the real event, so that when you go live your audience will have your full attention.

EXAMPLE: **ROOM LAYOUTS**

A poorly designed room layout

Fig 4.5

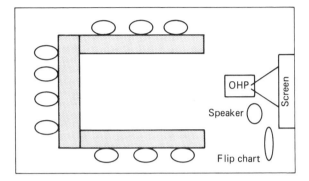

This presentation room has been badly designed. Used as it is, some members of the audience will have difficulty seeing the slides because the presenter will be in their way.

Making the best of it

Fig 4.6

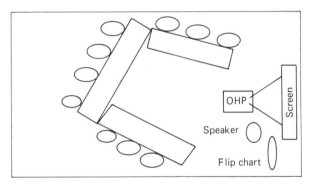

Here the organizer has rearranged the seating so that the audience focus mainly upon the presenter, turning their heads when they need to look at the projector screen.

A well-designed presentation room

Fig 4.7

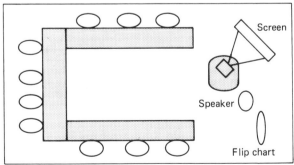

With this layout all members of the audience can see the presenter and the screen.
All of these layouts are for a right-handed presenter. For a left-handed person, position the projector on your left and move the flip chart to the other side of the stage.

4.6 OPENING, DEVELOPMENT AND CLOSING

First impressions are so important! A fumbled introduction can undermine your credibility and erode your self-confidence. So choose an interesting opening, and rehearse it thoroughly. Make sure you can easily get your tongue round the words. It's no fun stumbling, as once did a radio reporter, over a tongue twister like:

> '...at the scene of the fire at the Firestone tyre factory.'

After introducing yourself you *could* follow the well-worn approach of: tell them what they're going to hear; tell them; tell them what they've just heard.

You could indeed! But all too often this leads to a dull presentation, with the audience finding it hard to hide their impatience when it all comes round for the third time.

Openings that work

For a presentation where you know that your audience is anxious to receive the information you have to give, useful openings include:

- An outline of the scope you intend covering.
- A quotation from an authoritative source, or a relevant anecdote, setting the scene.

But where your intention is to influence the opinions of your audience or to change their attitudes, you might be better off with:

- A rhetorical question which sets them thinking from a different viewpoint.
- The statement of some fact or other which will come as a surprise to them.

A good selling presentation should open by capturing the attention. Avoid putting across the really interesting part of your message until you are sure everyone is listening. A simple 'Good evening', is not always enough. If necessary, use a more dramatic approach—the unexpected is often better than the traditional opening—and involve your audience right from the start. Refer to them directly:

> 'Have you ever wondered why...'

rather than

> 'I've often wondered why'

Features don't sell

People buy goods, services, and ideas too, not for their features, but for the benefits they offer. So, in developing your theme, remember to link each feature of your offer to benefits expressed from the audience's point of view. And if there are weaknesses in your proposal, spell them out yourself, but in such a way that the audience can accept the limitations as a reasonable price to pay for the benefits you are offering.

Make general points first; then home in on the specific. Take your audience in steps from what they know, understand and accept towards the conclusion you want them to draw.

Close quickly and cleanly

The final part of your presentation must leave a lasting impression with your audience, so rehearse the close as thoroughly as you do the opening. Whether you decide to restate the purpose of the presentation, to summarize, or to call for some action or other from your audience, don't ramble. Be brief. Finish, as you started, on an *up* note.

EXAMPLES Self-centred presentations are a real turn-off. Show your audience you have thought of *them* and what *they* need to get from your talk.

Opening windows

The double glazing salesman who begins his sales presentation with:

> *'Hi there! I'm really having a great day. I've made my monthly target in three hours, and still the orders come pouring in... which is what I want to talk to you about...'*

is unlikely to do well. A better opening might be:

> *'Hello. Your name was given to me as someone concerned about reducing waste and environmental pollution. Now I've brought some facts and figures to show how I could help. Can you spare a couple of minutes?'*

OK! Perhaps you've heard something along these lines before, but it stands more chance than the self-centred approach.

A benefit-based theme

Vanessa Tippet is talking about the auto-setting features of her new projector, but she is *selling* the benefits of ease of operation and more influential presentations.

> *'Notice every slide fills the screen with a pin-sharp image. This means your graphics have maximum impact, and any text is as large as possible. And you never need to break the flow of your presentation to fine-tune the focus.'*

The hurried departure

John Harman's talk on the site reorganization is lively and interesting, and it is put across with confidence. The problem is, John does everything in a hurry, never giving people a moment to absorb one point before rushing on to the next. He concludes with:

> *'So, there you are. It's all fairly cut and dried. But if you see any snags, let us know and we'll try to head them off. Just give my office a call on extension 276. We're always pleased to help; that's what we're here for.'*

Unfortunately, John is already halfway across the stage as he gives out his phone number, so the microphone doesn't pick it up. People get the impression their views are of no concern to him. He should have remained at the lectern, looking around the audience to make sure everyone had heard and understood his concluding point.

The reluctant departure

Janet has been nervous about her presentation to senior management. But as she gets into the detail she finds her audience is really interested in the talk. She soon warms to the occasion, and when it comes time to sum up she doesn't want to stop. She inserts extra, unplanned details, quite out of sequence, hunts back for a previous slide which has become buried, and pads out her conclusion, leaving a vague and woolly impression:

> *'Well, I think that's just about all I've got to say on this... unless of course... no, perhaps not... in view of the time I think maybe I'd better leave it at that.'*

How much better if Janet had concluded with something positive:

> *'So there it is. A sound idea. A well-planned project. And a team capable of turning the idea into reality. Now what we need is your approval so we can get things under way and be first into the market place. Thank you.'*

4.7 PRESENTATION SKILLS

The differences between you and your audience are barriers to communication. But, of course, if they were exactly like you, knowing what you do and having the same values and beliefs as you, what would there be to talk about? You use your unique encoding system to turn your intentions into messages; they use their decoding systems to interpret what they see and hear. Communication succeeds when the two systems match closely.

Breaking down barriers

If they aren't listening, try to find out why and put things right. Perhaps they are uncomfortable. Or maybe you have upset them, either by ignoring them—a self-centred introduction can do this—or by talking down to them. If necessary, ask!

Getting your message across

Once people are listening to you, use listener-friendly language. This means:

- Use simple, everyday phrases and avoid jargon or abbreviations with which your audience might be unfamiliar.
- Involve your audience. Rhetorical questions get people thinking:

  'Have you ever stopped to work out the cost of queueing for the photocopier?'

Direct questions get even more involvement, but they can lead to loss of control:

  'Has anyone present ever driven an amphibious vehicle?'
  'Yes... It all came about when my Uncle Charlie, who was very fond of...'

- Emphasize key points. Speaking a little louder helps underline the importance of a message, but you will get more effect if you also slow down. Insert a slight pause before stressing a key word; this will jog the daydreamers back to consciousness. Used skilfully, silence is a most powerful means of emphasizing a key point.
- Use the full range of your voice. In normal conversation you speak slowly and with a deeper tone when discussing bad news or passing on warnings, and you speed up and use a lighter tone when the message is positive. Do this in presentations, too. Show your audience how enthusiastic you are about an idea by exaggerating, compared with a one-to-one situation, the emphasis you put on key words.
- Be yourself. Let your natural body language echo what you say. Don't stand like a statue. Change posture as you move from one topic to the next. Make the occasional emphatic gesture. Look confident. Show with facial expressions how you feel about what you are saying.

The value of rehearsals

A video camera at the initial rehearsal can be a great help. Record parts of the presentation from different positions in the room. This will show whether you are involving the whole of your audience through eye contact.

You will probably be pleased with how you look, but you might not like how you sound. This is quite normal: you are hearing your voice as others hear you, via the air, rather than as vibrations transmitted through your skull.

The video should convince you that from a distance both gestures and facial expressions need to be exaggerated or they pass unnoticed. Practise this art of exaggeration; it will prove invaluable.

EXAMPLE

While describing her company's new automatic projector, Vanessa Tippet is interrupted by Dave Wellbrook, an American customer. Wellbrook asks:

> *'We do a lot of lecture tours. How does this kit stand up to being trucked about?'*

Vanessa's reply is factual and positive, but she misses the chance to tune in to Dave's communication style:

> *'During extensive proving trials, the equipment was transported in lorries for several hundred miles without any problems.'*

It would have been better if Vanessa had used the words *'kit'* and *'truck'* in her reply.

Nervousness and posture problems

While rehearsing her presentation for senior management, Janet used a video camera. She was dismayed to see how nervous and inhibited she appeared. In trying to improve her posture she found the position of her hands had a marked effect.

What helped Janet most in controlling her pre-event anxiety was the knowledge that she was well prepared and rehearsed. Deep breathing and relaxation just before speaking helped reduce chest muscle tension. The rest was largely a matter of experience, and that came from practice. She had joined a debating group, and volunteered to give talks about her work to local schools where she could practise at very low risk.

In the live presentation, Janet avoided non-assertive postures, using her right hand to count down the points in her lists, to make the occasional emphatic gesture, and to invite questions at the end of her talk.

Setting the pace

John Harman knows he will have a hard job winning the support of Keith West, Office Services Manager of FICO. But Keith's commitment to the planned move is essential to its success. Keith is a very serious, cautious and analytical manager, not easily swayed by emotional outbursts. John normally speaks very quickly; but, when he comes to the part of the plan that involves Keith's team, he slows down, leaving longer pauses than usual at the ends of sentences. In this section of the talk, John looks at Keith and his team rather more frequently, but still involves the whole of the audience.

John starts by recognizing the source of Keith's reservations:

> *'Now there* are *going to be problems. And if we don't get the details right, we could end up worse off than before the move. This is where we need help, particularly from those with first-hand experience of what was wrong with the layout of the old building.'*

Speaking off the cuff

When Sally was put on the spot with little or no notice, she asked a question to find out how much her audience already knew about the subject. This gave her a few moments to gather and organize her thoughts.

As well as listening to the answer, she arranged her ideas into some sort of structure, and rehearsed the opening sentence in her head. Having made a good start she soon slipped into a more relaxed, conversational style; this invited further participation by the audience and took more of the pressure off her.

4.8 MANAGING QUESTION TIME

Question time can be a nightmare. No matter how well you know your material, there is always a chance you will be asked a question you cannot answer. So invite questions during your talk only if you are confident of your subject and feel able to keep control. Questions at the end are easier to manage, but could mean people who don't understand an early point give up trying to follow your argument.

Plan ahead. What questions are likely to arise? Rehearse your answers, perhaps with a slide or two, to cover these points. Your audience won't think you have failed them if you have to admit you don't know everything. Honesty is usually the best policy.

Guidelines for answering questions

- Don't interrupt the questioner, assuming you know the rest of the sentence. Unless a questioner rambles on interminably, wait to hear the whole question.
- If the question is a complex one, or expressed in terms that not all in the audience will understand, paraphrase it before answering.
- If you don't understand the question, ask for more details, the circumstances involved or an example.
- Look towards the questioner to see if your answer has been understood, but also check around the rest of the audience.
- Facial expressions can tell you if people are confused or disappointed by the answer to a question. Try to act on this visual feedback.
- Don't ridicule someone who asks what appears to be an elementary question. If everyone knew as much as you, there would be no need for your talk.
- Don't let one or two people hog the questioning; involve as many as you can.
- If you don't know the answer, be courageous and say so. Maybe you can suggest another source of help, or offer to get an answer later. The audience will appreciate the extra trouble you are going to for them.
- At the end of question time, thank your audience for participating. The chances are they will respond with a round of applause: a positive note on which to end.

Leaving hooks

Some members of the audience will want additional details on certain points. One strategy is to leave selected aspects dangling inconclusively as you move on to the next topic. Keep an eye out to see whether someone jots down a note at this point; then open the question session by looking towards the person who seized your *hook*. You can then be reasonably confident of being able to answer at least the first question!

Planted questions

You may be able to arrange for a friendly questioner to quiz you on something you are well prepared for. If you do this, make sure the planted question is one which is helpful to the rest of your audience, or the strategy could backfire on you.

Managing awkward questioners

If you have to present a paper where your competitors are present, expect questions aimed at catching you out. Avoid getting into a slanging match with the opposition. Ask the questioner to be brief, give an equally brief reply and offer to discuss any detailed technical matters with the questioner in a separate meeting. Your assertive behaviour will win you the respect of the rest of your audience.

EXAMPLES   Vanessa Tippet is confident she will be able to answer any questions arising from her presentation to potential customers. Aware that she might use terminology some customers are not familiar with, Vanessa opens her presentation with:

> *'As we go through the main features of the Autojector, please ask questions as they occur to you. There will also be the opportunity for discussion and any further questions at the end. So, let's start with the technical details...'*

In contrast, John Harman has to put across his plan for a major site reorganization to managers who have worked for the firm for many years. He needs to win their support, but many of them will be concerned they might lose out from the changes. John knows that the event could turn into an unproductive free-for-all. He decides to open with:

> *'I'm sure you are all as anxious as I am to make the site reorganization a success. But change is rarely welcome, and even this one is only partly our initiative: the new town bypass has forced our hand.'*
>
> *'Can I suggest you first hear the whole plan before commenting on individual parts. Then we can discuss how to minimize any problems the move might cause your departments. So if I can have your attention for about twenty minutes, we can then go into a question and answer session. Ken will note down any problems we'll need to sort out before the move gets under way.'*

A baited hook

Janet Masters knows that her MD is always impressed by innovative thinking. She plans to intrigue him with an unanswered question when she presents her case for development funding. Talking about the market opportunity, she concludes the topic with:

> *'... a major customer benefit which none of our competitors can offer. This will enable us to break totally new ground in marketing this laminator. Next, let's look at the manufacturing implications. The new machine will...'*

At the end of her presentation, Janet's first question comes from the MD:

> *'Janet, I'm happy at the moment with your technical proposal, and Jim will no doubt comment from the manufacturing side. But can I follow up a point you made on marketing. What did you mean, "breaking new ground", exactly?'*
>
> *'Well, our existing customers have decided on their laminating requirements before leasing a particular machine. When their requirements change—and with exhibition people that's quite frequent—we have to swap the machine and take back unused consumables...'*
>
> *'I think I follow your drift. You're saying we cut our own costs, so we can offer a better deal and increase our profitability. I see!'*

The MD turns to the rest of the board:

> *'We'll need to go through the figures, of course, but I like this idea. It could be the opportunity we've been looking for to get into wider markets with our laminators. Let's work on it. Thank you, Janet. Now, who else has got a question... Jim?'*

The whole tone of question time became positive because Janet left a hook for the most senior person to seize upon, and she had a well-thought-out answer.

CHECK-LIST: PRE-PRESENTATION QUESTIONNAIRE

Use this questionnaire to define your presentation objectives and budget. The answers will help you decide what to say and what to show, in what order, in how much detail and in what style.

Complete one questionnaire for each audience group, so you can easily compare their needs and priorities.

Presentation title:	
Date:	
Presenter(s):	
Who is going to attend and why?	
Audience group (or individual):	
Organization/department/job title:	
What do they need to learn from attending?	
What should they do/not do as a result?	
What is the single most important point for them?	
Do they realize why it is important?	
Will they need hand-outs or further discussions?	
Are they familiar with my terminology and jargon?	
Do they encounter this subject frequently?	
What outcome do I want?	
What is my most important point?	
Whom do I most need to convince?	
What kind of argument will convince him or her?	
What do I want to happen as a result?	
What is my budget?	
How much time will they want to give up?	
How much time can I afford for preparing?	
How much will the venue and visual aids cost?	
How many rehearsals are necessary?	
What sort of venue will I need?	
On-site or off-site location?	
Seating arrangements and number of places?	
What types of audiovisual aids?	
Any other points which could help me when making my plan?	

CHECK-LIST: POST-PRESENTATION QUESTIONNAIRE

After your talk, invite members of your audience to assess your performance using this questionnaire. Use their answers to create an action plan for your next presentation.

	4	3	2	1
Presentation title:				
Date:				
Presenter(s):				
Please mark your assessment here using: 4 = Excellent: continue doing it well 3 = Good: scope for minor improvements 2 = Fair: considerable improvement possible 1 = Weak: considerable improvement essential	4	3	2	1
How well were the venue and administrative matters organized?				
Did you get sufficient notice of date, venue & subject?				
Was the room comfortable and suitable for the purpose?				
Were unnecessary interruptions avoided?				
Was the room set out properly?				
Were all visual aids and hand-outs ready in advance?				
How well did the content of the presentation suit your needs?				
Was the content relevant and at the right depth?				
Was the time spent appropriate?				
Did you find the structure logical and easy to follow?				
Do you feel well informed as a result of the presentation?				
Did the presentation style help you concentrate on the subject?				
Were you able to see the speaker(s) and to hear clearly?				
Was the pace varied to suit the subject matter?				
Were important points emphasized well?				
Did the speaker(s) use body language to good effect?				
Were distracting mannerisms kept to a minimum?				
How well did the speaker(s) involve you via eye contact?				
How well were visual aids used to help speaker and audience?				
Did the speaker(s) use notes or cue cards effectively?				
Were all visual aids clear, relevant and helpful?				
Did the visual aids achieve a lasting impact?				
Were visual aids and any audio equipment used well?				

Improvement targets for next presentation:	

IMPROVE YOUR BUSINESS MEETINGS
AND WASTE LESS TIME IN OTHER PEOPLE'S BADLY MANAGED MEETINGS

Meetings can be great for communicating ideas, coordinating plans, solving problems and making decisions; they can also be a major cause of frustration. Waste ten minutes in a business meeting and the cost to your organization can be the same as wasting an hour on your own.

The challenge

When you need the expertise of several contributors, with differing personalities, priorities and prejudices, to work out some solution to a problem, keeping both the process and the people under control is difficult. Whether you attend as chairperson or as a participant, there are important skills which can help keep the meeting on course for success.

You need to plan and manage business meetings well and to use the right decision-making processes, so that you:

- Get all who attend to participate fully.
- Make effective decisions more quickly.
- Gain group commitment to turn the decisions into actions.

The benefits

Business meetings are a forum for demonstrating to others your professionalism as a manager. And if they are run properly, your meetings can also provide cost-effective training for your team.

But what about the many more meetings you attend where someone else is in the chair? Perhaps, far from contributing to team spirit, many of these are tedious, irrelevant and thoroughly demotivating. Well, some of the ideas in this chapter should at least help you to spend less time in abortive meetings, to contribute more effectively when you need to be there and to influence other chairpersons to do a better job, too.

Get it right and you should find you call fewer meetings and attend fewer meetings chaired by others. But you should get more done, both in the meetings you do attend *and* in the time you will have saved!

SUCCESS OR FAILURE?

Meetings can fail to achieve their purpose because the contributors arrive unprepared. Often this is because they don't know what the purpose is. (Sometimes they still don't know when the meeting breaks up!) Yet, even when all are well prepared, success is far from guaranteed. A meeting could fail to make decisions or it could make the wrong decisions. And even when good decisions are reached, defeat can be snatched from the jaws of victory if there is no plan for putting into action the intentions of the meeting. These are all failures of the meeting *process*.

When things start going wrong in meetings, people often feel under pressure. Then the unity of the group is really tested. Aggression, self-interest and apathy are enemies of group unity. They are tough adversaries. So why leave the task of holding the group together to the chairperson alone? All participants can help.

Steps to success

Some meetings fail because they are over-controlled, others because they degenerate into undisciplined arguments. Good meetings require of all participants the flexibility to react to changed circumstances, as well as reasonably strict timekeeping and an understanding of decision-making or problem-solving processes.

Fig 5.1

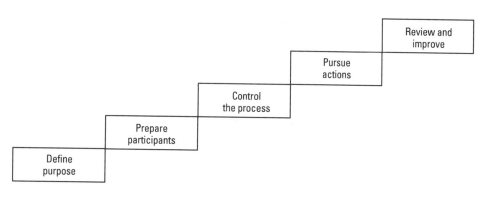

- **Before the meeting**
  Make sure you understand the problem you are trying to solve before you get together with other people to begin building a solution. And make sure everyone else understands: it is difficult to come to agreement on the solution if you are all aiming to solve different problems!

- **During the meeting**
  Things often go wrong right at the beginning of a meeting, either because the chairperson misdirects the group or because individuals behave in an uncooperative way. You need to make sure participants keep to the point and contribute in a constructive and cooperative way. This is a lot easier if the decision-making process has been agreed beforehand.

- **After the meeting**
  Turning decisions into actions requires clear concise minutes and an effective system for following up all of the actions agreed at the meeting. Then, critically reviewing achievements is the best way to improve future meetings.

TO MEET OR NOT TO MEET?

You have a problem to solve, information to share, people to persuade or consult. But is a meeting really necessary? Would getting together be the best way of dealing with the matter? There are several *wrong* reasons for holding a meeting. How about:

- But it's Friday morning, and we always have a meeting on Friday mornings...
- Well, we haven't got together for quite some time, so surely there must be things we ought to discuss...

But when there is a genuine reason for getting people face-to-face, what type of meeting should it be? Well, business meetings usually fall into one of the following categories:

1 **Meetings to inform**
   Here the purpose is to let others know of decisions already made or actions taken. For example, you may have had to make a hurried decision and now need others to know about it and, perhaps, to ratify it. The success of this type of meeting mainly depends on your credibility and your presentation skills.

2 **Meetings to persuade**
   Here one member puts a case to the meeting hoping to convince them to support a proposal. There may be conflict and counter-proposals, particularly where people come from different backgrounds and have differing priorities. Meetings between supplier and customer often fall into this mode at some stage. Your success in this type of meeting mainly depends on your influencing skills.

3 **Meetings to make decisions**
   These are information-seeking meetings where the chairperson encourages contributions from all present to build up a factual information base—for example before making decisions on targets or budgets. Success depends on all members preparing thoroughly, being willing to contribute and listening to the ideas of others.

4 **Meetings to solve problems**
   Ideally, the combined expertise of the group is brought to bear on a problem or a series of related problems. In reality these meetings often break down when participants discover that the chairperson has already chosen a solution and is merely trying to browbeat the group into agreement.

Decision-making and problem-solving meetings are the most difficult to manage. Unfortunately, the majority of business meetings seem to fall into these categories. They require careful planning and skilful control by the chairperson, and an understanding by all of effective problem-solving and decision-making processes—aspects we will concentrate on particularly here.

Problems bring with them problem people. When there are problems, many of us find it difficult to behave assertively. You can prevent your meetings, and those chaired by others, from breaking down if you recognize the symptoms early and take the right action to defuse conflict.

EXAMPLE

John Summers, FICO's training manager, had to to chair a meeting to arrange the training timetable for the year ahead. John was new to the job, and he wondered who to involve, what topics to put on the agenda, how long the meeting should take, and how the decisions should be made. Most of all John wanted to know exactly what the meeting should try to achieve. He needed to complete these sentences:

The purpose of this meeting is to...

This aim will have been met when...

John knew that all too often meetings are called with just an agenda—a series of topics for discussion. His meeting would have a clearly defined purpose; the agenda would then be the tactical plan for achieving this purpose. So John wrote the following and got the personnel director to approve it:

> *The purpose of this meeting is to make, and obtain commitment of department heads to, a plan for both customer training and staff development courses during 1994.*
> *This aim will have been met when we have answers to the questions 'What?' (courses), 'When?' (dates and times), 'Where?' (venues), 'How?' (training methods), and 'Who?' (trainers/delegates).*

How should he decide?

Two main factors influenced John's choice of decision-making process:

- Are some timetables better than others, or would any solution which fitted all the courses into the required time-scale be equally good? If not (and in this case solutions were not of equal merit), who has the expertise to produce a good enough timetable most quickly?
- Would trainers and delegates accept an imposed solution if they were not consulted? If not, who needs to be consulted in order for the timetable to gain acceptance?

Who should attend?

John knew an autocratic decision would not gain acceptance, even if he had the expertise to produce a good timetable. He needed to consult others who were both knowledgeable and sufficiently influential that their solution would be acceptable to all concerned. He needed help from:

- Those with the expertise to produce viable timetables.
- Those required to take actions and set up the courses.
- Those needed to approve decisions before actions can be taken.

That would have been a very large meeting. Instead, John invited four department heads responsible for different work areas and experienced in preparing previous years' training timetables. This team quickly produced a first rough plan, copies of which were sent to other senior managers, customers and training providers with a request that essential changes be marked and returned within two weeks.

There were few requests for change, and they were easily accommodated.

5.2 THE ART OF CHAIRING MEETINGS

The chairperson's job is extremely simple in principle, but far from simple in practice. The principles can be written in just a page:

1   Decide on the purpose and whose help you need. Call the smallest number of people possessing the expertise to achieve the purpose. If you need contributions from more than seven people, break up into smaller working parties. (Large groups are usually unproductive and always more difficult to control.)

2   Avoid multi-purpose meetings; they rarely succeed. If you have two or three unrelated problems to solve, deal with them in short separate meetings.

3   Give all participants enough notice and a clear statement of the purpose and the agenda—the steps towards meeting the purpose. Allocate time to agenda items according to how valuable (rather than just how difficult) their resolution is likely to be. And make sure if someone is required to bring information to the meeting that they know and accept this commitment.

4   Allow those invited to comment on the draft agenda. They may be able to suggest a valuable time-saving alteration, or know of something which should influence the ordering of items on your agenda.

5   Control the discussion so that it keeps to the agenda and time plan unless it becomes clear that the agenda is unsuitable—perhaps new information is available since it was drawn up—in which case get a revised agenda agreed.

6   Make sure that all participate; don't let the louder members of the group impose their views on the meeting or prevent less dominant members from contributing.

7   Make sure that the decision-making and problem-solving processes are agreed in advance for each agenda item; otherwise you may find valuable meeting time is spent arguing about the validity of the process rather than channelling energy into finding the best solution to the problem.

8   Summarize each decision and the basis on which it was made. Make brief notes (minutes) and provide copies to each member. Don't waste time and money on typing minutes if handwritten notes will suffice.

9   Follow up every action so that the decisions of the meeting are carried out effectively and on time.

10 Spend two or three minutes at the end of each meeting reviewing its effectiveness. Check on the timekeeping as well as the achievement, and agree actions to ensure future meetings are more effective. Write down these improvement targets so you can read them out at the beginning of the next meeting.

The most important points to remember are to have a *clear purpose* and a *proper agenda*.

That's what a good meeting is like. So why don't more meetings follow these principles? Here are three common reasons:

• Not all chairpersons know how meetings should be managed.
• Even those who do know often become so involved in the content of the discussion they forget about the meeting process.
• Contributors have their own motives, not always compatible with the meeting's aims.

EXAMPLE: # SETTING THE AGENDA

Here is an agenda circulated by Jim Salmon, commercial director of FICO Ltd:

Fig 5.2

MEETING, Conference Room A, at 9 a.m. next Monday, 7 October.
SUBJECT: Sales
   AGENDA
   1 Brochures
   2 Exhibitions
   3 Visits to customers
   4 Any other business
   Copies to
   J. Phillips; P. Van Kirst; V. N. Tippet   Signed: *J. Salmon*, **30 September**

What happens? Jean Phillips brings this year's results for review; Patrick Van Kirst plans brochures for next year's sales campaign; Vanessa Tippet prepares nothing, expecting to be *told* what is going to happen. The meeting takes three hours and gets nowhere.

A better approach

This is what Jim's agenda should have contained:

Fig 5.3

SALES MEETING, Conference Room A, at 9 a.m. next Monday, 7 October.

ATTENDANCE: J. Phillips; P. Van Kirst; V. N. Tippet; J. Salmon (chair)

The sales team needs to meet to plan next year's sales campaign and agree area targets and responsibilities. My suggestions for the agenda are as follows:

1 Brief review of this year's results to date on an area by area basis
Area managers: if your results differ from targets by more than 15 per cent please prepare a summary of the reasons, if known. 5 minutes per area, 20 minutes total.

2 Sales targets
To discuss and agree regional targets based on this year's results and trends. Note that divisional targets have been set; copies appended to this agenda. This is always difficult; any ideas on how we can streamline the process this year? I suggest a 30 minute slot for this item.

3 Brochure updates
All product managers please bring written outlines with changes prioritized as essential/desirable. 20 minutes on this subject.

4 Customer visits schedule
To discuss and agree a provisional plan and allocate responsibilities for each major client. 10 minutes should be enough.

Please let me have suggested additions/alterations to this agenda, and any ideas on item 2, by Friday 3 October at the latest, so I can circulate an updated agenda by the following Monday.

   Signed: _____*Jim Salmon*_____   Date: 30 September

Before you can make a decision you need options to choose from. Problem-solving is the way to discover what your options are.

New solutions or lost solutions?

Problems fall into two groups: those solved previously, where you need to find and reuse the previous solution, and new problems, where you are trying to find an as yet unknown way forward. Reading and consulting others will usually deal with the first type, which often amounts to logical fault-finding: 'it used to work, now it doesn't, so we need to find out what has changed'. Novel situations demand a more creative approach.

Brainstorming

Brainstorming is a powerful problem-solving approach for situations you come across for the first time. Here is how to manage a brainstorming meeting:

1 **Decide what outcome you want**
   Put the problem in a positive way, 'how can we...', and state the benefits of finding a good solution in '...so that...' form. Avoid suggesting a solution when you formulate the problem, as this can inhibit lateral thinking and narrow down your options. The more clearly you state your aims the easier problem-solving becomes.

2 **Generate ideas**
   Brainstorming meetings are a good way of maintaining motivation in the face of adversity. The chairperson invites the group to contribute ideas—possible solutions or suggestions which could trigger ideas from others. A recorder notes down the ideas on a whiteboard or flip chart. There is only one rule: *no analysis*. It is quite enough that most people play safe by analysing and censoring their own suggestions before they voice them. That's why it is better to complete the brainstorming session and have a short break before going into the analysis.

3 **Analyse the ideas**
   Where it is clear some suggestions are closely related, collect them into logical groups. To create a short list of ideas for further investigation, look for reasons for including each idea in the short list, not for excluding it. Initially, reject only those ideas which no one can see a use for. Now put your short list through an analytical decision process to see which are worth planning out in detail.

Problem-solving by analogy

This is a powerful technique for looking at a problem from a new angle. The group tries to find comparable situations, often in quite unrelated fields, and then analyses the problem in the comparable domain. For example, you might analyse a pilfering problem by comparing it with a cracked and leaking fuel tank which needs repair or replacement.

The power of competition

When faced with an apparently intractable problem, try splitting a group into two or three working parties, since small groups usually outperform larger ones when creativity and innovation are the keys to success. Not only will this avoid the effect where all go charging towards the first bit of firm ground which appears on the horizon (no matter how barren), but the element of competition spurs many people to strive harder.

EXAMPLES

Eliminating the impossible

Suppose a team of investigators are tasked with finding the cause of a plane crash. They will start by considering a very wide range of possibilities:

- Freak weather conditions, such as a direct lightning strike.
- Airframe structural failure due either to metal fatigue or to sabotage.
- Engine, control system or instrument failure.
- Pilot error.

...and so on. Then they apply a process of analysis: weather reports, flight data recordings and so on, gradually ruling out possibilities until, say, the failure is confined to the engines. Further investigations eliminate the fuel supply and lubrication, rotor blades etc., until the team are fairly sure a fractured shaft was responsible. At this stage other similar shafts could be inspected or subjected to fatigue testing. If no more shafts fail, the investigators go back a level and look elsewhere in the engine for a fault which could cause the same catastrophic results.

As Sherlock Holmes said, when you have eliminated the impossible, what remains is the truth—in this case, the solution to the problem.

Multi-solution problems

Now consider a team of designers, marketeers, manufacturing experts and accountants meeting to find a solution to their problem of falling market share in the 35 mm camera market. What can they do to recover the situation? The possibilities are virtually limitless, and most of them would have some effect on sales results. No longer are they looking for *the* answer, but one from a pool of many which vary in time-scale, cost, difficulty and risk. How will they know when they have found a good answer? Again, they put it to the test. If they fail, could the business afford another try? So here, cost of failure—financial, time-scale, market credibility—and the probability of success become key factors the meeting must feed forward to the decision-making stage. They must beware of the perpetual enemy of innovation—tunnel vision. They formulate a goal:

> *How can we increase our market share while maintaining return on investment at least at its present 28 per cent level?*

They come up with all sorts of ideas, some apparently nonsensical:

What could we change?	
Reduce our price?	Increase our price?
Reduce our costs?	Reduce our investment?
Use someone else's money?	Use someone else's customers?
Use someone else's factory?	Change the camera?
Sell more cameras?	Sell less cameras?

You may be able to imagine a scenario in which the company can move from any of these situations to the goal stated above. For example, what could you change about the customers? Their needs? Their preferences? Their knowledge? Their geographical location? Their wealth? And how could this help?

In this way, you fill in the steps between where you are now and where you want to be—a problem-solving process which relies on imagination. The analytical part, putting figures into spreadsheets, comes afterwards.

If you have more than one option (including leaving things as they are: the 'Do nothing' alternative), you need to make a choice of which one or ones to proceed with. If no one person has the expertise to make the decision, or if others need to be involved because it won't work out without their determination to succeed, then you will have to choose a group decision-making process.

Group decisions can be by consensus, where all support the choice, or by voting, where either a simple majority or some predetermined percentage decides which option is adopted. Voting is usually quicker, and works well where the success of the decision is little dependent upon the commitment of those outvoted. Consensus may take longer to achieve, but often talking through the pros and cons until everyone in the group is prepared to back the same option will lead to stronger commitment from members during the implementation stage.

Decision-making criteria

Consensus is more easily reached when the factors influencing a decision are objective and quantified, and when accurate data are available for each option. But it is easy to be misled by the style of presentation. For example, spreadsheet calculations of investment and return on competing projects may appear to show clearly which offers the best profitability, the most manageable cash flow or the shortest payback period. Often, however, the data are based on estimates or intelligent guesses. We cannot *know* how many units we will be able to sell into South America in three years' time, but the spreadsheet still has to contain an answer to this question. But using such a spreadsheet decision model, we can vary some of the unknowns through a range from our most pessimistic to our most optimistic forecast and see how this affects the attractiveness of each option.

Some decision bases may have to be subjective, with each group member rating the competing options as High, Moderate or Low against the various decision factors. (Star rating systems are a popular format.) The final ratings can be decided by consensus or by averaging the scores of all contributors to the meeting. Either way, it is best to get this process agreed *before* you start the analysis.

Building a decision base

Here are some guidelines for contributing to this type of group decision process:

- Decide on the decision factors and their relative importance before discussing any of the competing options. (Whenever possible, agree the decision factors and their weightings before you begin collecting data on competing options.)
- Present your views factually, without making emotional appeals for support.
- Don't browbeat others into submission. Reasoned argument is needed for making reasonable decisions.
- If others don't agree with you, try to find out why. What do they know that you don't?
- Avoid voting or averaging scores wherever possible, as these processes erode group unity.
- If a decision goes your way on one factor, don't feel you have to concede on something else. Do what you feel is right to get a good decision—a good option which will gain the support it needs to be implemented successfully.

EXAMPLE

A group of managers meets to choose the next generation of component test equipment. They list the factors they consider important in a compensatory decision base, where strength in one feature can offset weakness in another. The factors are given weightings, and members contribute their knowledge of possible products which might meet the need. In this example three options, A, B and C, are compared on cost effectiveness.

Calculating effectiveness

Each option is scored against the decision factors and compared with the ideal solution as an indication of its relative effectiveness. In the table below, option A is the most effective, scoring 31 points from a maximum of 40, or 77.5 per cent effectiveness. Option C is the least effective solution, providing only 55 per cent effectiveness. But before choosing, the team must also consider what value for money each option represents.

Decision factor		Weighting	Option A	Option B	Option C
1	Versatility	10	9	7	7
2	Throughput rate	8	5	7	3
3	Diagnostic capability	4	2	3	3
4	Statistics analysis	5	3	4	2
5	Upgrade facilities	3	3	1	3
6	Delivery	4	4	3	2
7	Maintenance support	6	4	4	2
Sum of factors:		40	31	30	22
X	Effectiveness	1.00	0.775	0.750	0.550
Purchase cost			£25 000	£36 500	£28 000
Annual running cost			£18 500	£12 000	£13 500
Y = Purchase cost/5 + Running cost			£22 500	£19 300	£19 100
Cost/effectiveness ratio (Y/X)			29 032	25 733	34 727
Relative cost/effectiveness			1.13	**1.00**	1.35

Weighing up the costs

Next, the annual cost of ownership—the purchase price divided by expected five-year life of the equipment, plus the estimated annual running cost—is calculated for each option. Dividing this figure by the effectiveness gives a cost/effectiveness (C/E) ratio. Finally, dividing all options by the lowest of these C/E ratios makes for easy comparison of options. Option B wins on cost-effectiveness, even though it is neither the most effective nor the least costly to purchase.

Alternative models

Consider the factor *versatility*—how broad a range of components the test equipment can handle. Equipment which cannot cope with any of the components currently being used in the factory should not be considered. The model can be made to reflect this by including a minimum performance threshold on some or all of the attributes, and awarding extra points for machines which exceed this minimum requirement.

Another approach which is sometimes useful is the lexicographic model. Here options are compared on the most important attribute. If two or more options draw, the next most important attribute is considered, and so on until there is a clear winner.

5.5 MAKING YOUR CONTRIBUTION

When you get invited to a meeting ask yourself:

- Do I understand the purpose, and what should be achieved under each agenda item? If the agenda is unclear—a series of headings, for example—ask the chairperson for more details and suggest any amendments to improve the meeting.
- What am I likely to be able to contribute, and what could I get out of this meeting? If the answer is 'not a lot', consider whether sending a written input and receiving a copy of the minutes would achieve much the same.
- What questions should I ask so that I can contribute fully to the decision-making? It's worth jotting these down as you prepare for the meeting.
- Do I need to be there full-time, or could I leave after making my contribution? You may want to influence the order of items on the agenda, so arrange this with the chairperson in advance.

If you do need to attend, prepare your contribution, turn up promptly, and be ready to take notes of any decisions and actions which affect you. Make constructive contributions to the discussion, and avoid dominating others who should be contributing.

It all sounds so simple, doesn't it? And so it would be, but for the presence of *other people*. If only *other people* were rational rather than emotional, business meetings would be so much easier. And boring.

Planning the people side

If you intend putting forward proposals which could raise conflict, be prepared. Plan strategically by asking yourself:

- What sore spots do I expect to find?
- Who will side with me?
- Who will oppose me?
- Who could be influenced by sound logic. (It's unlikely to be all of them!)
- What areas of agreement could be tackled first to create a more positive atmosphere? Bear in mind that most people have their best ideas early on in a meeting, so beware of dealing with trivial matters early on unless they are urgent.

Handling other people tactically (and tactfully)

If you do not get the expected reaction to your proposals then you must think on your feet. Here are some ideas to help you do this:

- Don't simply press on regardless; look and listen for signals of disagreement before they turn to aggression or resentment.
- Summarize your understanding of alternative points of view to clarify them if they appear confused. The others will usually appreciate being given time to think, too.
- Show firm but considerate (assertive) behaviour, don't become aggressive or resentful and don't cave in unless you really feel it is the right thing to do.
- Acknowledge when others are upset. Even though you don't agree with them, this often takes the heat out of the situation. Ignoring other people's frustration usually leads to increased tension or apathy, neither of which are helpful.
- If the chairperson doesn't summarize decisions and actions under one agenda item, do so yourself before the meeting moves on to the next item.

EXAMPLE

Dealing with difficult people

People usually take a more dominant stance when the issue is important to them and when they feel confident they have better information, greater expertise or more power than the opposition. They are more likely to cooperate if they respect or value their relationship with the person disagreeing with them, or if they recognize that they need the cooperation of their opponent to achieve a successful outcome. These attitudes will affect the behaviour of other people in the meeting:

- Aggression often provokes attack until one party or other backs down, usually with reluctance and resentment.
- Members who offer no contribution are often ignored by others.
- Accommodating people often get taken advantage of: familiarity breeds contempt.
- Assertive behaviour draws valuable contributions from those who would otherwise be disruptive, silent or volubly accommodating.

Meeting discipline can degenerate if the chairperson doesn't know how to manage difficult situations. Here are some common situations and ideas on how to manage them.

The latecomer

You *must* start on time, or people will drift in later and later to future meetings. If you can't deal with an item without inputs from latecomers then re-order the agenda so you can make a start. In the minutes, listing late arrivals as present *part-time* has a remarkable effect on punctuality for future meetings!

The talkative

If someone is taking too long to make a point, indicate the need for brevity. For example:

> Chairperson: 'Donna, can you explain—in about half a minute, which is all we've time for right now—the effects of this delay on our marketing plans?'

If Donna still insists on launching into a long speech, cut her short by latching on to a key phrase. For example:

> Donna: ... 'we see this as vitally important because...'
> Chairperson: 'Oh, I hadn't realized that. Er... Ted. Donna sees this as vitally *important*. From a publicity viewpoint, how significant are these changes?'

The silent

Silence can be difficult to interpret. Does it mean agreement, waiting to hear the views of others, or no contribution worth making? It could simply indicate tiredness, shyness or a hostile attitude to the meeting.

Wake up sleepers by asking them direct questions early on, and keep involving them.

Hostile behaviour often stems from resentment at having to attend or not being asked to chair the meeting. It is usually better to probe and allow affronted members to voice their feelings. You don't have to agree, but just listening can often help clear the air.

Encourage shy people by referring back to their contributions, showing you value their inputs. Junior participants often feel inhibited once their boss has spoken on a topic, particularly if they don't agree with the *official line*. Encourage their involvement by going up rather than down the pecking order when you call for ideas.

5.6 HOW TO SAVE TIME IN MEETINGS

If you attend only the meetings you *should* attend, and you leave once you have contributed and got all you can from being there, what more can you do? Well, how about cutting out some of the 40 to 50 per cent of irrelevant discussion which goes on in many meetings? (I got this figure from video recording business meetings and analysing them; what would the figure have been if people hadn't known they were being monitored?)

Spell out the time targets

If you are chairperson, mention the time allowance at the beginning of each agenda item:

> *'Well, the production targets took longer than planned, but let's move on to item four, maintenance schedules, where we might be able to recover some of the lost time. Jim, got a brief report for us?'*

As a contributor, you can show a sense of urgency by prefacing your inputs with:

> *'I'll keep my report brief; if anyone needs more details I'll be pleased to provide them outside the meeting without taking everyone else's time...'*

Be a clock watcher

If someone is rambling on, don't be too covert in checking your watch, particularly if the chairperson shows no sign of stepping in and taking control. And if you feel the meeting is going out of control, consider intervening with:

> *'Chairman, I can see we're not going to fit everything into the time slot we budgeted. (Was there a time budget?) I suggest we re-plan the rest of our agenda so we get the most important things finished.'*

When you get to the end, stop!

When a meeting has done its job, stop. Some people will continue talking even though they have nothing constructive to say. The chairperson should prevent this.

Of course, you shouldn't terminate a discussion just because you youself are getting confused. Nor should you close a meeting because it looks as if the outcome will be unpopular or not what you would have wanted. But there *are* good reasons for closing a meeting without resolving all matters on the agenda—for example when:

- You need inputs from people who are not present.
- Those present need time to gather more information or to consider something which has emerged during the discussion.
- The matter is more complicated than you thought, and it needs much more time than can be spared in the present meeting, or is simpler than expected and can be resolved by one or two people outside the meeting.
- The situation has changed and a decision is no longer required.

Finish on a positive note

Many people feel their time is being poorly spent in meetings—even in those which go well—so do end on a positive note, referring to the meeting's worthwhile achievements.

Next time...

If you need another meeting, get participants to check their diaries and agree the date and time. But before they leave do also check that the venue is available. This will save time phoning round later.

Finally, take a few extra seconds to thank participants for contributing!

EXAMPLES   Many of the interactions between people in meetings are no more than rituals where the outcomes are predetermined and quite irrelevant to the job in hand. Eric Berne, in his book *The Games People Play*, lists a great many of these time-wasting rituals. Here are two common examples (there are many more).

'Why don't you... Yes, but...'

Peter's project is falling behind schedule, and he feels powerless to prevent this. Ruth has some ideas which could help:

> Ruth: 'Well, Pete, how are things?'
> Pete: 'Hopeless. Every month we slip at least a week. My people are fed up with being criticized when it's not their fault. We're five short right now.'
> Ruth: 'Couldn't Personnel arrange a special recruitment campaign for you?'
> Pete: 'Yes, but it would be months before we would get anyone and we'd have missed the launch date by then.'
> Ruth: 'Well, what about internal transfers.'
> Pete: 'Yes, but you know the sorts of people you get: nobody worth their salt would ever be made available. Look, Ruth, if you can't come up with something sensible, don't waste my time with stupid suggestions!'

'Oh gawd ain't it awful'

This is the ever popular complaining game, where *they* are responsible for all wrongs:

> 'D'you know what they've done now? They've rearranged the lunch rota so a different department starts lunch every fifteen minutes. It'll never work, you see!'
> 'Yes, and another thing... why don't they get some decent letterheads, anyone would think they didn't need to win any more orders.'
> 'Even worse than that... d'you know what I heard they've decided now...'

Game roles

In most of these games there is a Victim and a Persecutor. There may be a Rescuer, too. Indeed, sometimes the Rescuer ends up being attacked by both Persecutor and Victim!

How to stop games

In moderation, games can make a positive contribution. The 'Oh gawd ain't it awful' game can help unite a group. But there is little point in unity unless it can be turned towards something positive, so it's worth knowing how to stop a game before it gets out of hand and somebody gets hurt (emotionally, at least). Games are spoilt by adult behaviour:

> 'What ideas have you considered so far, Pete?' calls for a positive response, and makes it more difficult for Pete to slide into the childish 'Yes but...' ritual.
> 'How can we prevent these problems...' takes the impetus out of the 'Oh gawd ain't it awful' game.

Rather like a joke the second time round, once you point out you recognize the game and know its outcome, few will want to continue playing.

5.7   MINUTES — WHY SPEND HOURS?

Minutes are the written *results* of a meeting; they are not meant to be a verbatim transcript of all that happens. Record the attendance, date, venue and apologies for absence where appropriate, and then keep the minutes to a brief summary of the agreements reached on each agenda item. Minutes of internal meetings can usually be handwritten; rarely is typing necessary. A pre-printed *Internal Meeting Minutes* form can save a lot of time.

At the end of discussion of each agenda item, the chairperson should summarize any decisions and list the actions which have been agreed. The person appointed to take the minutes can play an active role in the meeting, knowing that all that is needed is to note down these inter-item summaries. This way the minutes are ready for copying as soon as the meeting is over. In fact, if you hold a two minute post-meeting review the minutes could be copied and issued to participants before they leave the room. This should put an end to such lame excuses as:

> *'I couldn't get on with my actions: I hadn't received the minutes.'*

Actions

Actions are the way you get the decisions of the meeting carried out. Not every minute will have an action; some are for noting only. For example, a meeting may decide not to proceed with a proposed project. The minute would record this decision with a brief statement of why the project was cancelled.

Actions should be specific tasks, not general policies. They should be things which would not happen if the meeting had not been held. And avoid open ended commitments like:

> *Mr Jones to make sure this sort of breach of security never happens again.*

All actions should only be placed on people who are present at the meeting. If you need others outside the meeting group to undertake work defined by the meeting, then a member of the group should be actioned to arrange for this work to be done.

Every action should have an owner—*one person only*. There should be no shared responsibilities. If an action needs the expertise of two or more people, one of them should be the owner of the action, empowered by the meeting to call upon the resources of the others.

Make actions obvious

Actions can get overlooked if they are hidden in paragraphs of text. For example:

> *The matter of a venue provoked much debate. Eventually it was agreed that Mr Gable would investigate the availability of 'A' block conference room for this series of seminars, and he agreed to prepare a draft timetable before the next meeting.*

can be written so that the person actioned and the date by which the task must be completed are more conspicuous:

Minute ref	Decision	Action by	Completion date
94 / 21	Investigate the availability of A Block conference room for the TAG seminar series and circulate a draft timetable to steering committee members.	A. J. Gable	27/7/94

Meeting of: _____

Held at: _____ On _____ (Date)

Present _____ (Chairperson)

_____

_____

_____

_____

Apologies were received from: _____

Purpose of the meeting: _____

_____

Minutes

Minute ref	Decision	Action by	Completion date

Page No. ____ of ____

TURNING AGREEMENT INTO ACTION

All actions *must* be followed up. The credibility of the chairperson is soon eroded if nothing happens as a result of his or her meetings. Often the chairperson or minutes secretary has to chase members to ensure their actions are completed on time. This, however, is an inefficient method of progress chasing. It is better if the participant responsible for an action lets the chairperson know when it has been satisfactorily completed or if they find they are unlikely to be able to complete their actions by the agreed date. The chairperson may then be able to arrange extra help, or to transfer the action to someone who can meet the deadline.

Once all actions are completed, participants rarely need keep their copies of minutes of internal meetings. Instead they can rely on the minutes secretary to file a reference copy. (Sales of filing cabinets would plummet if managers followed this advice!)

What about actions not completed?

At the beginning of a meeting, hold a review of the minutes of the previous meeting. Go through each action in turn, thanking those responsible for completing on time. Be assertive; don't let renegades get away with it! Ask questions of the type:

> 'What has prevented you from completing this action, Jim?'
> 'What special measures did you take to try to recover the lost time?'
> 'How will you prevent the delays in completing this action from upsetting the rest of the programme?'

Don't give a new reference number to actions which are carried over. Include them, together with their *original* target dates, in the minutes of the next meeting. That way it soon becomes clear who repeatedly lets the team down. Group pressure may pull the delinquents back into line; if it does not, then warn them—privately, not in front of the whole group—that you will have to speak with their managers and get them replaced by someone who is more committed to the aims of the meeting. Remember, if the meeting fails to achieve its purpose, the chairperson must take responsibility. So the chairperson *must* stamp his or her authority on the meeting. This is particularly important in the following up of the actions.

Closing the loop

Measure the effectiveness of your meetings if you want them to improve. One way is to circulate a review questionnaire to all participants, asking for their assessment. Review the preparation, the meeting process, and the follow-up. Discuss with the group what improvements you want. Then, as you begin the next meeting, remind everyone of the aspects you intend improving this time round.

As a further refinement, why not get an independent observer to provide feedback to the group before you disperse? Although more costly, this might be worthwhile if your meetings frequently overrun or fail to achieve their aims. An alternative is to leave a video camcorder running in the corner of the room. People soon forget that the camera is there. Afterwards members of the group can review both the content and the process of the meeting at their leisure.

CHECK-LIST: HOW GOOD WAS THAT MEETING?

Use this questionnaire to review the effectiveness of your meeting and to set improvement targets for future meetings.

	4	3	2	1
Meeting title:				
Venue, date and time:				
Chairman:				
Please mark your assessment here using: 4 = Excellent: continue doing this well 3 = Good: scope for minor improvements 2 = Fair: much improvement is possible 1 = Weak: major improvement is essential	4	3	2	1
How well were participants briefed/prepared before attending?				
Was there appropriate notice of date, venue & subject?				
Was the room comfortable and suitable for the purpose?				
Were unnecessary interruptions avoided?				
Was the room reserved and set out appropriately?				
Was the aim of the meeting understood in advance?				
Were agendas and attachments sent well in advance?				
Did participants have a chance to influence the agenda?				
Were time allocations stated in the agenda?				
Were participants' contributions well prepared?				
Were the right people present?				
How well was the meeting managed?				
Did all participants turn up on time?				
Was time managed well during the meeting?				
Did the meeting stay on the agenda?				
Were problem-solving/decision processes appropriate?				
Was the discussion controlled assertively?				
Did participants listen attentively to other contributors?				
Were conflicts resolved without bullying?				
Were key points questioned and summarized?				
How effectively were decisions turned into actions?				
Were all decisions minuted clearly and concisely?				
Was each action, with date, accepted by one person?				
Were the minutes produced quickly (within 24 hours)?				
Were all actions completed on time?				
To what extent was the purpose of the meeting achieved?				

Improvement targets for next meeting	

DEVELOP YOUR INTERVIEWING AND NEGOTIATING SKILLS
AND LEARN TO CREATE WIN–WIN SITUATIONS

With the right people working together in a team, great achievements are possible. But for this to happen you must make the right selections in the first place, and then motivate and develop your team members. Selection interviews and performance appraisals are vital elements in your strategy for achieving this. They require careful planning and skilful execution. It's also likely you will need to use negotiating skills during these interviews, so we should cover this topic, too.

The challenge

Some of your most important management decisions will be made in selection interviews. Get them wrong and you may be made painfully aware of your mistakes for years, as you try to live and work alongside them. No amount of training can correct a really bad recruitment decision.

The benefits

Do you dread having to interview people almost as much as you dread being interviewed? Learn to create an atmosphere of cooperation and you will have no reason to fear being an interviewer.

Do your staff treat appraisal interviews as an opportunity to argue their case for a higher performance assessment? Turn the appraisal into a forward-looking process and you will find people more ready to discuss difficulties and ways of overcoming them.

Do you think negotiating is such a 'black art' that you can only 'play it by ear'? It needn't be so. There are well-proven negotiation processes to help you achieve an outcome favourable to you and to your organization. This need not necessarily be at the expense of those on the other side of the negotiating table; in part, at least, negotiations can also be turned into 'win–win' situations.

COOPERATION OR COMPETITION?

All too often, an interview is like a boxing match. At first the opponents circle cautiously, one stabbing out unexpected questions, the other covering up where possible, each looking for a chance to get the opponent against the ropes. Points are scored fairly evenly by both sides until one makes a tactical error, exposing a weakness. This is the signal for an all-out assault, with the victim, defeated and demoralized, perhaps spared total humiliation only by the time limit—saved by the bell.

But it need not be like this. With careful preparation, and use of assertive interviewing skills, you can confront the issues that matter without insulting or injuring the interview candidate. Both parties in a selection or an appraisal interview can benefit from the experience, provided the atmosphere is constructive and cooperative.

Negotiations need not be battles

Negotiations begin in a competitive way, sometimes even in a hostile environment. This barrier must be dismantled before real progress is possible. Successful negotiations end in harmony, with both sides committed to turning the agreement into reality. And for this to happen there must be some element of cooperation, at least in the later stages. Each party should feel that in the circumstances they have made worthwhile achievements in closing the deal.

Steps towards success

Frequently in interviews and negotiations there is a need to confront issues which one or the other party would prefer not to discuss. Here is a process which starts and finishes on a positive note:

Fig 6.1

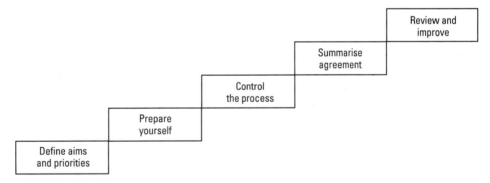

- Be clear what you hope to achieve and what your priorities are; and try to discover what those on the other side are likely to want.
- Gather and study information beforehand so that during the interview you can concentrate on listening and observing reactions.
- Discuss and agree the process before discussing the content.
- Remain flexible without losing control, and ensure the necessary content is covered.
- Look for common ground which can help you move towards solutions which benefit both sides.
- Summarize all agreements and get explicit commitment before leaving the interview room.
- Quickly follow up agreements with actions; don't leave it to the other side to take the initiative.
- Analyse successes and failures, and set improvement targets for the future.

6.1 DO INTERVIEWS WORK?

Interviewing a job applicant is just one stage in the selection process, and there is plenty of evidence that interviewing is an unreliable and unpredictable process. Research shows that, in general:

- The application form and the appearance of the candidate carry more weight than responses to interview questions.
- The offer/reject decision is usually made in the first four minutes, the rest of the time being spent gathering information to substantiate the decision.
- Interviewers tend to probe weaknesses and failures more than strengths and successes.
- Candidates are more often compared one with another, rather than against the job specification.
- Interviewers' prejudices and preferences influence not only their interviewing style but also their selection decisions: candidates with more in common with the interviewer get more favourable treatment.

So why bother?

It is precisely *because* interviewers and interviewees are human, with the human failings suggested above, that good interview techniques are necessary. Usually, people *need* to meet face to face before they will commit themselves wholeheartedly to a recruitment decision. Then if the interviewer chooses a candidate or the candidate chooses a job that is less than ideal, they usually work hard to overcome the resulting problems. There is little doubt, however, that skilful interviewing can increase the chance of selecting a candidate who will fit in and learn to cope well with the job.

Courses for horses

Before you can check whether a candidate matches a job vacancy, you need a clear idea of what the job involves, how it needs to be done, and how it interacts with other jobs within and outside the organization. This means gathering information about the job and deciding what sort of person would be best suited to doing the work.

Sources of candidates

Many vacancies are caused by promotion or retirement of people within the organization, and so it is natural to look internally for their replacements, too. However, people also leave to join other organizations, and it is equally important to bring in new talent with fresh ideas from outside. The optimum staff turnover figure is not zero!

You could find candidates for a vacancy in your department or team through:

- Internal advertisements and requests for transfer.
- A search through your organization's personnel records.
- Educational establishments.
- Local or national advertising.
- Government employment offices.
- Private employment bureaux.
- Recruitment consultants.
- Executive selection agencies.

EXAMPLE: **AN INTERVIEW PROCEDURE**

The system FICO use for approving and filling staff vacancies is shown below in flow chart form.

Fig 6.2

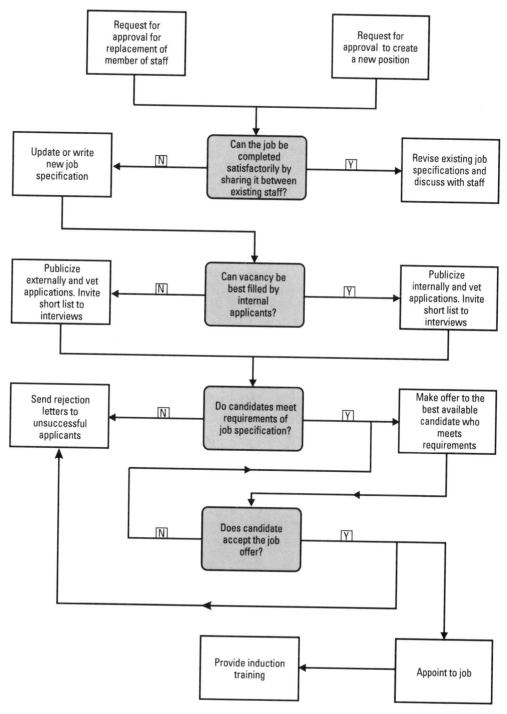

6.2 DEFINING THE REQUIREMENTS

The first step in recruitment is to define the requirements that job applicants should satisfy and the terms and conditions of employment you are able to offer.

Analysing the job

Collect information about the purpose of the job, and the tasks and responsibilities it entails. For this you may need to interview other people with whom the successful applicant will have to work, because you need to create a job specification which contains both a 'job description' and a 'person description'. You will probably have to include a summary of your findings in any job advertisement.

Writing the job specification

A job description should start with the purpose of the job. From this you can define the work which must be done to fulfil the purpose. In addition, for most jobs you will have to define:

- The division, location and department where the job holder will be based.
- The job title and level in the organization.
- The reporting structure both upwards and downwards from the job holder.
- Main responsibilities and duties.
- Any special tools or equipment the job holder will have to use, and any special requirements for communicating with people inside or outside the organization.
- Any other unusual requirements, such as hazardous working conditions, heavy lifting, shift work and so on.
- The support systems and resources which will be available to the job holder.

Next you need to describe the type of person who is best suited to the job. In the person description you will normally include:

- Qualifications and experience, with specific rather than general reference to specialist knowledge.
- Special skills and aptitudes. For example:

  'The job holder should be a skilled written and verbal communicator, and should be capable of planning and preparing customer training courses on existing and future product ranges.'

- Age or other special requirements of the job. For example:

  'This job is likely to appeal to persons under thirty who enjoy travel: periods of up to six months' overseas working may be involved.'

- Personality. For example:

  'The job holder must be decisive, with proven ability to impose his or her authority in times of crisis.'

Finally, make a note of the terms and conditions of employment, including salary range, fringe benefits, hours of work and holidays.

The information in the job specification is also used when drawing up a 'job vacancy' notice or advertisement.

EXAMPLES   This is the job specification form used by FICO for both internal and external recruitment.

FICO (UK) Ltd — Job specification	
Division	
Department	
Job title/grade	
Part I — Job description	
Job holder will report to	
Reporting to job holder	
Purpose of job	
Main responsibilities with duties and approximate time percentages	
Monetary and other decision making responsibilities	
Staff development responsibilities	
Relationship responsibility (customer/supplier liaison, etc.)	
Special requirements (Use of tools, equipment; shift/night work, travelling, etc.)	
Support systems and other resources available	
Part II - Person description	
Qualifications	
Skills and experience	
Special abilities (numerical, verbal, etc.)	
Physical requirements	
Personality (self-reliance, leadership, etc.)	
Circumstances (mobility, housing commitments, etc.)	

6.3   PLANNING THE ASSESSMENT

The interview is just one component—often the final one—in your decision base. Many applicants may be eliminated without interview because the information on their application form shows them to be unsuitable for the job. You could also invite candidates to take some sort of suitability test, of which there are several types.

Psychometric assessment

Psychometric assessment involves the use of tests and questionnaires to gain an insight into a candidate's abilities, preferences and personality, and so to predict the likelihood of the candidate succeeding in a particular job.

Ability tests are designed to measure specific job performance factors, such as numerical interpretation, word reasoning, abstract reasoning or manual dexterity.

Personality questionnaires are designed to assess behaviour traits, attitudes and preferences. Simple questionnaires are easily 'faked', but professionally designed questionnaires, often with computer analysis of responses, are capable of reliable results. Personality dimensions include Extrovert–Introvert; Dominant–Submissive; Autocratic–Democratic; Aggressive–Friendly; Imaginative–Realistic; Venturesome–Cautious; Flexible–Rigid; Optimistic–Pessimistic; Trusting–Cautious; Tough-minded–Sensitive; Radical–Conservative; Forthright–Tactful; and many more. The needs of the job determine where along each scale the ideal candidate would sit.

Properly constructed psychometric assessments have the following advantages over interviews:

- They provide a fairer process, less dependent on assessor bias.
- They generally give a better prediction of success at the job.
- They clearly discriminate between different abilities, such as verbal and numerical skills. (Interviewers often rate more highly applicants who communicate well, regardless of whether such skill is required in the job.)
- They can be more cost-effective if several candidates are tested at the same time.

Situational interviews

This is a means of assessing a candidate's ability to do a particular job based on his or her response to a series of hypothetical situations which might arise in the job. For example, an applicant for a supervisor position might be asked:

> *'One of your subordinates is repeatedly late for work. What would you do?'*

or

> *'When allocating work to your team, what factors would you consider?'*

Situational interviewing is a particularly useful process where a candidate has no track record in a similar position in the past.

Assessment centre selection

This assessment technique usually involves a combination of interviews, ability tests, personality questionnaires, and individual and group exercises. The process, which can take one or more days to complete, is most commonly used for filling senior management positions.

EXAMPLE: AN ASSESSMENT PROCESS

In their assessment centre selection of senior managers, FICO use ability tests and personality questionnaires, comparing individual applicants with stored data on 'group norms'. They also ask candidates to undertake individual and team exercises.

Some of the individual exercises take the form of 'in-tray' exercises, in which candidates deal with a range of typical job tasks by analysing them, setting priorities and stating what actions they would take in each case. Other individual exercises involve job simulation—for example financial decision-making.

Group discussions, problem-solving and decision-making exercises are used to see how candidates relate to other people. The purpose is to assess the social and communication skills, persuasiveness and determination of each applicant.

Outdoor exercises, such as getting a team across an obstacle course by devising and constructing rustic structures, provide candidates with the opportunity to demonstrate their creativity, leadership and teamworking abilities.

The performance of each candidate is recorded and compared with the requirements outlined in the job description, as well as with the performance of the other candidates.

FICO—Group exercise assessment record		
Vacancy:		
Candidate:		
Scale:	4 = Excellent; 3 = Good; 2 = Fair; 1 = Poor	**Score**
Participation	How much did the candidate contribute to the achievement of the group?	
Determination	How strongly was the candidate committed to the success of the task?	
Leadership	How effectively did the candidate direct, motivate and control the other group members?	
Teamworking	How well did the candidate consider and work in harmony with the other group members?	
Creativity	To what extent did the candidate contribute original ideas or find new approaches to problems?	
Analysis	How logically did the candidate analyse problems and structure information?	
Oral expression	How clearly did the candidate express ideas and check understanding of the other group members?	
Influence	To what extent were the candidate's views accepted by the other group members?	

The raw scores are not simply added together. Instead, they are multiplied by a factor ranging between 0 and 10 according to their relevance to the job. For example, 'Analysis' would be weighted more highly for a finance manager than for a chef.

Aware that selection centre techniques can be stressful for candidates, many of whom do not perform in their normal way in such a competitive environment, FICO use only trained assessors who can usually differentiate between natural and forced behaviour.

PREPARING FOR THE INTERVIEW

The job specification is a summary of what you are trying to achieve; now you need a plan for achieving it.

Preparing yourself

The better prepared you are, the less likely it is you will allow your decision to be influenced by factors which bear little or no relevance to the job specification. So the first step is to make yourself familiar with the job specification. Be clear whether you should give qualifications higher priority than experience; ability higher priority than personality.

Preparing the plan

Study the application form and make sure you understand the information the candidate has provided. Write down questions not clearly covered in the application. For example:

- Why couldn't the candidate's career aspirations have been met by their present employer?
- Does the candidate see this vacancy as a step towards some other role?
- Are there any family circumstances which could limit the candidate's ability to fulfil the role?
- Does the candidate hold offices in societies or sporting bodies which might limit their ability to move location or work 'in the field' if the job so required?
- Does the candidate have special needs or health limitations for which you will have to make provision. (For example, effects of sight, hearing or mobility limitations can often be reduced by adapting the work place accordingly.)

None of these are reasons for rejecting a candidate, but it is wise to raise the issues during the interview.

Have a file of information available to hand to the candidate towards the end of the interview if you feel they match your requirements. Depending on their personal circumstances this could include:

- An organization tree showing their position in the reporting structure.
- Copies of recent staff newsletters, house magazines or press releases.
- A local map.
- Local newspapers with housing advertisements and estate agents' details.
- A list of schools and colleges in the area.

You may think of other ways in which you can help applicants. All this goes towards creating a good impression so that, when you find a candidate you really want, they make their decision in your favour, too.

How long?

It's difficult to obtain the information you need in less than about 20 minutes, and experience shows that much more than an hour of questioning can become unproductive. So, if you need longer, organize two sessions with breaks in between. In practice most interviews consist of around 45 minutes of questioning the candidate, followed by 15 minutes presenting the organization and answering questions posed by the candidate about the job and what help you can provide in relocation.

EXAMPLE: A TYPICAL INTERVIEW PLAN

Here is a plan for a one-hour interview. You should be prepared to adjust the time allocations to suit the particular circumstances, however.

Activity		Budgeted time (minutes)
Before the interview		
1	Prepare the job specification.	60
2	Study application form and prepare questions.	30
3	Prepare information pack for candidate.	10
4	Prepare the room and arrange for no interruptions.	10
During the interview		
5	Welcome the candidate; offer tea/coffee; put the candidate at ease.	2
6	Explain structure of interview and/or selection process, and check that the candidate understands and accepts it.	3
7	Check that you both understand and agree what job the candidate is being interviewed for, and ensure that the candidate would be willing to undertake that kind of work.	3
8	Discuss candidate's qualifications, experience and ambitions so you can assess how well suited he or she is to the job vacancy.	20
9	Assess the candidate's personal qualities and ability to fit in with the other team members, if appropriate.	10
10	Ascertain that the candidate's family commitments and leisure interests are compatible with the demands of the job vacancy.	5
11	Sell the job, the organization and the prospects to the candidate if you deem him or her to be a suitable applicant for the position.	5
12	Invite the candidate to ask questions about the job, the organization and the opportunities available to the successful applicant.	5
13	Answer the candidate's questions about accommodation, transport, shopping, schools, recreation and leisure facilities, etc., (assuming the job would involve moving to a new area).	5
14	Summarize and conclude the interview, ensuring that the candidate understands when he or she will hear the results of the interview and what the next step in the selection process will be.	2
After the interview		
15	Complete interview record summary.	10
16	Make decision and notify successful applicant; seek acceptance.	10
17	Write 'regret' letter thanking unsuccessful applicants for attending.	5

Note

Use this as a basic interview plan, but don't let the plan rule you: it is only a guide. If you find you need more time on one section, be flexible, and then curtail the discussion slightly on another aspect so that you don't make the candidate late for a train or another appointment.

6.5 QUESTIONING TECHNIQUE

Questions and answers are the substance of interviews. Questioning the candidate and listening attentively to the answers allows you to:

- Check that statements in the application form are correct and complete.
- Get the candidate to focus on issues important to you both.
- Assess the verbal communication skills of the candidate.
- Check the reasoning and decision–making skills of the candidate.
- Discover the knowledge, experience and opinions of the candidate.
- Check that the applicant understands sufficient about the vacancy and your organization to make an acceptance decision if offered the job.

Getting the balance right

When questioning a candidate, you should normally spend at least twice as long listening as talking. If not, change your questioning style. Similarly, when answering questions about the job or about your organization, the answers you give should be more detailed than the questions you receive.

Grading the questions

Remember, your organization will only gain from what the candidate knows and can do, so don't spend much time trying to discover the negatives of these. And in the early stages of the interview, when you want to put the candidate at ease, ask questions of fact. For example:

> *'I see from your application you studied three A levels. What subjects did you decide on?'*

Later you can probe into the opinions and decisions of the applicant with questions like:

> *'What made you embark on a career in finance?'*

Finally, you may need to discover the attitudes and prejudices of a candidate, if the job involves working in sensitive areas:

> *'Tell me how you feel about research which involves carrying out tests on animals.'*

As you move from one topic to the next, you will often need to shift back to questions of fact before probing the opinions and attitudes of the candidate.

Dealing with difficult candidates

Nervousness makes some people voluble; others become withdrawn and over-cautious. With the chatterbox you may have to interrupt. Do so politely but firmly to direct the discussion where you want it to go. For example:

> *'That's interesting. Now can I ask you to jump ahead to your university days. Your project... whose idea was it?'*

Shy and reserved candidates often need more time to settle in to the interview. Initially, seek areas of common interest. Discuss non-threatening topics and be prepared for the candidate to illustrate answers by sketching with pencil on paper if this helps them explain more clearly what thay have achieved in the past.

Later, if all you are getting are Yes/No answers, switch to open questions of the type:

> *'What does a typical day's work involve you in doing?'*

CHECK-LIST: INTERVIEW QUESTIONING DOS AND DON'TS

Technique	Example	Use it
Yes/no questions	'Are you a Chartered Engineer?'	Rarely. The answers are usually stated in the application form, and you are likely to get a bald re-statement. It's usually better to seek more details by asking an open question such as: 'Could we talk about your professional qualifications?'
Closed questions	'What is your current salary?'	To check or gather facts
Open questions	'What aspect of the work did you find most interesting?'	To discover opinions and values
Probing questions	'How did you feel when the department was closed down?'	To discover feelings and motivations
Leading questions	'I'm quite sure you wouldn't expect to have full budget responsibility right at the outset, would you?'	Rarely if ever. You won't find out other people's opinions and values by trying to force your own upon them.
Pauses	...	To give candidates time to consider your question and gather their thoughts. Show you are comfortable with the silence, or you may invite rash and ill-considered responses.
Repeat previous answer in questioning tone	'You enjoyed the travelling?' 'Yes. At that time I wasn't married and it was a chance to see more of the world. I wouldn't want to spend much time away from my family nowadays, though.'	If the pause technique gets no response. This is a useful means of getting a candidate to expand on a terse or incomplete answer.
Critical comments	'It was rather short-sighted of you to drop computing at the end of your first year.'	Never. If you show disapproval, don't be surprised if candidates are reluctant to open up to you.
Trick questions	'From your experience as a gamekeeper, I'm sure you know a lot about wildlife. Tell me, do peacocks lay their eggs in nests on the ground or up in trees?'	Never. Humiliating a candidate is a poor way to sell a job vacancy if you decide later this is the right person for the job. Be forthright! (The hens lay the eggs.)
Multiple questions	'Did you meet any reliability problems with this approach; if so what did you tell your project supervisor, what did you do about it, and what would you have done differently with hindsight?'	Never. If you confuse the candidate with multiple questions, don't be surprised if the answer bears little relationship to your line of questioning. Keep questions short and straightforward.
Showing interest	Smile, nod approval, stay alert.	To encourage the candidate to discuss matters of importance. Don't intervene just for appearance sake.

AVOIDING UNLAWFUL DISCRIMINATION

The purpose of a selection interview is to discriminate between candidates. However, to stay within the law you must not discriminate unfairly on grounds of gender, race, colour, religion or ethnic origin.

Sex discrimination

In the UK, the Sex Discrimination Act, 1975, 1986, requires that a woman should not be treated less favourably than a man because of her gender. Although discrimination against women is more often encountered, broadly the same requirements apply in respect of discrimination against men.

Racial discrimination

The UK Race Relations Act, 1976, makes it unlawful for an employer to treat one job applicant less favourably than another on the grounds of race, colour, religion or ethnic origin.

To stay within the law you must not:

- Draw up the job description in a way which unfairly disadvantages one group of applicants.
- Ask different types of questions of one group of applicants so that they are unfairly disadvantaged.
- Make your selection decision on a subjective basis favouring one candidate over others on grounds of gender, race, religion or ethnic origin.

Exemptions from the discrimination laws

There are situations in which gender, race or colour are 'genuine occupational qualifications'. It is not unlawful to discriminate on such grounds, but you should make all potential candidates aware of such special requirements before the interview. The tables below list examples of genuine occupational qualifications (GOQs).

GOQ—Gender	Example
Physiology	Modelling women's clothes
Decency/privacy	Supervising or maintaining sanitary facilities
Living in	Where premises cannot reasonably be equipped with sleeping or sanitary facilities for both sexes
Personal services	Social counselling which is best provided by a man (or a woman)
Dramatic performance	Portrayal of a male (or a female) character

GOQ—Race	Example
Authenticity	Portrayal of a well known historical character or creation of a picture or film for which a person of a particular racial group is required for authenticity
Restaurants	Waiter/waitress in an Indian restaurant where food and drink are provided in a particular setting for which a person of that racial group is required for authenticity
Personal services	Social counselling which is best provided by a person of a particular ethnic background

EXAMPLES

Direct sex discrimination

Jim's secretary is due to retire in three months time, so Jim advertises the vacancy. He receives applications from Mary and Jill, both aged 22, Stephanie, aged 55, and Mark, aged 23. All are well qualified and have sufficient experience to cope with the job, but Jim believes a pretty young secretary would brighten the office and create a better impression with clients. He short-lists Mary and Jill.

Is this unlawful discrimination?

Yes. Jim would have a hard job convincing an industrial tribunal that he was not discriminating unfairly against Mark. Stephanie would not be able to claim unlawful discrimination, however. Age discrimination may be short-sighted, and Stephanie's experience might well make her the more effective secretary, but Jim is entitled to discriminate against older applicants provided he treats men and women equally.

You could also show indirect discrimination against one sex—for example, by asking a female job applicant:

'Do you intend starting a family in the near future?'

You must have a valid reason for asking such a question—for example, the job involves long periods away from home—and then you must ask this question of both male and female applicants.

Direct racial discrimination

Paul advertised two vacancies for machine operators. He received applications from Peter Stevens, Janet Strong, Mahmood Hishami and Gabriella Pinot. At the interview he gave each applicant a passage from Shakespeare and asked them to summarize it in their own words. Mahmood and Gabriella found this test difficult because English wasn't their first language. Peter and Janet performed well in the test and were offered jobs.

Is this unlawful discrimination?

Yes. All applicants were subjected to the same treatment, so Jim thought he was being fair to all applicants. But he used tests which could not be linked to job success, and these tests discriminated against those applicants whose first language was not English.

It is also possible to discriminate less directly against racial minorities—for example, by asking only of those applicants who come from ethnic minority groups:

'How long do you intend staying in this country?'

Avoiding problems

You will find it easy to avoid unfairly discriminating against applicants on gender or racial grounds if you treat all applicants equally, asking them all similar questions and appointing on the basis of matching the person to your pre-defined requirements.

Be wary of appointing someone whose experience and qualifications are much inferior to those of other applicants, even if you feel they have the personality you are looking for. Subjective arguments carry little weight in industrial tribunals.

6.7 SELECTION INTERVIEW — NOTES AND FOLLOW-UP

During the interview you will need to take notes. Keep them brief so that you can spend most of your time concentrating on what the candidate is saying.

Note taking affects motivation

It is quite natural for a candidate to assume you place greatest importance on those points at which you make notes. So, if a candidate is apprehensive you can use note-taking to build up his or her confidence. For example:

> Candidate: '... and that was really the turning point, when I decided to go back to college and study for a Diploma at Birmingham.'
> Interviewer: 'Interesting... I'll just make a note of that... 1989, wasn't it?'

But contrast that with the effect on a candidate discussing a career set-back:

> 'So, despite all that hard work, the customer decided he couldn't wait any longer, and he cancelled the contract. My team and I were left high and dry. We had nothing else in the pipeline.... I suppose if I'd been more strategic in my thinking I would have seen it coming, but at the time...'
> Interviewer: 'Yes, I'll need to make a note of that... should have seen it coming...'

A more sensitive interviewer would have moved to another subject, making a note about the lack of strategy while the candidate was discussing some positive achievement.

What happens now?

Occasionally it becomes clear early in an interview that the job and the candidate are poorly matched. There is no benefit to either party in continuing for the planned duration with what could become a charade. Thank the candidate for attending and close the discussion on as positive a note as you can.

If, however, there is a real prospect of your offering the candidate the job, explain the next stage in the process. For example:

> 'We will be writing to you within three days letting you know if we wish to take your application further. It then takes a further two weeks to get a formal offer to the successful candidate.'

Interview records

After the interview, convert your cryptic notes into proper records. A simple interview record form can reduce the work involved, especially if you are seeing several candidates.

The most important point is to compare candidates against the job specification, and not just one against the other.

The follow-up

Once you have made up your mind—normally this should be after you have interviewed all on your short list—you need to send an offer letter to the successful applicant and a rejection letter to those who fail to meet the standard you are looking for. If your first choice applicant accepts then you will need to send rejection letters to the others who met your requirements.

You may need to obtain work, character and medical references before confirming an offer. Pursue these urgently; delay could cost you a first-class candidate.

CHECK-LIST: HOW EFFECTIVE WAS THAT INTERVIEW?

Either the interviewer or an independent observer can use this check-list to identify opportunities and set targets for improving future interviews.

	4	3	2	1
Candidate:				
Interviewer:				
Date:				
Please mark your assessment here using: 4 = Excellent: continue doing it well 3 = Good: scope for minor improvements 2 = Fair: much improvement is possible 1 = Weak: major improvement is essential	4	3	2	1
How well was the interview prepared?				
Was the candidate given adequate notice of date/venue?				
Was the duration agreed with the candidate in advance?				
Was the room reserved and set out appropriately?				
Was the room comfortable and suitable for the purpose?				
Were unnecessary interruptions avoided?				
Was a job specification adequately defined in advance?				
Had the interviewer studied application forms in advance?				
Was the candidate interviewed by the right person?				
Overall: How well prepared was this interview?				
How well was the interview managed?				
Did the interviewer turn up promptly and keep to schedule?				
Was the interview well structured and purposeful?				
Did the interviewer begin by putting the candidate at ease?				
Was the candidate allowed to demonstrate what he or she had to offer?				
Was the interview controlled assertively?				
Did the interviewer probe adequately?				
Did the interviewer listen to and note the candidate's answers?				
Did the interviewer invite and answer the candidate's questions?				
Overall: How well managed was this interview?				
How effectively were decisions turned into actions?				
Did the interviewer gain the necessary information to make an offer/reject decision?				
Was an offer/rejection letter sent out promptly?				
Were references checked urgently?				
Overall: How effective was this interview?				
Improvement targets:				

6.8 APPRAISAL INTERVIEWING — PURPOSE AND PROCESS

Many organizations, in both the public and private sectors, now use a system of performance appraisal as a means of improving business performance. Unfortunately, the purpose of appraisals is often obscured by the process. A line manager reviews his or her staff, just as a manager must occasionally discipline staff; so, the appraisal interview can become a battle in which the manager tells people what is wrong with them, while they defend their actions and claim greater achievements than they have actually made.

This adversarial, backward-looking approach is not constructive. The real purpose is:

- To discover and document how a person is performing, and the reasons for this.
- To agree how that person can do better in future, and what help or other resources will be needed to secure this improvement.
- To provide valuable benefits to the person concerned, to the manager and to the organization.

Appraisal systems can fail because people are unclear what they are for. Appraisal is not meant to be:

- A disciplinary system. Although poor performance may lead to disciplinary action, you should not leave such matters to the annual appraisal interview.
- A means of identifying people with high potential. This is part of your job, but you need to motivate *all* your staff, and a fair appraisal system can help you do that.
- A salary negotiation forum. You might become involved in pay negotiations, but don't use the appraisal system alone for worth assessment, or you will not get people to discuss openly any difficulties they are having with their work.

Self-appraisal

Effective performance appraisal means confronting problems and agreeing solutions. But you will find many people become defensive if you suggest they have weaknesses which affect the quality or quantity of their work. Why not, then, ask your staff to prepare a draft appraisal of their own performance over the past year? Give them a structure so they can make notes of the targets they were set, the achievements they made and any circumstances which made achievement more difficult or easier than expected. You may be pleasantly surprised to discover how objective most people can be about their achievements and failures, provided they know they won't be penalized for their frankness.

Target-setting

Appraisal interviews cannot affect the past, so spend most time on actions which will improve future performance. Wherever possible, *agree* targets for the year ahead. Many will be job targets—cost reductions, increased quality and so on; but others may be to do with behavioural skills—communication, for example. Targets should be realistic for the individual, specific rather than vague, the circumstances clearly stated and, most important, the individual must understand what he or she is taking on. For example:

> 'Make sure we never again have trouble with suppliers.'

may be what you want, but it is not a realistic, quantified and clear target. This is:

> 'Write to each of our materials suppliers once per month updating our estimated requirements over the year ahead. And get them to fill in a reply slip so we know in advance if they can't meet our demand.'

CHECK-LIST: APPRAISAL PREPARATION AND RECORD FORM

Here is the appraisal interview summary form used by FICO. Their personnel department issues copies to both the manager and the appraisee. Each is encouraged to complete the form in draft before the interview. After the interview the manager issues a final version containing the agreed targets and action plan resulting from the interview.

Job holder:	
Job title:	
Appraising manager:	
Period of review:	
1 Key objects set over review period:	Assessment of performance against each objective:
2 Circumstances affecting performance	

3 Job performance factors
    Use the following ratings:
    4 = Exceeds requirements
    3 = Meets requirements
    2 = Needs improvement
    1 = Unacceptably weak - act now!
    N/A = Not applicable to this job
	Job knowledge:
	Ability to get results:
	Planning and preparation:
	Analytical ability:
	Creativity:
	Communication skills:
	Relationships with others:
	Teamworking:
	Financial awareness:
	Commercial awareness:
	Reliability & timekeeping:
	Control of subordinates:
	Development of subordinates:

4 Overall assessment of performance	
5 Key objectives for next year	
6 Longer term career objectives	
7 Training needs	
8 Other actions to help appraisee meet key objectives and career objectives	
9 Job holder's comments	
10 Manager's comments/ recommendations	
11 Senior reviewing manager's comments/ recommendations	
Signed by appraisee:	Date:
Signed by appraising manager:	Date:
Signed by reviewing manager:	Date:

6.9 APPRAISAL INTERVIEWS —AGREEING THE ACTION PLAN

All too often good appraisal schemes lose credibility because the agreements made in the appraisal interview are not turned into action:

> 'My boss promised me all sorts of training and development opportunities. She said I'd get increased responsibility this year, too, but just look... here I am, a year older, and nothing has changed. Our appraisal system's a farce!'

Well, if nothing changes the appraisal system *is* a farce. To some extent we could blame the appraisee for not chasing the manager to get something done, but the main onus must reside with the manager who carried out the interview. Maybe the circumstances changed so that it wasn't possible to provide the opportunities expected at the time of the interview. If so, then the appraisee should have been invited to another interview where the new circumstances could be discussed and new, more realistic targets set.

Making realistic promises

You can help prepare people for opportunities, but it's unreasonable to promise that those opportunities will necessarily arise just when they are needed; so don't make rash promises. People will respect you for your forthrightness, and so come to trust you.

This doesn't mean you mustn't make plans and projections, however. Rather, you should state clearly any assumptions on which your plans depend:

> 'If we get the Weavers contract within the next three months, I would want you to manage it, David.'

Training budgets are always limited, so prioritize training needs and consider, before the appraisal interview:

- What you can achieve by on-the-job coaching.
- What the appraisee can reasonably be expected to achieve by self-development—correspondence courses or distance learning, for example.
- What development needs are best fulfilled by off-the-job training courses.

Following up the actions

It's likely that most of the actions from an appraisal interview require only the agreement of yourself and the appraisee. Occasionally, however, you will need the help of others, and it's best to get their commitment before making promises. For example:

> 'To help prepare you for the position of project manager, I've asked Jim Peterson if you could work alongside him when he plans the launch of Remflow 400. Jim's quite keen and says he will need your help all next month, Avril. So, if you're still keen on a career in project management, I'll arrange a secondment right away. I've checked with William and Carol; they say if you can clear the inventory check before you move over, they should be able to cover for you while you're away. What do you think?'

Then keep a copy of the action plan, with target start and finish dates, so you can check on progress and take any action necessary to remove obstacles.

Of course, if circumstances change you may need to revise the action plan. A good way of doing this is by holding an interim appraisal interview. Explain how things have changed, agree new targets if necessary, and then re-prioritize the action plan so that both the appraisee and you get a fair deal in the new circumstances.

CHECK-LIST: AN APPRAISAL ACTION PLAN

Use the following action planning check-list to record the actions agreed at the appraisal interview and to check on the progress of those responsible for carrying out the actions.

Job holder:		Period of action plan		From: To:	
Job title:					
Appraising manager:		Start date		Finish date	
Action agreed	Person responsible	Plan	Actual	Plan	Actual
1					
2					
3					
4					
5					
6					
7					
All actions completed	Signed (Appraisor):		Date:		
	Signed (Appraisee):		Date:		

NEGOTIATING PRINCIPLES

A deal can be struck only when two parties have differing views on the cost and value of something which is to be exchanged. Business depends upon this process of exchange. Defining and agreeing exactly what will be exchanged is a negotiation.

The different values and beliefs of each side in a negotiation provide the opportunity for agreement. They also represent barriers. Uncertainty about the motives and beliefs of the other side causes many negotiators to feel pressured, and when under pressure they do not always behave assertively. However, progress to agreement and action is only possible when both sides are behaving assertively.

Viable solutions

Normally, a negotiating impasse can only be resolved if:

- Both parties genuinely want to reach agreement.
- Negotiators avoid taking up fixed positions at the outset.
- Negotiators discuss the conditions on which they are prepared to negotiate before examining alternative outcomes.
- There is some overlap between the ranges of outcomes acceptable to the two parties.

Negotiating guidelines

While flexibility is important in negotiation, it is possible to set out guidelines:

1   Plan the sequence in which you would prefer issues to be discussed, even though you may have to concede some changes in structure when you meet the other side.
2   Plan your position on each item, deciding what you would like the outcome to be, what you expect the other side to ask for, and what you would be prepared to accept.
3   Make sure you are clear on your own priorities, and try to discover beforehand, or early on in the negotiations, which points are most important to the other side.
4   Knowledge is power. You have more leverage if you know more about their problems than they do of yours. Homework pays dividends in negotiating.
5   State your demands clearly and firmly. Don't shy away from conflict; resolve it.
6   Don't allow yourself to be picked off item by item. If you try to create a constructive atmosphere early on by conceding in areas where you are strong, you may find yourself backed into a corner later, when you may have nothing to bargain with.
7   Nothing is for nothing. A negotiated deal should be a package of costs and benefits for both sides. Don't concede a point because it has no value to you; it might be high on the priority list of the other side.
8   Make all offers conditional:

   'If you can guarantee to deliver 200 a month for the next three months, we might be able to look again at the matter of some sort of advance payment.'

9   Don't make 'take it or leave it' demands unless you mean them. Every bluff which gets called undermines your credibility and makes it more difficult to rebuild the relationship of trust and cooperation which will be needed to put the agreement into action.
10 Depart from any of these guidelines if it helps you get a result better for both sides!

EXAMPLE: A NEGOTIATING PROCESS

Sally Quinn, chief buyer at FICO UK, is negotiating with Charles Leman, product manager of Optico Inc., for the supply of optical components for FICO's new 35 mm projectors. Charles is aware that FICO have the option of producing lens systems at their own factory, and he knows that there are German and Japanese companies capable of meeting FICO's specifications. Sally knows that Optico are the only supplier capable of meeting her delivery requirements, especially for the sales demonstration prototypes, which are running behind schedule due to last-minute design changes. Below are extracts from the negotiations.

Stage	Sally Quinn, for FICO (UK) Ltd	Charles Leman, for Optico Inc.
1 Opening	Welcomes Charles, offers coffee, offers visit to factory later.	Thanks Sally for hospitality, states wish to achieve mutually beneficial agreement.
2 Stating the principles	States requirements: products, specifications and possible quantities of each.	Confirms Optico's ability to meet these requirements.
3 Stating the demands	Specifies price, delivery and terms required.	States Optico's standard terms and conditions.
4 Identifying areas of conflict	Defines areas of conflict: price and payment terms plus call-off delivery. (Deliveries made as and when required by FICO's factory.)	Agrees to discuss these as a package. Suggests that call-off might not be a problem if FICO were prepared to make an initial down payment. Cannot meet all of FICO's delivery requirements at such short notice.
5 Exploring possible solutions	Indicates that it might be possible to reschedule pilot production provided at least 100 sales demonstration units could be completed within four months.	Agrees that 100 kits could be provided if FICO will accept an initial tooling charge.
6 Finding common ground	Makes a counter-offer that if the tooling charge be spread over the first year's production, and if this would keep the kit price below $15, then it would be worth discussing the full production schedule.	Concedes the spreading of tooling charge over 12 months in order to gain the chance to negotiate for supply of lens kits for full production.
7 Packaging the offer	Negotiates towards a package of price, terms and conditions attractive to FICO and acceptable to Optico.	Negotiates towards a package of price, terms and conditions attractive to Optico and acceptable to FICO.
8 Working in cooperation	Discuss improvements to the package which could increase the benefits to both parties. (e.g. Using Optico's shipping subsidiary.)	
9 Agreeing	Agree on a package deal covering price, delivery, terms and conditions for both pilot run and production quantities.	
10 Turning agreement into action	Summarizes the purchase agreement, gets it typed up, and signs it or agrees to present it for senior management signature.	Signs the supply agreement or agrees to present to senior management for signature.

CHAPTER 7

IMPROVE YOUR WRITING SKILLS
A STRATEGY FOR SUCCESS IN THE INFORMATION AGE

In conversation, people will accept the occasional slip of the tongue, the incomplete or fuzzy explanation. You might even be forgiven an inaccuracy when quizzed without notice. But go into print, and people expect you to think it out before you write it out. If you get your facts or figures wrong or don't make your meaning clear when writing, you get pounced upon.

And why not? After all, you do have the opportunity to check over what you write and to correct any mistakes before sending it.

The challenge

Much of what you do as a manager remains invisible to others: you are judged on the part other people know about. Some of what you achieve may be tangible—a well-run administrative system or a productive processing plant—but perhaps much more is in the form of ideas put across to others, some of these spoken, others written.

The more important the idea, the more likely it will have to be put in writing. All too often the quality of the writing is taken as a measure of the quality of the idea, *and* of the person putting it over. So, if *you* are going to be judged by the quality of your writing, it had better be good!

The benefits

Do you ever compromise on quality because you run out of time? See how you can write less, and so have the time you need to do the job properly *and* meet your deadlines.

Do you enjoy your job *except* for the paper work? A structured approach will help you get your writing done quickly and painlessly. Who knows? Once you have an efficient system you may even come to enjoy writing!

Do the people who read your letters and reports have to call you to find out what you *meant* to say? Follow the guidelines in this chapter and that should never happen again. I promise no easy route to a Nobel prize, but you will find ways to cut your word count, use more powerful language, and get your message across so people remember it.

WHAT IS EFFECTIVE WRITING?

Effective writing is purposeful writing. It fulfils defined aims—aims of both writer and readers. You might want to amuse or inform your readers, or to influence their attitude. They, in turn, might require information to make a decision. But they may also be assessing your competence! Without clear aims, you will find it difficult to decide what to include and what to leave out, and you will probably produce a document larger than is necessary, including material *just in case*.

Effective writing is also stylish. But your choice of style must depend upon your target readership, their reading ability and their vocabulary.

Above all, effective writing is time-efficient. With an effective process you will write quickly just what is required, and in a style your readers can quickly assimilate.

Benefits for all

For the reader, your writing will be:

- **Accurate**: factual and objective.
- **Brief**: taking no more time to read than it deserves.
- **Clear**: understandable, complete and to the point.

For you there are advantages, too:

- **Avoid writers' block**: you need never be stuck for words.
- **Be more productive**: rapidly write only what is needed.
- **Convince others**: win their support by your enthusiasm and directness.

Steps towards success

Break the task into stages:

Fig 7.1

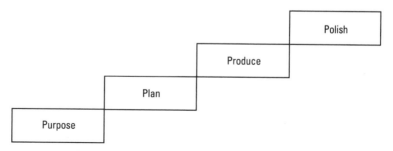

- **Define the purpose**
  Find out who your readers will be and what they really need. Meet their needs, and you have more chance of achieving your own objectives.
- **Plan both content and style**
  Very little of your writing will be wasted if you make a structured plan and choose a style which suits your readership.
- **Produce without pain**
  Use a rapid writing technique to produce quickly a draft which is 95 per cent right first time.
- **Polish till it sparkles**
  Structured editing will quickly transform your rough draft into stylish finished work. Then get the benefit of an independent review of your most important documents.

7.1 SETTING THE OBJECTIVES

The first step is to get to know your readers in terms of:

- What they will need to get out of the document.
- Their views on the relative importance of topics.
- Their prior knowledge of the subject.
- How long they are prepared to spend reading your document.

You may have objectives, too. You might want to impress people with your knowledge and ability, or to win their support for your proposal. Only if you give people a fair deal for the effort they put into reading your writing can you hope to achieve your own objectives.

Beware the multi-purpose document

Where groups of readers each require only part of the information, produce a common core with specialist appendices. But if there is no common core, you will have to produce two or more smaller documents, each tailored to specific needs.

Don't compromise. Where you have one decision-making reader group, design your document to meet their needs. Accept that it will not be ideal for the other reader groups.

Do you really need to write?

Ask about every letter or memo: 'Why am I writing this; wouldn't it be better to telephone or go and see them?' Some of these alternatives take less of your time but require more time from other people. Would they be prepared to give up the extra time?

With face-to-face communication:

- It's easier to show how you feel about your subject, so you need fewer words and less time to put across your message.
- You can see what response you are getting, and take corrective action if your audience doesn't seem convinced.

But a written message has advantages, too:

- You can hide your emotions.
- You can check and correct complicated messages before sending them.
- The readers can read at their own time and at a pace which suits them.
- Any questions are usually in writing, so you can research your answers.
- It's easier to prove you have sent information when it is in writing.

The best of both worlds

For your most important messages, use a combination of written *and* face-to-face communication. Maybe you should send a report and follow it with a personal visit. Or perhaps your presentation should be supported by hand-outs to be studied afterwards.

Agree on the order: should you write to them first, or talk first? Only then can you decide what to say and what to put in writing.

How much of your time is it worth?

Ration the time you spend writing. Decide how much time each job is worth, ensuring that key documents—in particular those which go to customers—are most carefully planned, edited and reviewed.

CHECK-LIST: WRITING OBJECTIVES

This check-list will help to clarify the purpose of your document *before* you plan how you will achieve that purpose. Use it to define the objectives and budget for any document of more than three or four pages. The answers will help you decide what to write, in what order and in how much detail.

If you have to write for more than one reader group, with different requirements, complete a check-list for each; compare the answers to decide whether a single document could be successful.

Document title and date:	
Author:	
Date:	
Who is going to read it, and why?	
Reader group (or individual):	
Organization/Department/Job title:	
What do they want to learn from reading it?	
What should they do as a result?	
What topic is most important to them?	
Do they realize why it is important?	
Are they familiar with this subject matter?	
Are they familiar with my terminology and jargon?	
What outcome do I want?	
What is my most important point?	
Whom do I most want to convince?	
What kind of argument will convince him or her?	
What do I want to happen as a result?	
What is my budget?	
How much time will they be willing to give up?	
How much time can I afford to spend writing this?	
How many words/pages does this correspond to?	
Can I achieve what's wanted in this space/time?	
What illustrations do I need?	
What sort of binding should I arrange?	
Are there any other special requirements?	

7.2 THINK IT OUT BEFORE YOU WRITE IT OUT

Whether you have to write a one-page memo or a five-volume user manual, you will find it easier if first you choose a structure. For the memo you need only to decide what belongs in paragraphs one, two and three, but for the user manual there will be several levels in the structure, from volume and chapter down to subsection and paragraph.

Avoid the trap of plumping for the first solution that comes to mind. Try to find a structure which will help readers to follow the logic of your argument. Build upon their prior knowledge by linking new concepts to those explained earlier. You might choose:

- Historical: recording what happened in chronological order.
- Progressive: working from the familiar to the novel.
- Logical: each step building on the previous one.
- Importance: following a descending order of value to the reader.

Choose the structure which best suits the needs of your primary reader group. Additional information for other groups can be slotted in lower down the structure or included as an appendix.

The detailed plan

The next step is to decide, right down to individual paragraph level, what you need to include. Allocate space (numbers of pages or words of text, and numbers of diagrams) to each main section based upon the priorities of the primary reader group.

Numbering the sections, subsections and paragraph headings gives a clear view of the balance of material in your plan: have you provided too much detail of low priority subjects at the expense of shallow treatment of areas more important to your readers?

Computer-based outliners

For documents running to many pages, chapters or even volumes, a well-planned outline is essential. But if you plan right down to paragraph level, you can end up with an outline running to many pages. It's hard to check the balance of such a large outline, especially when working from the computer screen. This is where computer outliners win over hard copy: you can view your document as headings alone, and choose the number of levels you want to see. You might start by viewing your document as a set of chapter headings. Once you are happy with the chapter titles you can switch in the next level—section headings—and view them one chapter at a time. Finally, switch in the sub-section or paragraph headings.

Each level in the outline is numbered, so you know immediately what part of your document is on screen. And if you don't want to retain paragraph headings in the finished document, the numbers can easily be switched off once you have drafted the text.

Use helpful headings

Choose meaningful section and subsection headings. When writing the text they will remind you what point you intended to make, leaving you free to concentrate on making the point clearly and concisely. And if you leave these headings in your final text they will help your readers to find their way around your text, too.

EXAMPLES: PLANNING THE STRUCTURE

Jane Symonds is FICO's customer services manager. She needs to reply to a customer who has complained that a slide projector, manufactured by her company, broke down when connected to the battery supply of a mobile exhibition vehicle. The message of Jane's letter is that the projector should not have been run from a vehicle supply, and the customer has invalidated the warranty.

Jane is concerned that the letter should have an assertive tone. She chooses this structure:

1 Thank customer for reporting problem, and assure him that the company wants all its customers to get reliable service from their projectors.
2 Point out that labels on the projector and warnings in the front of handbook expressly state it must only be connected to an a.c. mains supply, and that battery operation invalidates the warranty.
3 Make a special offer to repair the projector at parts cost only, provided the customer arranges its return and collection.

So the structure of the letter is: good news; bad news; good news. It is usually best to end on a positive note, especially when you could be involved in future correspondence with the same person.

Reader-friendly headings

Now let's look at part of the outline of a larger document, a user manual for a personal computer system.

What do you learn from reading this section heading?

> *3 Laser printer*

Such a vague heading gives little idea what the topic covers. It means 'don't look in Section 3 if you want to learn how to make cheese'. But not much more! The section might be about:

- How to use your laser printer
- How to repair your laser printer
- How to make your own laser printer from an old photocopier

These are reader-friendly headings:

> *3 Installing and using your laser printer*
>   *3.1 Setting up procedure*
>   *3.1.1 Connecting up the cables*
>   *3.1.2 Setting the DIP switches to suit your PC*
>   *3.2 Installing and changing the toner cartridge*
>   *3.2.1 Installing standard (black) cartridges*
>   *3.2.2 Installing colour cartridges*
>   *3.3 Loading and unloading the paper tray*

7.3 PRECISELY WHAT DO YOU MEAN?

As managers, we often have to make decisions based on incomplete information. That's one reason we sometimes make poor decisions. Another reason is that information isn't always communicated in a precise form.

Be specific

At each transmission, part of a message can get altered. The sad thing is, it's the factual core which so often rots away first. A precise quantity, date or location becomes generalized. Later, someone takes a guess at what the original message must have been, and often they get it wrong.

So don't write *some* or *several* if you mean four, or between fifteen and twenty. Why say *soon* when you mean *by next Friday*?

Check your facts and figures

Facts come from factual sources; everything else is rumour or guesswork. If you can't trace and examine the source, it's not a fact, but hearsay. If you deal in doubtful data, it's just a matter of time before you let someone down, and once they make an important decision on your information, taken on trust, you will find it hard to regain their confidence. So, if you quote a figure check its source. If you haven't been able to trace the origin, make that fact clear to your readers and state the basis for your information.

Food for thought

I've heard it said that spinach is a recommended food for people suffering from iron deficiency. For years, figures for the iron content of spinach were copied from report to report, all based on values in an earlier publication in which the decimal point had been shifted one place to the right. In fact, spinach is no higher in iron than most other green vegetables.

At least, so I heard somewhere!

Separate fact from opinion

When reporting on an investigation, distinguish clearly between the facts, your opinion of what they mean, and what you recommend should be done. You can even have sections headed Findings, Conclusions and Recommendations.

Regularly or frequently?

Some words are so often used incorrectly that perhaps we should trust them no longer. What, for example, would you understand from:

> *Check the oil level regularly.*

Would you check it most days? Every month or two? At exactly ten year intervals? The dictionary says regularly means recurring at fixed intervals. So every ten years is correct. It may be correct to write:

> *Check the oil level frequently.*

But precise communication requires something like:

> *Check the oil level every week.*

Write the numbers right

When you include numbers, dates or quantities with units, double check them. Usually they are the second most important items in a document (second only to *yes* or *no*). Get the numbers right or failure is inevitable.

EXAMPLES

Vagaries of interpretation

How are you to make decisions on information like this?

> *It is very important to give reasonably fast responses to customer enquiries. Major customers—*
> *essentially this means those who submit frequent orders or require high value products—*
> *normally deserve a more rapid response.*

You are left to guess what numerical values satisfy the implied instruction. But is *any* information conveyed by the words *very, reasonably rapid, major, essentially, frequent, high, normally* and *more*?

Here is the message as it should be, worded precisely:

> *Reply within three days to every customer enquiry. For customers who send us more than three*
> *orders a month, and for those who order goods priced at £1000 or more, reply within 24 hours.*
> *Allow an extra day for replying to enquiries received the day before a bank holiday.*

Here are a further six vague words which allow writers to hedge and avoid specifics:

> ...appreciably *better...*
> ...considerable *improvement...*
> ...essentially *unchanged...*
> ...slightly *worrying...*
> ...significant *deterioration...*
> ...very *important...*

The most over-used of these vague words is *very*. It adds very little meaning, and should be used very, very sparingly.

Assumed facts

Here are three phrases used to raise the status of assumption towards that of fact:

> *It is well known that...*
> *For obvious reasons...*
> *It is perhaps true to say that...*

All can be replaced with:

> *In my opinion... but I've no evidence for this.*

A number of possibilities

What would you do if you received this order?:

> *Dear Sirs,*
> *Please supply 15 400 metre lengths of your type RT-22 cable.*

Now, are you to send fifteen long pieces or a whole load of little bits? If you take a guess and cut the cable into metre lengths you could end up with a lot of scrap. Avoid ambiguity by writing:

> *Please supply fifteen 400 metre lengths...*

7.4   WRITE AS YOU WOULD TALK

If you want to be convincing, write as you would talk to your readers if they were sitting opposite you. Keep it simple and direct. Show you're alive, and friendly.

When they've something important to say, most people use short sentences. For the less important details they may add an extra clause or two. Even so, most spoken English sentences contain fewer than 20 words. So why do so many people write in old-fashioned language, instead of as they talk?

One reason, I suggest, is that they write as they were taught to, by people much older than themselves, whereas their speech is continually being influenced by people of all ages. But formality, long sentences, obscure words—these are instruments of conflict: they undermine trust and arouse suspicion. Pompous writing will not convey your enthusiasm or the sincerity with which you want to help your readers.

Shun the passive voice

What would you think if someone spoke to you like this?

> *It has been found that a less persuasive message is provided by, and insincerity more often inferred from, letters which have been written in the passive voice with avoidance of the use of personal pronouns. The sincerity of one's personality is more effectively transmitted by use of the active voice.*

Something has been done to something by something else. Hard going, isn't it? See how you have to extend each sentence to show who did the something. But some people do write like that. Let's try it again, this time in an active, personal style:

> *Write letters using the active voice. Use personal pronouns—you, they, us. This way you show concern for your readers, and sincerity comes across in your writing.*

Make the active voice your default style, but be prepared to switch to the passive voice when appropriate:

> *A helpline has been set up for relatives of victims of the disaster.*

It's not important *who* set up the help line. Its existence is what matters to your readers.

Don't be self-centred

If you want someone's attention, show an interest in them and in things that matter to them. Make *yourself* the subject of too many sentences and you risk losing your reader's attention. Reword your writing so that *I* appears less frequently. *You* and *your*s are more influential words than *I* and *mine*.

Move on from the nineteenth century

Many of the conventions of letter writing were established more than a hundred years ago. Phrases such as:

> *I hereby gratefully acknowledge receipt of your esteemed correspondence of 17th instant.*

do little to suggest your sincerity. Why not write what you mean?

> *I was pleased to get your letter dated 17th.*

Fewer people study Latin in school than was the case forty years ago, so why not replace such terms as *per pro, viz,* and *ex gratia* with their English translations. Why risk being misunderstood by writing i.e. or e.g.? Not everyone knows the difference.

EXAMPLES Maybe your great grandparents had time to decipher letters like this:

> Dear Professor Booksearch,
>
> I write in reference to your communication of 29th ultimo. In respect of your esteemed order for a copy of volume IV of General Sir Charles Grimsby-Trawler's Memoirs, it is with deep regret I must advise you of the non-availability of said volume; this being due to its cremation, along with the corpus delicti of the said late General, in accordance with the instructions of the executors of the estate of the same in which expressly it was required that the volume in question should so be disposed of.
>
> We trust you will continue to favour us with your instructions, and we hope to be able satisfactorily to fulfil your expectations in future transactions.
>
> I remain your humble servant.
>
> I A M Crusty
>
> Per Pro Crusty, Dusty and Dry, Antiquarian Bibliologists

Your readers haven't time for such puzzles. Give it to them straight:

> Dear Professor Booksearch
> YOUR REQUEST FOR GEN SIR CHARLES GRIMSBY-TRAWLER'S MEMOIRS
>
> Thank you for your letter dated 29th March. I'm sorry, we can't provide a copy of Volume 4 of these memoirs. The late general's executors tell us the last copy was cremated with the author's body.
>
> Thank you for contacting us; we hope to be more helpful in future.
>
> Yours faithfully
>
> I A M Friendly
>
> for The Personal Bookservice
>
> PS I've checked, and there is a copy in the War Museum. They have a personal loan service— Tel: 012 345 6789

Not for Latin lovers

Here are eight Latin abbreviations which are often misunderstood; use them at your peril!

Latin abbreviation	Latin in full	English meaning
c.	circa	in approximately (followed by a date)
c.v.	curriculum vitae	career record
e.g.	exempli gratia	for example
ibid.	ibidem	in the book/section mentioned above
i.e.	id est	that is
p.p.	per procurationem	for and on behalf of
q.v.	quod vide	which see
viz.	videlicet	namely

7.5 PERSUASIVE WRITING NEEDS POWERFUL WORDS

Have you met the word-hog? She finds a new word each week—the more obscure, the better—and flaunts it as a status symbol. Driving her new word recklessly through meetings and memos, she causes communication congestion and undermines other people's confidence. But this selfish behaviour can also lead to poor decisions, as others try to hide their embarrassment by guessing the meaning.

Word-hogs would be better advised to use everyday words more effectively.

Active verbs

Verbs are the engines of communication. If you want to move people, use powerful verbs—action verbs such as make, send, draw—and use them in an active way. Write:

> *We recommend you scrap the machine and buy a more modern one.*

rather than:

> *Our recommendation is that the machine should be scrapped and that purchase of a more modern machine should be effected.*

See how you lose the persuasive power of an action verb by turning it into a noun—a nominalization. *We recommend,* becomes *Our recommendation is.* The verb *to be* is a weak verb. It says something is the same as, or equivalent to, something else. No action there!

Use down to earth language

Ask a group of managers each to write their understanding of the words *charismatic, conceptualize,* and *scenario,* and then to discuss and reach a consensus on a single definition for each. Arrange plenty of coffee! But ask what they understand by *square, throw* and *cement mixer,* and there's no problem reaching agreement.

Abstract words like charismatic make reading hard work. Concrete words (like cement mixer!) are easily converted to pictures in the mind: they are reader-friendly words.

Cut out the fog

It's not clever to use obscure words which leave people guessing at their meaning. Sentences with many subordinate clauses can also cause confusion. When writing safety notices, letters to people whose first language is not English, or complex instructions for those whose skills are manual rather than intellectual, don't take such risks.

> *In order to obviate any deleterious effects, ensure that the primary supply is disconnected from the prime mover prior to selection of alternative transmission velocity ratios.*

means:

> SWITCH OFF MOTOR BEFORE CHANGING GEAR.

So why not say so?

The long and short of stylish writing

Stylish writing contains a mixture of short sentences—fewer than ten words—and longer ones—up to 30 words. Use short sentences for important points. Expand on these points, if necessary, by providing extra details in longer sentences containing subordinate clauses, such as this one; but never use a long word where a shorter, more commonly understood one will do the job.

EXAMPLES THE POWER OF PLAIN ENGLISH

Here is a selection of weak expressions and redundant sentence preambles, with suggested alternatives:

Foggy and weak language	Direct and more powerful language
If and when we receive ...	If we receive ... When we receive ... (But not both)
At the present time ...	Now ...
At this point in time ...	Now ...
Absolutely perfect.	Perfect. (Can anything be *slightly* perfect?)
Due to the fact that ...	Because ...
First and foremost ...	First ...
The end result was ...	The result was ...
In the course of ...	While ...
In the event of ...	If ...
The vast majority of ...	Most ...
With reference to ...	About ...
With a view to ...	To ...
In order to ...	To ...
In my own personal opinion ...	In my opinion ...
As explained earlier ...	Omit this sentence altogether; no one needs it.
It is not necessary to stress the fact that ...	So don't stress it! Omit this preamble.
It is of interest to note that ...	Of interest to whom? Omit this preamble.
In all sectors of the environment ...	Everywhere ...
I am under an obligation to ...	I must ...
At this juncture it is worth pointing out ...	Just point it out if it's worth doing.
In order to keep things in perspective, we would like to emphasize the fact that ...	You achieve more emphasis without the preamble!

And now a few foggy words with everyday ones which will usually do the same job:

Pretentious word	Plain English equivalent
Subsequently	Later
Initiate	Start
Termination	End
Implemented	Done
Commencement	Start
Anticipate	Expect
Accomplish	Do
Modification	Change
Utilization	Use

7.6 MAKE THE PAGE SAY *READ ME*

One glance at some of the reports which land on your desk is enough to tell you they're going to be hard work. Nothing springs out at you; if you want to know what's there you've got to read the lot! Three or four large paragraphs cover each page. While reading, you'd better keep a finger on your place: if you look away you'll have a hard job finding where you were. And as your eyes get tired the page fades into obscurity like closed Venetian blinds. It looks boring; you feel bad; it *is* boring!

Headings are signposts

Use attention-grabbing headlines for your letters and memos. Let people know at a glance what you are writing about. In longer documents use subheadings (meaningful ones, remember!) to help readers find specific topics.

You don't need a multiplicity of typefaces in a desk top publishing system to make a letter look inviting; **bold**, underlined and CAPITAL LETTERS will do the job. Indeed, a warning to amateur DTP fans: many people find letters typeset in a multitude of fancy fonts a real turn-off.

Bullets keep you on target

Use bullets to:

- Identify the separate items in a list.
- Call attention to a single sentence.

For lists longer than seven items, numbers are usually preferable to bullets, especially if readers might want to refer back to individual items.

Charts and pictures

Graphics can liven up your text. Be clear about the purpose of each, and choose the graphic style best suited to that purpose. With a meaningful caption, a diagram can sometimes do a better job than a page of text. Keep your sketches and line drawings simple, showing just enough detail to illustrate your point.

Bar charts, pie charts and line graphs all have their places in business communication. Choose the style that puts your main message across most clearly.

White space

White space is not necessarily wasted space; it is the visual equivalent of silence. Leave spaces between subsections, around diagrams, beside bullet lines. And leave wide margins where readers can add notes. Business documents are for working with, and in management, this includes thinking. Many people believe they think better with pencil in hand and somewhere to jot down their thoughts.

House style

Through its reports, proposals and other written communications, an organization projects an image to its customers, its suppliers and its employees. For this reason many standardize on one or more style sheets. So all product specifications, for example, would use a standard format—typestyles, margins, numbering system, binders and so on—which customers get to recognize.

If you think your organization is anaesthetising itself and boring its customers with venetian blind documents, why not crusade to get the format changed?

EXAMPLES

Fig 7.2

> MEMORANDUM
>
> 16th September 1993
> From I.A.M. CRUSTY
> To U.R. Dusty
>
> I write in reference to your communication of 29th ultimo. Having given careful consideration to the points you make concerning our expenditure in the area of advertising, I would just like to document my views on possible ways in which we might blah blah and lots more blah blah. And more and yet more blah blah. Blah blah blah blah blah blah blah blah blah. And more blah blah blah blah blah blah blah blah blah blah blah blah blah.
>
> At this stage it might be worth adding the observation that blah blah. And more and yet more blah blah. Blah blah blah blah blah blah blah blah blah. And more blah blah blah blah. And more and yet more blah blah. Blah blah blah blah blah blah blah blah blah. And more blah blah blah blah. And more and yet more blah blah. Blah blah blah blah blah blah blah blah. And more blah blah blah blah blah blah blah blah blah.
>
> Finally I would add that blah blah blah blah. And more and yet more blah blah. Blah blah blah blah blah blah blah blah. And more blah blah blah blah. And more and yet more blah blah. Blah blah blah blah blah blah blah blah. And more blah blah blah blah blah blah blah blah blah blah blah.

This memo looks heavy and dull. This suggests reading it is going to be hard work. It won't be surprising if it goes straight into the pending tray, there to decay to irrelevance.

Fig 7.3

> **MEMORANDUM**
>
> 16th September 1993
> From B E M Odern
> To U.R. Dusty
>
> **HOW WE CAN CUT OUR PUBLICITY COSTS**
>
> Last year we spent £40 000 on publicity - twice the industry average (ADPLAN Figures, Jan - Dec). Our costs were as follows:
>
> * Newspaper and magazine advertising £12 000
> * Sponsorship £28 000
>
> Our sales analysis report (SR47 dated 4th March 1993) shows the effects on costs and revenue of switching 50 per cent of our sponsorship budget to magazine advertising.

> **Recommendation**
> We should not sponsor next year's mud wrestling grand prix; but we should increase our advertising budget by £14 000, transfering the balance to profits.

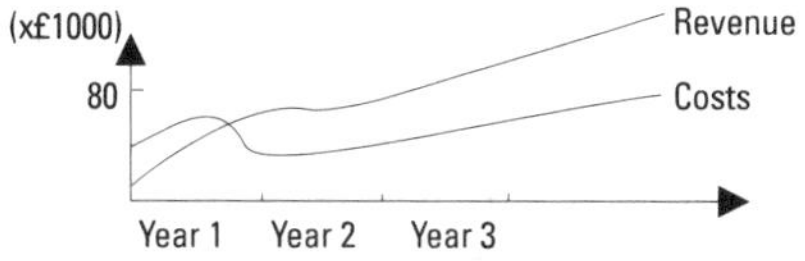

In contrast, this layout is inviting. The message is easier to understand, because:

- The heading makes it clear what the memo is about.
- Bullet lines make the three findings stand out.
- The graph shows the benefits the writer is forecasting.
- The recommendations are signposted with a bold subheading.

This is just what the reader needs to make a decision.

7.7 A PRODUCTIVE WRITING PROCESS

If you have followed the planning process suggested earlier, you will now have an outline of your document, or at least of a chapter of a larger work. Now all you have to do is write one paragraph under each heading in your outline and insert the illustrations. There are several advantages in this approach:

- You don't have to think about *what* to write, as your helpful headings remind you what you intended to say; so you can concentrate on *how* to put it across accurately, briefly and clearly. (That's quite enough of a challenge for most of us.)
- You can write the paragraphs in any order. You don't have to worry whether the sequence is logical: you've sorted all that out in your plan. So there is no need to start at the beginning of your document—often the most difficult place to start.
- If you are held up for information to complete a section, you can skip it and return later to fill in the missing details.
- When you are tired, but under pressure from an approaching deadline, write some of the more straightforward paragraphs on which you can make rapid progress. The progress you make can help lift your motivation so you are soon able to return to those difficult aspects.

Get quickly to 95 per cent right

You need a rapid writing process to complement your efficient plans. I have been able to plan, produce and edit ready for publication up to 8000 words per working day, depending on the complexity of the subject matter, using the following approach:

- Put down your ideas without stopping to correct any typing errors. If you go back to correct an error you will probably re-read the sentence in which it occurs; this will break your train of thought and slow you down.
- When stuck for a word, don't allow this mental block to distract or demotivate you. Simply enter ?? and continue typing. During the editing phase you can search out all occurrences of ??, calling up the thesaurus in your word processor if necessary. But often these are temporary blocks, and once you read your complete draft you are able to insert the majority of missing words right away.
- If you feel that a word is wrongly chosen or a sentence badly expressed, type ?? and move on. It is quicker to deal with these second thoughts all in a batch during the editing phase. And there is another important advantage in editing some time after you type in the initial text entry: you are then much less likely to read what you intended to write, rather than what is actually on the page!

This rapid writing technique will help you produce a draft almost as quickly as you can type. So suppose you are a 'few fingers' typist capable of just 30 words per minute; then an hour's work should give you about 1500 words. The beauty of this system is that 90 to 95 per cent of those words will be the right ones. The editing stage takes more than another 5 per cent of the time, of course. A realistic allowance for a 'few fingers' typist is:

Task	Time allowance (%)
Defining objectives	10
Making the detailed plan	30
Writing the draft	30
Editing and revision	30

EXAMPLE

Most modern word processors contain outlining facilities which are useful for planning multi-chapter documents. If a subsection is moved to another location, the numbering is automatically adjusted throughout the book. Once the writing stage is complete, it is a simple matter to modify the outliner rules so that the lower level headings are printed without their numbers.

This screen shot shows the outliner in Lotus *Ami Pro* being used:

Fig 7.4

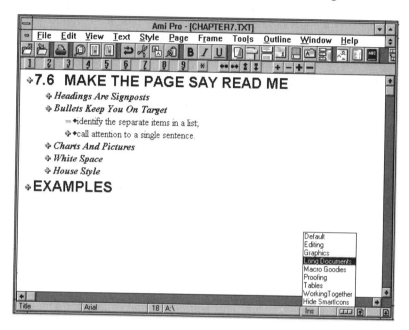

Once the chapter is complete, the spelling checker and thesaurus are used to fill in the missing words and correct the typing errors.

Fig 7.5

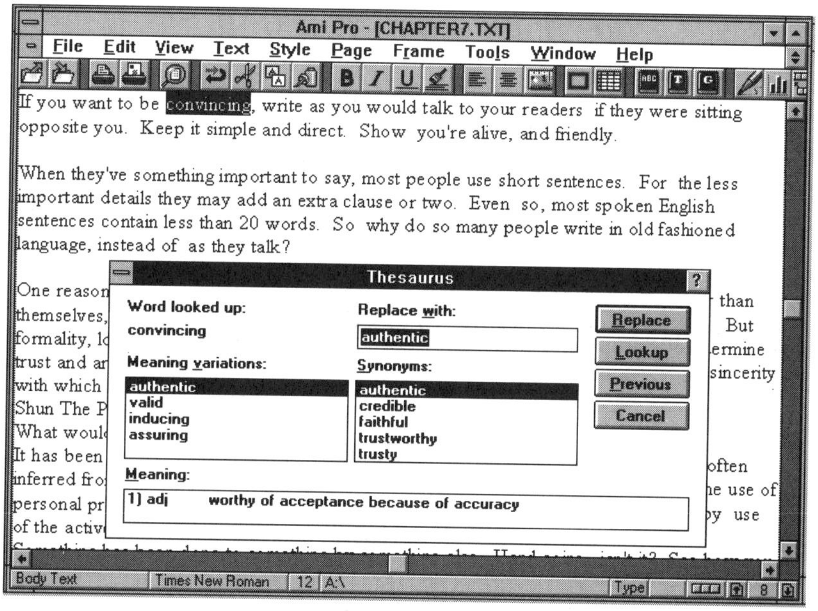

7.8 EDITING — THE QUALITY CONTROL STAGE

The amount of time you spend checking and editing will depend on:

- How important the document is (and how senior the people receiving it are!).
- How closely your publishing deadline looms.
- How keen you are to develop your writing skills.

For a memo to the catering department asking them to arrange working lunches for a meeting, you need only check that you have correctly typed the time, date and number of lunches required. But a report to a client deserves more thorough checking.

A structured editing process

You soon learn what kinds of errors you make most frequently. Then you can adjust your editing process to match your *fault spectrum*.

Here is a checking process suited to someone whose typing is erratic, with words joined together, letters swapped around, etc:

1 Check that all numerical values are correct (especially the position of decimal points) and that the correct units are quoted (cm or mm, g or kg, etc.).
2 Check that numerical values in illustrations and their captions agree with those stated in the text.
3 Check that factual statements have been typed correctly. For example, has the word *not* been omitted or has *we must now* become *we must not*?
4 Now run the spelling checker and correct typing and spelling slips.
5 Print the document double spaced. (Few people are able to spot mistakes as readily from a screen as they can from hard copy. The advent of large, high-resolution monitors with paper-white screens has helped, but you may still prefer to give your eyes a rest from the screen.)
6 Read through and mark in red any errors of the following kinds:

- **Omissions**. Are all sections present and complete, and are tables complete with column and row headings?
- **Subjectivity**. Are there any unsupported statements or opinion expressed as fact? If so, include a reference to the source of your information.
- **Grammar**. Watch out for incorrect changes of tense, person, number and gender.
- **Punctuation**. It's easy to type ':' instead of ';'.

7 Mark suggested improvements where your writing is vague, passive or verbose.
8 Make your corrections and then take a break—two or three days would be ideal, but at least an hour—so you can come back to your work and read it as if you were one of the people for whom it was intended. Be ruthlessly self-critical. Mark any sections which are too detailed, unclear or which contain confusing terminology or abbreviations.
9 Re-run the spelling checker and correct any typing errors introduced while editing.
10 Make a final printout and read it aloud. By now your work should sound good, but you may decide to alter the wording here and there before sending it to your readers or, for your most important documents, to an independent reviewer.

EXAMPLE: Here is part of a draft report before editing:

Fig 7.6

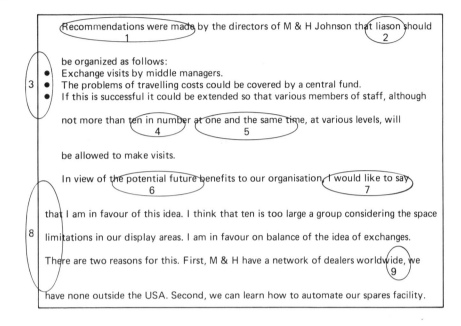

Editing comments

1   Use the active voice.
2   This is a common spelling error. The correct spelling is: 'liaison'.
3   Put listed items in the same (parallel) form: all as sentences or questions, etc.
4   They couldn't be ten in colour! Omit *in number*.
5   ...*at a time*... is better.
6   *Potential* implies *future*. (This is termed *tautology*.) Say either *future* or *potential*.
7   Just say it!
8   Re-order these sentences. Make the most general statement before the more specific, and build from the familiar towards the novel.
9   Use a semicolon to link closely related sentences, not a comma.

The edited version

Fig 7.7

> The directors of M & H Johnson recommend that:
> - Middle managers should make exchange visits.
> - We should set up an exchange visit travel fund.
> - Exchanges by groups of up to ten staff could follow later.
>
> I am in favour of these proposals for two reasons. First, M & H have a worldwide dealer network; we have no dealers outside the USA. Second, we could learn from M & H how to automate our spares facility.
>
> We may have to limit staff groups to six people or fewer, as space is tight in our display areas.

7.9 INDEPENDENT REVIEW

Get a colleague to review your most important documents. If possible, ask someone whose knowledge of and interest in the subject is similar to those of the intended readership. Explain what you are trying to achieve, and give them a copy on which to mark recommended changes and comments. They may also need background material, such as a letter of complaint or a report on the previous phase of a project.

A good reviewer is a rare animal

Some people are good at reviewing; others provide little more than a second-rate spelling check service. Get to know who in your organization will do a good job, because a good reviewer is a valuable ally in your campaign to improve your writing skills.

Beware of the 'delay lines'. These are the people who, when asked to review a document, never refuse; but they leave it in their pending tray until you chase them for its return. Only then do they skim superficially the first few pages, desperately seeking some trivial point which might suggest they had read through the whole thing.

Do check that your reviewer can spare the necessary time. A thorough review takes about five minutes per A4 page. Work out when you need the reviewer's comments by, and arrange to deliver the draft in time to meet the deadline—not forgetting to leave time for corrections resulting from the review.

Using the feedback

When the reviewer returns your marked-up typescript, it's usually best to read through *all* the comments before making any changes to your document. You may not agree with some of the recommendations, but don't criticize the reviewer with:

> *'Ah yes, but you don't understand. It's not as simple as that...'*

A defensive response like this could make your reviewer less willing to help you in future. Indeed, it's quite likely there *are* things the reviewer hasn't taken into account. That's no problem: it's still your decision what, if anything, to change. Often a suggestion by a reviewer will prompt you to find a better way of putting across a difficult point, and the final version may be nothing like either your draft or your reviewer's suggestion. If the result is a more effective document, the review process has been successful.

If you don't understand a comment or criticism, ask for clarification. But no matter how your pride may have been hurt, thank your reviewers for their work. In the long run, both you and your organization will benefit from this effort.

Two-stage reviews

Occasionally the reviewer may suggest an alternative structure, layout or style. This can pose serious problems if you are working to a tight schedule. Try to arrange a two-stage review. In the first stage you provide your outline and a sample page, together with brief details of who your readers are and what you are trying to achieve. Follow this with a second stage where the full text is offered for review.

When you are battling to meet a deadline, it's tempting to omit the review stage. Don't! An important report issued without independent review is as unlikely to be effective as an unrehearsed presentation.

REVIEWER'S CHECK-LIST

Complete the header section of this check-list before passing it, with your draft report, to an independent reviewer.

		Y/N
Report title:		
Author:		
Reviewer:		
Intended readership:		
Is the report complete? Does it contain (as appropriate)		
Title page, with issue date, report number, copyright statement?		
Distribution list for the full report and any executive (separately issued) summary?		
Amendment record with date panel?		
Summary?		
Contents list?		
All pages of every chapter and appendix?		
Is the report presentation of good quality?		
Pages set out with adequate margins		
Meaningful headings and subheadings throughout		
Illustrations adjacent to relevant text where practicable		
Printing legible throughout		
Headers and footers consistent throughout		
Spelling check completed		
Are the contents accurate and clear?		
Structure clear, complete and understandable		
Facts substantiated and information sources stated		
Numbers unambiguous and units consistent throughout		
Is the writing style appropriate?		
Tone sufficiently personal and conversational		
Passive voice used only where necessary		
Obscure words and jargon avoided		
Short sentences, especially at beginnings of topics/paragraphs		
Unnecessary detail, superfluous words avoided		
Powerful verbs used and abstract terms minimized		
Any other points?		

IMPROVE YOUR COMMERCIAL AWARENESS

YOUR CONTRIBUTION TO SALES, MARKETING AND CUSTOMER CARE

Few business decisions are purely technical; most have commercial implications. That is why all managers need to understand marketing concepts and how the commercial side of their business works.

Marketing is more than simply satisfying customer needs. It is devising the means of doing so profitably. Long-term success comes from investing part of today's profits in new products and capabilities for the future. Without this investment objective the business would be unable to meet future needs profitably.

The challenge

To succeed, a business must satisfy its customers, for the cost of finding new customers and earning their loyalty is usually greater than that of winning repeat business. In any case, disgruntled customers spread a bad reputation which is difficult to repair.

> *'But we have a marketing department and a sales department. Surely that's enough? After all, someone's got to produce the goods and deliver the services. The more we spend on customer relations the higher our prices will be.'*

Perhaps! But if you want to know *why* you are asked to take on particular tasks, you need to know what your organization is striving for—its marketing strategy.

The benefits

Understanding the commercial aspects of your organization can help you to:

- Appreciate your organization's commercial position: the strengths and weaknesses of your product range, and your financial and technical capability.
- Realize when your competitors are pursuing business opportunities you need to win, and decide how you can stop them.
- Know your competitors well enough to be able to predict their actions better than they can predict yours.
- Understand how your customers make their buying decisions.

COMMERCIAL AWARENESS — WHAT CAN YOU DO?

A commercial organization must make reasonable profits, or its owners will move their financial backing to more lucrative ventures. Profitability depends on providing just the right level of customer satisfaction—high enough to win and retain the business, but not so high that the costs of doing so erode profit margins excessively.

But there is another requirement for a long-term future: the organization must have a strategy for winning new orders. Some of these new opportunities may be with entirely new customers and based upon new systems, new techniques, and new ranges of goods and services.

Start with the customer

To delight your customers with service beyond their expectations, and to do so at sufficient profit, you need to know your customers. The things you do, whether based on white heat innovation or super-efficient production, should all stem from your knowledge of your customers and their needs. You need answers to questions like:

- What do your customers think of your existing products?
- How satisfied are they with your present standard of service?
- What unfilled requirements have they currently which you might be able to satisfy?
- What could they be influenced to buy in future?
- What budget have they got, and what are the trends—upwards or downwards?

Get to know how your markets operate. Then you will be able to contribute to the strategic planning and management of your organization.

Your contribution

The basis of commercial decision-making is market intelligence. The more complete and up to date your market data, the better your decisions should be. So how can you contribute to your organization's commercial database?

Maybe you can tap sources not readily accessible to your marketing people: trade reps can be a mine of commercial information. But remember, commercial intelligence is a two-way flow. You want to know more about your competitors, but you also need to limit their access to your plans, and so safeguard your position for winning further orders.

Every employee contributes to the image the company projects to its customers. How, for instance, do your staff deal with incoming calls?

> *'Sorry! She's not 'ere and her job's a complete mystery to the rest of us, so I can't help you. You might have better luck if you ring tomorrow!'*

The caller might be one of your most valued customers, and far from impressed with the image of your company. But most people only need guidance in telephone technique and they will do a good job:

> *'This is Jane Symonds. Janet won't be back until two o'clock. May I take a message or get her to call you back?'*

And when visitors walk around your area, what do they see? Are notice-boards cluttered with out of date information? Are workplaces littered with back issues of trade magazines? Or is the image that of an up-to-date, efficient organization?

8.1 MARKETING CONCEPTS

Like most jobs, marketing has its share of jargon. So, before looking further into how you can contribute to the commercial success of your organization, here are some terms your marketing colleagues might use:

Market segmentation

Technical requirements, buying method, location, size of budget—these and many other factors make buyers unique. Segmentation means grouping together similar opportunities and adjusting your strategy so your offer is most attractive to that group or segment of the market. You might decide to go into head-on competition with a powerful market leader. More likely, however, you would look for a niche—a market segment the dominant player has overlooked or is ill-equipped to exploit.

Marketing mix

This is marketing jargon for getting the right combination of:

- **Product**—goods or services with the right features, quality, after-sales support, etc.
- **Promotion**—advertising, sales promotions, public relations, etc.
- **Price**—including settlement terms, discounts, etc.
- **Place**—sales area coverage, distribution methods, stock holding policy, etc.

Marketing strategy

A commercial organization might have a long-term plan to regain a former position, to retain its present position, or to move to some new position in the market it serves or would like to serve.

A strategic analysis must define:

- The strengths and weaknesses of the organization and those of the competition.
- The commercial opportunities, their risks and potential benefits.
- The markets which best match the organization's capability and resources.

Marketing plans

The outcome of a strategic analysis of business opportunities is a marketing plan. The plan should be to make effective use of the resources of the business to define, design, produce and sell a range of products (goods or services) that sufficient customers will buy at prices profitable to the business. It must justify a choice of market segments and marketing mix, and will contain a schedule of marketing and sales activities with staff responsibilities and cost estimates.

The marketing plan says:

- What goods or services should be designed and produced.
- How they should be designed and made available.
- How they should be promoted.
- How they should be sold.
- How they should be distributed.
- How they should be supported after sales.
- What future enhancements could extend the saleable life, or improve the cash flow and profitability of the product.

EXAMPLE

Here is the outline of FICO's marketing plan for their new Autojector, an automatic image centring and scaling overhead projector:

FICO Industries, Visual Aids Division
Product range: Autojector overhead projectors
Models: Table and portable models, with wall and free-standing screens
Market information
Market research data—segmentation, price sensitivity, market shares
Customer files
Competitor files
FICO product specifications
FICO customer support facilities
Autojector product plan
Quality plan—reliability, maintainability, audit and review procedures
Safety plan—policy, audits, testing and review procedures
Development plan—human, capital and materials resources, schedules and costs
Production plan—human, capital and materials resources, schedules and costs
Promotional plan—advertising, publicity, PR—with schedules and costs
Product launch plan—venue, timing and cost estimates
Sales plan—territories, responsibilities, sales brochures, schedules and costs
Warehousing and distribution plan
Product support and enhancement (maintenance, new features' etc.) plan
Human resources plan
Recruitment plan, schedule and cost estimates
Staff training programme and schedule
Incentives—performance measurement criteria, timing and costs
Financial plan
Development, manufacturing, marketing, sales and customer support budgets
Pricing policy—home and export markets, direct and/or via distributors
Discount policy—quantity discounts, badged products, educational sales policy
Cash flow forecast
Return on investment analysis
Financial/commercial risk analysis

All areas of the plan are drafted during a feasibility study. Once full development is under way, the initial estimates are refined every six months. Market forecasts are also reviewed so that the financial appraisal can be brought up to date.

HOW BUYING DECISIONS ARE MADE

People buy your organization's products for the benefits they provide. And even if you sell to other organizations, it is still *individuals* who make the buying decisions. Each of these buyers seeks benefits—to acquire a reputation as an orator, for example—and will be led by beliefs—a better overhead projector would improve the quality of their presentations—to define wants—a new projector.

You can't always discover why individual people make particular purchases, but you can look for patterns of behaviour in the buying of your products or services. You may find several criteria form the basis of decision. These might include:

Economic factors

- Purchase cost.
- Running cost.
- Credit facilities.

Technical performance

- Functionality.
- Extendability.
- Reputation for reliability.

Other commercial factors

- Relationship with your company representatives.
- Confidence in your ability to deliver on time.
- Confidence in your after-sales service.
- Political pressures, such as buying home-produced goods.
- Safety standards and other regulations.

Customer relations

Is it realistic to get to know your customers personally? Do you have a small number of high-value accounts or are you supplying thousands of people, perhaps via a distributor network?

The general public usually make buying decisions on a less deliberate, often subjective, basis. This makes it difficult to produce a meaningful decision model, and so the persuasiveness of advertising, public relations, sales promotion campaigns, and in particular salespersons' skills, become more important.

For a one-to-many supplier–customer relationship you may have to rely on advertising and other forms of publicity. But if you rely on repeat orders from a few customers, you will need to cultivate a more personal relationship. Think of them as clients, in the same way an accountant or legal adviser would. And treat them that way. Get close to your clients and find out what selection criteria they are using. You need to know how they will weigh up the purchasing decision factors, so you can make trade-off decisions in your marketing plans. For example, should you spend money improving the reliability of an equipment or the frequency of a service, or would it be better to reduce the price? Put the factors and their weightings into a decision table to compare alternative strategies and see which are likely to give best results.

EXAMPLES

A birthday present for Aunt Lucy

Vanessa is looking for a present for her Aunt Lucy. She goes window shopping with no clear objectives. She sees a pair of leather gloves. No, she gave gloves last year. (Criterion: must not be similar to last year's gift.) Next she considers flowers. No, Aunt Lucy has a fine garden. (Criterion: must be something she hasn't already got.) She looks at a make-up box, but decides £150 is too expensive. (Criterion: must not cost more than £50.) Finally, she spots a pendant watch at £45. It's within her budget; it's different; Aunt Lucy needs a watch; and it's unlike last year's present. So Vanessa buys the watch.

Vanessa bought the first thing she saw which satisfied her (unvoiced) criteria. This is common in personal buying. Prominent displays ensure potential buyers see your products; this can even allow you to outsell competitors whose products are superior.

A major account sale

Things are usually different in business-to-business selling, where buyers are trained to seek alternative suppliers and evaluate offers more objectively. Even so, the relationship between buyer and seller is often a key factor in the decision base.

The table below shows how a professional supplier mirrors the customer's activities leading up to a sale, and so improves the prospect of securing an order.

Stage	Customer action	Supplier action
1	Unaware of any specific needs.	Research into customer organization. Write stating capability; follow up by phone, requesting a meeting.
2	Meet supplier. Try to shift supplier's work towards solving your problems.	If requirement vague, try to shift it towards your capability. Find out budget and who is key decision taker.
3	Liaise with supplier to learn what is feasible. Prepare a cost-benefit analysis. Draft an internal proposal to win budget for purchasing.	Provide customer with discussion papers which help them draft their internal proposal.
4	Secure internal approval for budget. Identify possible bidders. Write request for proposal.	Discuss terms and conditions. Try to discover basis on which bids will be judged and budget available.
5	Publish request for quotation.	Study request for quotation. Prepare proposal and quotation.
6	Vet proposals and create short-list. Ask for best and final offers from favoured bidders.	Fine tune bid and adjust price (downwards or upwards according to your knowledge of other contenders).
7	Choose supplier and negotiate contract.	Negotiate on quantities, price, terms and conditions; close the deal.
8	Monitor progress of supplier.	Supply according to contract, keeping customer informed of any unavoidable departures from plan.
9	Use product, monitor the benefits obtained and compare with initial predictions.	Monitor customer's use of the product, providing assistance so results match expectations.
10	Consider future enhancements and eventual replacement.	Discuss future requirements. Develop capability to meet future needs.

8.3 CONTRACTING — DEVELOPING A WINNING STRATEGY

If your business is based on contracting there's a lot you can do before jobs come up for tendering. You won't win unless the customer thinks yours is the best bid. And how will you know *what* your customer is thinking if you don't stay in touch?

This is too big a job to be left to the sales team. People at all levels—in research, development and customer support, for example—should help. Maybe that includes you; in which case find out who is your opposite number in each key customer organization and allocate part of your time to building close links with them.

If you are the project manager designate, you will need to coordinate all this effort. Arrange planning and review meetings with your key players. They should have targets: who should visit whom; how often; with what objectives?

Influencing the requirement

Wouldn't it be great if you could get the customer to ask for things you are good at, but which your competitors would find difficult? Well, why not team up with your customers so the products you develop closely match their needs? Here's how:

- When you visit, take along discussion papers setting out your ideas on what matters most to your customer. Make sure these are written from the customer's point of view. Invite comments. Invite customer representatives to visit you to see how things are coming along. (Yes, there *are* commercial risks. But you show *what* you have to offer, not *how* you do it—at least, not in too much detail.)
- Listen to your customers. Let them influence the direction of your development. And let them *know* they have had an influence. When you take up a suggestion, write and thank the customer, and maybe arrange a demonstration.
- Whenever you send outline specifications for comment, you are training your customers to use your jargon. Get it right and you could find the customer uses your wording when drawing up the request for quotation (RFQ). What could be more depressing to your competitors than to find they don't even understand what the customer is asking for? It must undermine their credibility when they have to ask the customer what the tender document means!

Your proactive investment brings your capability closer to your customers' needs. It also draws their requirement specifications closer to your capability, so when the RFQ arrives you get fewer surprises and have less work to do to put together a winning bid.

Sounds simple! But your strongest competitors will be trying to do much the same thing, so there will still be work to do. A lot depends on how the tenders are judged—the basis of decision. That's something else you will have been trying to influence, of course.

Influencing the basis of decision

You can't just invent a win strategy once the RFQ has arrived; it has to be earned by proactive marketing and innovation before the customers know what they want. Winning is not simply a matter of being better than your competitors. You must also influence the customers' perceptions of what you have to offer and their criteria for choosing between bids. Try, during this pre-bid phase, to get the customer to ask for responses on points where your competitors are weak. In this way you can emphasize your own strengths and ensure that the weaknesses of competing bids are highlighted.

EXAMPLE

Bid/no-bid decision

FICO have kept closely in touch with the National Conference Centre during the past 18 months. Technical, sales and customer support managers have made frequent visits, providing assistance in drawing up specifications and working to influence both the NCC requirements and the basis on which competing tenders will be judged.

Now the RFQ has arrived and FICO's bid team meet to study the documents and plan their campaign. One of their first decisions is whether FICO should bid for the contract.

Here is the check-list FICO use to assess the risks and the financial viability of these types of contracts.

Contract: NCC refurbishment	Review board's assessment of FICO position			
RFQ received: 14 September				
Tender closing date: 31 October	Strong	Weak	Value	Comments
How closely is this contract aligned to our business strategy?				
How serious is the tender? (Some RFQs are frivolous, with no resulting contract.)				
What are the technical risks, and their cost implications?				
What are the commercial risks (for example, is the customer financially secure)?				
What are the currency exchange risks (if being paid for exports in foreign currency)?				
What is the value of this contract?				
What is the value of follow-on opportunities?				
What is our probability of winning?				
How profitable is the deal likely to be?				
Could we fund the cash flow?				
What will it cost us to prepare our bid?				
How will bid preparation affect our existing work?				
What effect would winning this contract have on our other work?				

If they decide to bid, the review meeting must also agree:

• What form the bid will take—full or partial compliance.
• Whether to offer alternative bids.
• What budget will be available to the bid team.
• Who will present the proposal.
• When to present the proposal. (Normally, for security reasons, this will be close to the tender closing time.)

8.4 MANAGING A PROPOSAL

If you are appointed Project Manager designate you will probably manage the bid preparation. Break the work into stages. Decide what help you need and make sure the bid team can be freed from their other work at the right time. Try this approach.

1 Study the RFQ
Before planning your response, go carefully through every clause of the RFQ to make sure you and your team members understand the requirement.

2 Make a work schedule
Working back from the submission date, plan your schedule for the bid preparation work. Note how many copies (and volumes if applicable) are required, and forewarn your reprographic services supplier. If a presentation is required, include its preparation, rehearsal and review in the schedule. Leave time for review and revision of the proposal documents before printing and binding.

3 Structure the proposal
Don't antagonize your customer by using an arbitrary or inappropriate structure. If the RFQ states the structure to use, then adhere to it. If not, can you structure your proposal to match the scoring system? Otherwise, choose a logical structure which presents your proposal in the best possible light.

4 Agree the topic themes
These are your means of highlighting more attractive claims than your competitors can justifiably make. To ensure credibility, you must substantiate every claim you make. You should also aim to undermine the claims of your competitors.

5 Provide a layout and style guide
Draft and edit one topic in the style and at a standard you can offer as a guide to others who will contribute to your proposal. Call your writers together and talk them through the topic, pointing out why you are using a low fog index, a personal style, graphics in place of long descriptive passages, and so on.

6 Draft and edit the proposal
Get all the material drafted and edited by your writers, with roughs of all graphics. Work through each topic checking for completeness, accuracy and directness of style. Make all corrections and print draft copies for the final stage of checking.

7 Arrange a red team review
Brief a shadow customer vetting team so they understand the background and have studied the RFQ. Give each a copy of your proposal so they can mark up weaknesses, mistakes, omissions and irrelevant material.

8 Update and publish
Discuss the red team criticisms with your writers. Agree what changes are needed and update your proposal. Make a final check that all red team comments have been taken into account, before sending the proposal for printing. Check that everything you send to the printer does, in fact, get put into the proposal. Make sure the right number of copies are delivered to the customer.

EXAMPLE: # USING STORYBOARDS

Vanessa Tippet is contributing to FICO's bid for re-equipping the National Conference Centre. She has been asked to respond to the section of the RFQ that asks for proposals for audiovisual aids equipment. Having already made several visits to demonstrate the new Autojector, a self-centring and scaling overhead projector, Vanessa knows this is her trump card. The budget for her topic is just two pages, and she needs to bring out this win theme while showing compliance with all the other requirements.

Vanessa uses a storyboard to discuss her plans with the bid manager and to explain to the illustrator what graphics she will need:

Fig 8.1

7.12 AUDIO-VISUAL AIDS

Thesis: Autojector facilities on all OHP and 35 mm projectors give clearer images and improve quality of presentations.

Points:
1   FICO can supply complete range of audio and visual aids for conference and syndicate rooms.
2   FICO's field service team provides 4 hour response to requests for help.
3   FICO's unique Autojector gives superior images for all sizes of OHP slides.
4   Our Autojector-35 is now available for 35 mm slide projection.

Graphics: To show typical OHPs with standard projector and Autojector facility.

Standard OHP

Autojector

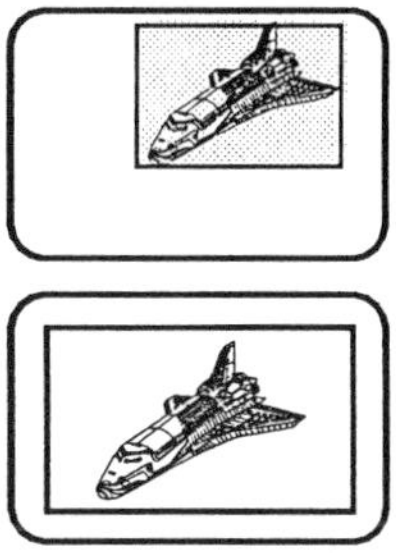

Selecting persuasive themes

Price is not the only key factor, particularly where the cost of ownership is mainly incurred after initial delivery. Vanessa knows that the conference centre manager wants to impress potential clients with superior facilities which would help them achieve more impact with their customer presentations.

Vanessa realizes that in the competing proposals there will be many topics in which there is nothing to choose between bidders. The discriminating factors may amount to no more than 10 per cent of the requirements. She must focus on these key issues. If FICO are to win, most will be areas of strength where they can go on the offensive. But there may be other areas needing defensive work.

In this example, Vanessa chooses to highlight two points where her bid is superior to *some* of its competitors, and two where she can beat them *all*. In other parts of the proposal FICO may have to defend itself in areas of relative weakness.

Choosing persuasive graphics

An aerial photograph of the FICO factory might look pretty, but does it help put across the message 'FICO can do it better'? Vanessa decides not! She asks the illustrator to show two conference screens, one with a poorly centred, under-sized image and the other with a clear, full-screen display benefiting from the Autojector facility.

WRITING PERSUASIVE SALES LITERATURE

Your brochure or proposal must sell the advantages of your offer to the customer. So you need to show how your offer is superior to those of your competitors, and to get the customer to value your offer above all others.

Use customer terminology

If the RFQ uses one term, don't substitute your own preferred alternative. Make it easy for your customer to read and understand your proposal. If the RFQ spells something out in full you should do the same, even if there is an accepted abbreviation.

Build win themes into every paragraph

Padding reduces impact. If a message doesn't support your bid, it shouldn't be in there. Every paragraph should carry a message—one of your win themes—strengthening your bid for the order. Most of your win themes will come from your strategy. These messages appear throughout the proposal, underpinning your claims to uniqueness and superiority. They are influential messages directed at specific individuals in the customer decision-making group. So, you could have major themes on your technical superiority, proven track record, environment friendliness, better after-sales support, less costly upgrade path than your competitors, and so on.

Don't neglect the occasional persuasive message which is not related to your strategy, but which is of benefit to some or all in the customer decision group. You may have a smaller product which fits in a standard briefcase. Even though the product may be transported very occasionally, this factor could carry some weight. (Literally!)

Make the discriminators sparkle

There will be many parts of your document similar to those of your competitors. You still need to do a good job on these, of course. But on the handful of topics where you are ahead of the field, and on those (even fewer, if you are to win) where your competitors' offers could be seen as superior, you must do an even better job of presenting your case. These topics are the discriminators. Every sentence must put your message across persuasively.

Give proof for your claims

To be credible, you must show you have considered the alternative approaches taken by your competitors, and have sound reasons to provide something different. If the customer will be making a careful assessment of alternatives before choosing a supplier, make sure your literature contains trade-off justifications of your chosen approach.

Sell the benefits

Fig 8.2

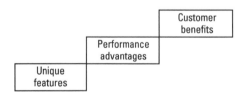

Briefly describe each feature of your offer. Explain the advantages over alternative approaches your competitors may offer, and show how customers benefit more by choosing your solution. Remember, it may not be obvious to your customers how they will benefit from your technical superiority.

EXAMPLES

A sales brochure

Here is part of the text of a sales brochure advertising a fast print service. Notice how each paragraph contains a selling message in customer benefit language:

DOESN'T A QUALITY BUSINESS LIKE YOURS DESERVE QUALITY BROCHURES? NOW SIMULPRINT MAKES SUPERB COLOUR AFFORDABLE

The new **SIMULPRINT** process. The marketing breakthrough your business needs:

- **Process colour printing at spot colour prices**. Put your competitors in the shade with full colour printing, even for small quantity circulars and mailshots.
- **Standard turn-round only 3 days.** SIMULPRINT works directly from your colour slides or prints, so you avoid the time-consuming and costly colour separation stage. And if you need super-fast turn-round, you don't have to settle for low quality photocopying. Call our 24 hour hot line on 071 234 5678 and we will collect your original and get finished prints to you **within 24 hours.**
- **Perfect colour registration every time.** No more blurred end-of-run copies, because **SIMULPRINT** is a one-pass process.

BOOST YOUR SALES WITH QUALITY PRINTING AT BUDGET PRICES DIAL 071 234 5678 NOW AND CLAIM YOUR INTRODUCTORY DISCOUNT

A proposal

Here is part of FICO's proposal to supply their Autojector range to the National Conference Centre. Notice how FICO have given evidence for each claim they make.

THE AUTOJECTOR OHP PROVIDES UNSURPASSED RELIABILITY, AND ITS MODULAR CONSTRUCTION CUTS SERVICING TIME TO A MINIMUM

1 In independent tests on 50 Autojectors, ITS Assessment Services measured a mean time between failure of 16 000 hours—over six years' life at seven working hours a day.
2 FICO will provide a three year parts and labour warranty (except lamp bulbs). So there is no additional cost of ownership for three years from the date of installation.
3 Autojectors contain sealed-for-life bearings and self-cleaning filters. So there are no maintenance costs or down-time: the Autojector is always operational.
4 The Autojector uses Extra-life lamps with average life of 2000 hours. (A copy of IECT Test Report 497/32b is included in Appendix 4 of this proposal.) A carousel of three lamps rotates automatically when one lamp wears out, so avoiding the serious disruption to presentations caused by manual lamp changing.
5 Light emitting diodes at the rear of the Autojector indicate the number of functioning lamps remaining. Lamp replacement does not require the removal of covers, and so avoids any risk of electric shock. The carousel plugs into a slot in the side of the Autojector, and can be changed in less than thirty seconds.

Unique self-aligning and scaling facilities, *and designed-in reliability* won for the Autojector the coveted Audiovisual Product Of The Year award at the 1993 AVP Exhibition.

8.6 BRING ON THE RED TEAM

While the preparation of the proposal or brochure is under way, set up an independent red team. Their job will be to carry out the final review of your selling documents. Choose red team members to shadow your customer's vetting team. For example, if you are submitting a proposal in response to an RFQ, you might need a technologist, a project manager, an accountant and someone with user experience. Each of these people should review the proposal from the point of view of a specialist in the customer organization. A sales leaflet for direct mailing to the public could be vetted by a range of people from the social and income groups to be targeted. It is also worth having a non-technical person check the document for readability. The non-specialist will often notice aspects of quality—poor or misaligned printing, inconsistent header or footer wording between volumes, etc—which those involved in the contents might miss.

Briefing the red team

Give the red team all available customer information—the RFQ, the scoring system if it is known, reports on previous phases, details of competitors and their products or systems— anything the customer is likely to have access to. They will need time to study all this material and to set up their own evaluation criteria. Remember, they are trying to compare your proposal with what they believe the customer ideally wants.

Beware of involving the red team too early. If they help with your rough drafts they could become prejudiced. Let them judge your final draft as the customer will—seeing it for the first time when you make your submission.

Review sequence

Don't use the red team as spelling checkers. Give them something good so they can help you make it even better. Hold your own reviews as your preparation work proceeds:

- Review your understanding of the RFQ. Make sure you get clarification of any points on which you are uncertain; then test the understanding of the bid team.
- Review your proposal outline and make sure it covers everything the customer has asked for, and nothing else.
- Give your authors a chance to review their own work.
- Let the proposal editor make any revisions of style.
- Now you are ready to hold your final red team review.

Red team review

The red team must be constructively critical. They should look at every aspect, from structure, accuracy and completeness of response, to layout, typestyles and quality of reprographics—in fact, anything which could improve the value of your bid in the eyes of the customer.

Red team comments are best put in writing on copies of the documents. Once the bid team have studied these comments it's usually worth calling a review meeting where any comments which aren't clear can be resolved before the bid team get back to work to meet their deadline.

Red teams have an unenviable task. In doing a good job they are unlikely to win many friends. But they will help your organization win more business.

RED TEAM PROPOSAL CHECK-LIST

Use this check-list to provide a critique on a section of a proposal, a sales brochure or other sales support literature sent to customers.

	4	3	2	1
Proposal/brochure title:				
Volume/section:				
Reviewer:				
Please mark your assessment here using 4 = Excellent: continue doing it well 3 = Good: scope for minor improvements 2 = Fair: considerable improvement possible 1 = Weak: considerable improvement essential	4	3	2	1
How well do the content and structure suit customer needs?				
Does the structure follow the RFQ (if appropriate)?				
Are all customer requirements adequately covered?				
Have unnecessary details been avoided?				
Are all subheadings relevant and meaningful?				
How persuasive is the document?				
Is the writing in customer language?				
Are any new terms clearly explained?				
Is the writing active and easily readable?				
Does the emphasis match customer's basis of decision?				
Are selling themes and messages included throughout?				
Are trade-offs presented clearly?				
Are features linked through advantages to benefits?				
Are graphics relevant and supportive of topic themes?				
Is evidence provided for all claims?				
How well is the material presented?				
Are page layouts attractive, with adequate margins?				
Are headings and other captions clear?				
Do customer requirements precede company capability?				
Are graphics used to full effect?				
How good is the quality of reproduction?				
Is the document bound to a high quality?				
What is your overall impression of the document?				
Impact				
Readability				
Credibility of claims				
Persuasiveness				

CONTRACTS

Legal contracts and contract law support the process of exchange—the exchange of goods, services, work or money for other goods, services, etc. There is national and international legislation covering the many types of contracts neccesary for commercial transactions. There are laws governing:

- Sale and carriage of goods.
- General Agreement on Tariffs and Trade (GATT).
- Consumer protection.

All this legislation is designed to safeguard the rights and to provide a basis for enforcing the obligations of contracting parties.

What is a contract?

Someone may agree to clean your car as a favour to you. If they later renege on the agreement they do so with impunity (in law, at least!), because there is no contract between you. A contract is more than an agreement by two parties. For a contract to exist there must be:

- An offer by one party, and acceptance by the other.
- Something returned in consideration—payment in cash or kind.
- An intention to create a legal relationship. You cannot enter into a contract by accident.
- A purpose which is clear to both parties. This implies that both parties must be competent to contract.
- Capability to execute the contract. You cannot contract to do something which is patently outside your capability.
- No intention to break the law. Contracts to 'liquidate' people are illegal and not, therefore, contracts in law.

What constitutes an offer?

The offer must contain the following:

- A clear Statement of Work, with quantities, dates, locations, etc.
- A statement of the Proof Of Performance—for example, specified acceptance tests which an item must satisfy.
- Commercial terms and conditions. These include price, payment terms, arrangements for the transfer of title, warranties, assignment of intellectual property rights, etc.

Contract negotiations

Although a contract may be for the supply of goods or services to a stated standard or specification, the technical aspects are not what we negotiate. Technical performance is something both parties must agree. Negotiations are over terms and conditions, including quantities, price, payment terms, shipping, insurance and so on.

Negotiating is a special skill. The unwary can be picked off item by item, conceding what they value little only to find it has far greater value to the other side. So if you have to get involved in contract negotiations, first attend a negotiating skills training course and then spend a day or two observing experienced negotiators at work.

EXAMPLES

Suppression depression

Janet Masters urgently needs interference suppressors, following problems with radio interfering with prototype Autojectors during the product launch. She has difficulty finding a suppressor to fit in the space available, until the ULC rep shows her a neat unit which fits behind the On/Off switch.

> *'Great! I began to think I'd have to get the housing changed. How much?'*
> *'Well, I guess for your quantities we could come down to... say, £4.50 each?'*
> *'It's more than I expected. Still, the alternative is an expensive tooling charge to change the housing. OK, if you can get me 500 units real quick, I'll get our buyer to fax an order through.'*

Inadvertently, Janet may have negotiated a contract to which FICO could be held. She has also undermined the negotiating position of her firm's buyer. The ULC rep now knows he alone can supply suppressors to fit the space available, so he has quoted the full list price and can stick to it.

The National Conference Centre contract

As part of a major refurbishment programme, NCC issue a tender for supply of visual aids equipment throughout their conference suites and syndicate rooms. The initial order will be for 145 projectors of various types (OHP, 35 mm, video and cine film), as well as screens, public address and lighting equipment.

The contract calls for all electronic equipment to be tested for susceptibility to radio-frequency interference. Not only must projectors meet international standards for interference and susceptibility, but a clause in the draft contract states:

> *All projectors must operate satisfactorily when situated within one metre of NCC's UHF mobile security radios and within 5 metres of NCC's base station. NCC will make available radio equipment for testing purposes during the equipment development programme.*

Vanessa Tippet, FICO's bid manager, feels the matter is adequately covered in the contract. But, to be quite sure, she consults her contracts manager who wants the terms made clearer. In particular:

- **What** radio equipment will be available? Mobiles *and* the base station?
- **When** will FICO be able to use it? Maybe, to avoid disruption at NCC, access would only be available outside normal conference hours.
- **Where** will the equipment be available? It would be expensive to do the tests at NCC, but it's unlikely NCC will allow their base station to be moved to the FICO factory.
- **Who** will operate the radio equipment? If only NCC staff are allowed to use the radios, who will pay for their time during the test programme?

Vanessa discovers it would be cheaper and more convenient for FICO to hire UHF security radios for the evaluation period. She gets NCC to agree that evaluation using hired radios of the same type will satisfy their requirement.

8.8 INTELLECTUAL PROPERTY RIGHTS

The creative work you produce as part of the job for which you are paid is intellectual property. When you work for an employer, your contract of employment assigns to your employer all intellectual property rights (IPR) resulting from your work. IPR includes copyright, registered designs and patents.

What form does IPR take?

IPR can reside in:

- A technical report, sales proposal or brochure.
- The design to which a piece of equipment is manufactured.
- The underlying know-how by which a technique is exploited.
- The ownership of an invention.
- The design form of a product (for example the shape of a Coca-Cola bottle).

What about sponsored work?

If yours is a contracting company, the sponsor—for example, a government agency—will normally seek the right to exploit any IPR generated under the contract. But to undertake the work at all you may need to use IPR you acquired through previous work, and in particular work which you funded. So there are two categories of IPR:

- **Foreground IPR** means information, inventions and expertise first generated in carrying out the contract—specifications, design data, software, etc.
- **Background IPR** is information needed to fulfil a contract, but which was not funded by the contract.

How can you protect your organization's IPR?

Your sponsoring customers will want to own the IPR arising from work done under their contracts, whereas your organization will want a license to use the IPR developed as a result of contracts, and if possible to be allowed to license it to other parties. For example, you may secure an export contract to help an overseas organization set up a manufacturing facility and to produce equipment and systems to your designs.

Often your sponsoring customers will expect to own any foreground IPR, or at least to have the right to exploit it, and you may have to pay royalties as an exploitation levy if you sell to other customers products which exploit this foreground IPR. With a government sponsor, you may be able to negotiate a reduced or waived levy if you can show the levy would make you uncompetitive in world markets. The sponsor would monitor the profitability of an order so secured and could claim an increased royalty if the project became more profitable than your forecast.

In your contracts, you will want conditions which ensure any background IPR you release to your customers is properly safeguarded. You could seek royalties if the sponsor were to decide to get the product manufactured by another contractor.

Quoting from published work

In quoting from someone else's work you could be infringing their copyright and damaging their interests—for example by reduced sales of a book. Brief quotations, duly referenced, which recommend other works to your reader are rarely a problem. If in doubt, write requesting permission. The publisher may request a fee if you ask to quote extensively from copyright work.

Copyright

You automatically own the copyright of all your written work, and others may not copy it without your permission. The copyright is yours throughout your life and remains in your estate for 50 years after you die. But when an organization owns the copyright—as your employer will own what you create at work—death of the author doesn't have the same consequence.

Copyright refers not to ideas but to the way they are expressed. So if you write what someone has previously written, but use different words, you are not infringing copyright. But the laws of copyright are not restricted to text. Photographs, diagrams and other graphic information are also covered. So is computer software, where you pay for a licence to use the program on a specified number of terminals or machines.

All FICO sales literature, specifications and reports carry a copyright claim of the form:

> © FICO Industries 1993
>
> *The information in this publication is the property of FICO Industries, and it may not be copied in whole or in part, either in its present form or into any other medium, without the prior written permission of the copyright owner.*

Patents

Patents protect inventions or improvements to existing inventions, processes, etc. Inventions can only be patented if they are novel and not obvious.

Janet Masters invented a technique for automatically adjusting an overhead projector image so the image is centred, in focus, and fills the display screen irrespective of the distance between projector and screen. Before publicizing the Autojector—a product exploiting this idea—Janet's company, FICO, took out a provisional patent. (You cannot obtain a patent after you have publicly announced how an invention works.)

By the time the provisional patent was granted it was clear the Autojector was commercially viable, so FICO applied for full patent cover in all countries capable of copying and exploiting the invention. As the cost of maintaining the cover increases throughout the life of the protection, FICO must review the value of its patents annually, only paying for those inventions which justify the expense of protection.

Registered designs and trade marks

All Autojectors carry a badge which FICO include in all their advertising and publicity material. To ensure other makers of projectors don't benefit from the Autojector publicity campaign, FICO registered the Autojector symbol. Their literature carries the statement:

> *FICO* ™*, Autojector* ™ *and the Autojector device are trade marks of FICO Industries.*

Fig 8.3

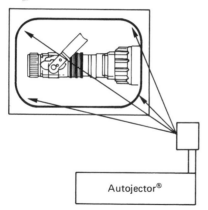

Autojector®

8.9 SAFETY MANAGEMENT

When people are killed or injured at work, or their health is impaired, the employer may be taken to court. Similarly, when customers suffer from using a product they, too, have recourse to the law. In recent years courts have greatly increased the value of damages awarded, most particularly in the USA. But the cost to industry and commerce is not limited to compensation payments: absence through work-induced illness or injury and loss of public goodwill further justify management attention to health and safety matters. As a manager you are personally liable if your negligence puts other people's health and safety at risk.

A safe working environment

You are responsible for monitoring and controlling the work environment of your staff and ensuring they are not put at risk. Make them aware of any special hazards in your work area, and of fire and other safety procedures. Make your own hazard list and check it frequently. For example, are all exits clear? Have combustible materials accumulated? Is all machinery guarded? Are electrical equipment safety tests up to date?

Product liability

It is the duty, under the UK Health & Safety At Work Act, of 'any person who designs, manufactures, imports or supplies an article for use at work' to ensure 'as far as is reasonably practicable, that the article is so designed as to be safe and without risks to health when properly used'.

It may not be sufficient to show that the purchaser had misused your product, so you need to minimize the hazards associated both with its proper use and with its abuse.

Product safety programme

Evaluate new designs to discover what risks exist, both to operators and to the product itself—a process called hazard and operability analysis. Then, during development, review how the product could go wrong and what effects each failure could have on the user and on the product itself—a process called failure mode and effect analysis.

Data from these safety reviews will help you choose safer materials, processes and methods of use. Where hazards cannot be removed, fit clearly visible labels and insert prominent warnings in the user manual and in any assembly, transportation, storage, testing and maintenance documentation.

The simple product safety questionnaire opposite will help you list the potential hazards associated with goods or services you provide. This is not a complete check-list. You will have to amend or extend the list to suit your type of work.

Safety hazard priorities

In your safety reviews, grade risks according to their seriousness:

- **Critical hazards or incidents** are those threatening injury or serious damage. Immediately recall any products in use and allow no further development or production until you have corrected the fault.
- **Major hazards or incidents** are those requiring immediate action, such as informing users of the risk and advising them how to avoid it.
- **Minor hazards** are those not threatening personal injury, but whose correction will extend the life of the product. Incorporate without seriously disrupting production.

PRODUCT SAFETY CHECK-LIST

Use this questionnaire to check that safety requirements have been considered. (You may need to add sections to cover other hazards special to your product.) Inform people involved (in writing) of any unavoidable hazards, and seek professional advice on safe procedures for handling, use or disposal.

Update the questionnaire whenever design or manufacturing processes change.

	Y/N	Comments
Product:		
Development stage:		
Origin (purchased/manufactured in-house):		
Person responsible for safety of product:		
Hazards from toxic/corrosive chemicals		
Are substances hazardous to health used in manufacture?		
Are toxic/corrosive materials incorporated in the product?		
Are carcinogenic substances used in manufacture?		
Are all staff briefed on handling and disposal procedures?		
Are toxic warning labels/procedures clearly displayed?		
Could production or use cause environmental pollution?		
Are proper disposal procedures included in user manuals?		
Electrical hazards		
Are high voltages (>50 volts) used in the product?		
Are high voltage connections screened and labelled?		
Are protective devices fitted to minimize risk of shocks?		
Are fuses fitted to ensure safety during fault conditions?		
Do earthing and/or insulation give adequate protection?		
Does the product meet stray radiation specifications?		
Fire and explosion risks		
Are any explosive materials used in manufacture?		
Are combustible materials incorporated in the product?		
Are safety labels permanently fixed and clearly visible?		
Are safety warnings/procedures prominent in manuals?		
Mechanical hazards		
Are sharp edged or moving parts adequately guarded?		
Are high pressure points adequately protected?		
Are lifting points secure and adequate?		
Are safety aids (goggles, clothing, etc.) required?		
Are safety aids available, and recommended in manuals?		
Are high temperature surfaces adequately guarded?		
Failure effects		
Has a failure mode and effect analysis been completed?		
Have failure effects been minimized in the design?		
Has a failure reporting and review procedure been set up?		
Other safety points		

HOW TO MANAGE INFORMATION
AND AVOID BECOMING A DATA DUMP

To make management decisions you need information. Good decisions need good information—accurate, up to date and relevant. Then you may need to store this information in a form you can use later, or to communicate it to others in a form they can understand. This is what information management is all about.

The challenge

Information technology (IT) can help you process data and present the results in a form you and others can easily understand. Computers can provide you with powerful decision-guidance systems, and lightweight laptop and notebook computers can be invaluable when you are away from your office. (They can also provide rapid communication, via modems and networks, with databases and people back at the office.)

The key to using IT effectively is strategy. Just as your organization needs a strategy for its investment in IT systems so, too, should you plan your own investment in training time. Learn to use the most appropriate IT tools efficiently so you reap the rewards of improved effectiveness.

The benefits

Are you in danger of becoming a data dump for other people? Reports, memos and magazines; television, phone and fax; laptop, desktop and networked computers—all are sources of business data. These data can only become useful information if you know how to convert them to a form you can understand.

Should you be more selective in the information sources you access? You can improve matters by *choosing* how and when you receive data.

Do you spend too much time converting data into a form you can use? There are computer-based tools to simplify the conversion process.

INFORMATION IN BUSINESS

You act upon feelings and information. How you feel is determined by your personality, the circumstances, and what has been happening recently. You might be feeling insecure, confident, anxious or relaxed; and these feelings will affect how you react to information you receive. But the trigger for action—for decision-making—is information, most of which you receive through sights and sounds, and in particular, pictures, words and numbers.

What is good information?

It is good to be well informed, but this does not mean gathering as much information as you can. The most valuable information you can have is:

- **Relevant**: making a worthwhile contribution to solving serious problems.
- **Correct**: accurate and as specific as possible.
- **Up to date**: incomplete information on time is often better than complete information later.
- **Understandable**: in a form you can use, or easily convertible into that form.

Data, information and decisions

Much of the information used to make decisions is numerical—costs, quantities, delivery dates and the like. These are termed data. You use analytical thought processes to decide what these numbers really mean. In so doing, you convert the data into information, which in turn can provide the necessary understanding of a situation to allow you to make decisions. You may decide to communicate your understanding to others so that they will feel as you do and will decide to take action themselves.

Fig 9.1

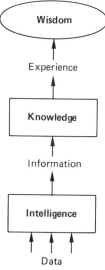

Data for decision-making can be classed as either **primary**, where you spend your own time and money investigating a situation, or from **secondary**, where you gather data from previous investigations.

Secondary data is usually more complete than primary data, but it may not be as relevant or as up to date. It is invariably less costly to gather secondary data, and sources include:

- Specialist journals and newspapers.
- Government legislation.
- Technical books.
- Learned society journals and conference proceedings.
- Survey reports by market research organizations.

9.1   **DATA REPRESENTATION**

The way you present information can affect its value, both to yourself and to others. For example, if you were to tell your staff that you feel the organization 'did reasonably well last year, considering the difficult circumstances', what would they think? That their future prosperity is assured? That financial collapse is imminent?

They don't need your opinion; they need facts—as precise and specific as possible. Numbers are the answer! And you need to present the numbers in such a way that the message people need is most easily understood.

Brighten up tables

Most people find a sequence of more than seven numbers difficult to remember. Tables add structure and make priorities clearer. You can design the layout of your tables to highlight those numbers of most significance. For example, in a table of sales or production results you could include bold headings, highlight important values and add a comment column.

Use the right graph style

When communicating with people who understand graphs, your choice of style can determine what message the data convey. Useful styles include:

- **Data tables**. Use these when the exact numerical values are needed.
- **Bar charts**. These allow people to read off approximate values at a glance. Bars can also be stacked upon one another to show the sums of two or more sets of data.
- **Gantt charts**. Here the bars are printed horizontally rather than vertically. The horizontal axis represents time, and the bars show the duration of each activity.
- **Pie charts**. Here the relative proportions are immediately visible—useful for displaying market share, etc.
- **Line graphs**. Trends are best communicated by line graphs. They are preferable to bar charts when presenting four or more sets of data together.
- **Pictograms**. Use these instead of bar charts. They are ideal for people who aren't familiar with graphs.
- **Organization charts**. These can be used to display hierarchies and family trees.

Create clear and simple graphs

A few simple rules will help you to communicate data in graphical form:

1. Choose the style which best conveys the message.
2. Include only essential information; omit all irrelevant details.
3. Include meaningful captions.
4. Label all axes, ensuring the units are stated.
5. Mark the zero line and clearly differentiate between positive and negative values.
6. Use colour or shading to distinguish between two or more sets of data in one graph.
7. When displaying sets of data with different scale ranges, make this clear—if necessary by adding an explanatory comment.

EXAMPLES

In the summary of his annual Sales Support Review—a document required by the Vice President, Sales and Marketing, in the USA, and copied to all FICO's UK directors—John Scarman has to include a table of figures:

Region	Order intake ($k)	Deliveries ($k)	Comment
UK	4710	4350	
France	614	650	Deliveries include $20k of re-exports
Germany	1325	1400	JBK order excluded as it is not yet ratified
Japan	58	42	
USA	975	975	
Other	24	29	Effects of new outlet in Delhi not included
Totals	7706	7446	

In the main body of the report, John makes use of graphics to show market share and trend information.

A pie chart is fine for showing at a glance the proportions of sales support business coming from each region.

Fig 9.2

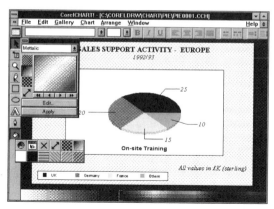

Trends and actual values are more easily seen from a bar chart. This is the style John chooses when presenting monthly order intake in graphical form.

Fig 9.3

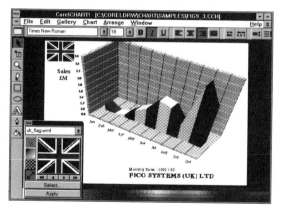

The information on which we make management decisions rarely comes *when* we want it and *in the form* we need it, so it must be stored and processed. Management information systems (MIS) provide a means of capturing, storing, processing and communicating information.

Fig 9.4

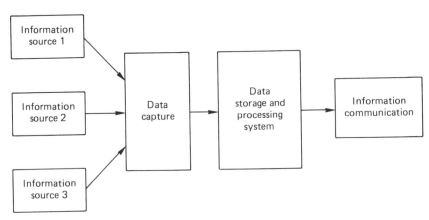

Information technology has greatly altered both our ability to capture and process information and the speed at which we can share information with others. It has also raised expectations and led to some false assumptions. For example, a marketing plan may be based upon sweeping assumptions about political and economic trends and the actions of competitors; yet the resulting sales forecasts are often presented as precise numbers rather than as bands. These predictions, which may be printed to three or more significant figures, are sometimes treated as facts. In reality they are but considered guesses.

Data capture

Data can be entered into an MIS manually, often by a combination of keyboard and mouse. The human–machine interface has changed recently with the introduction of the graphical user interface (GUI). Programs run in windows on a display screen. You control the processing by means of a mouse, moved across your desk surface; this is mirrored by a pointer moving around the screen window. Clicking the mouse button when the pointer is on an icon selects particular functions and reveals menus of commands from which you can select. GUIs are of greatest value when you need to process information in graphical form, with the keyboard being used mainly to enter text.

Data may also be entered into an MIS automatically, either by electronic transfer from another computer or via a data capture device such as a bar code reader.

Data storage and processing

Accounts, personnel, manufacturing and sales information are all examples of systems you may have in your organization. However, unless you are a specialist in one of those disciplines you are unlikely to need to operate these systems yourself. But there are several computer applications commonly used by managers, and these are described in the following topics.

UNDERSTANDING MICROCOMPUTER JARGON

Even if you don't have a microcomputer of your own, or a terminal to a larger machine, you will certainly come across people who expect you to be computer literate. This summary of common terminology will help you understand the jargon they use.

Bits and bytes

Computers use binary arithmetic. One *binary digit* is called a *bit*, and can have a value of 1 or 0. Bits are assembled into sets of eight, called bytes, which can have values in the range 0 to 255. Larger ranges are achieved by combining bytes. Depending on its complexity, a computer can process one or more bytes at a time. Currently most microcomputers work with either 16 or 32 bit 'words', while powerful supercomputers, such as those used in weather forecasting, may have to work with 64 bit words.

ROM

Inside the computer, data is held in electronic form within silicon chips. ROM—read only memory—is the storage place of the permanent instructions which control the internal workings of the computer. Data are safely retained in the ROM even when you switch off.

RAM

Programs and data you feed into your computer will be held in random access memory (RAM). If you disconnect power from your computer without saving your data, everything in the RAM will be lost. Personal computers generally have one to eight megabytes of RAM. One megabyte = 1 048 576 bytes.

Disk drives

Your personal computer will probably have one or two floppy disk (or diskette) drives and a hard disk. They store data as magnetic dipoles on the surface of a rotating disk. Floppy disk drives have removable disks, typically storing 1.2 or 1.44 megabytes. Hard disks can store many tens or even hundreds of megabytes. They allow faster data retrieval than floppy drives.

Operating system and user interface

This is a set of instructions, usually stored on disk, controlling the inputs and outputs of your computer. You may also have a graphical user interface (GUI) such as Microsoft *Windows*.

All application programs which operate with a particular GUI will use the same screen layout, icon designs and menu format.

Fig 9.5 shows the Microsoft *Windows* GUI running three applications.

Fig 9.5

WORD PROCESSING

A word processor allows you to create, store, edit and modify the layout of documents. Word processor software is available on microcomputers and, via terminals, on minicomputers or mainframes. With the move towards graphical user interfaces, most modern word processors offer the ability to generate simple drawings and to import more complex graphics into documents as they are being created.

Most modern GUI-based word processors provide the following features:

1 Input

- Insert or overwrite text entry.
- Load or merge text from other word processors or as ASCII files.
- Accept graphics in data formats such as .PCX, .TIF, .PNT and .IMG.

2 Processing

- Left justified (straight left edge), right justified, fully justified and centred text layout modes.
- Bullet, number, indent and large first character paragraph indicators.
- Search and find or replace words or phrases, with the ability to switch on sensitivity to upper and lower case characters.
- Block copy, move and delete facility.
- Facility for shrinking a document to its outline by temporarily discarding all text below a required level of heading—for example chapter and section headings only.
- Ability to reformat text to fit another layout style—changing the number of columns or the size of type, for example.
- Facility for including mathematical symbols and formulas.
- Header and footer function, which can include chapter and page numbering, with different headers or footers on left and right pages.
- Ability to open more than one file, either for *browsing* for ideas or so that data can be cut from one and copied into another.
- Context-sensitive help menus which present information relevant to your task.
- Built-in spelling checker and thesaurus.

3 Output

- WYSIWYG display—What You See Is What You Get, including screen fonts which closely match the printed output.
- A range of character styles and sizes (fonts) in normal, bold and italic.
- Ability to send data to the printer via a buffer or print manager, so you can continue working on your document while waiting for a print out.

Word processor performance

Always try out a program on your kind of computer. GUI-based software can be slow in responding to commands if used on a low-power machine. Test for:

- Response time when you ask for a new layout style.
- Speed of moving through a large document using the **Go To** command.
- Time to feed a file into the print manager so you can continue working.

MIXING TEXT AND GRAPHICS

John Scarman prepares his monthly report using the Lotus *Ami Pro* word processor. As the headings are the same each month, he loads a standard outline and makes a few minor changes.

Page layout

John calls up his REPORT style sheet, a pre-defined set of rules for page layout. This defines page size, margins, number of columns and the typestyles to be used for headings, subheading and text paragraphs.

Ami Pro comes with more than 50 style sheets, including designs for memos, reports, invoices and OHP slides. All may be modified and saved as new styles if required.

Fig 9.6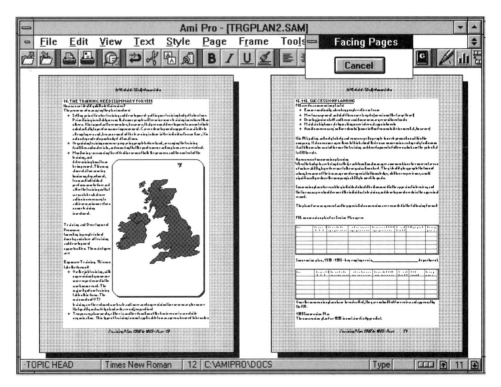

Tables and charts

John lists all customer enquiries with dates received and responded to. The table headings are the same each month, and can be *Protected* so they can't be accidentally changed while editing the data. Simple formulas can also be programmed in, so when John changes the data the totals are updated automatically.

Tables and charts are ideal for communicating numerical information, such as enquiry dates and order values. Tables are created by defining the number of rows and columns, and what line styles and background fills are required.

GRAPHICS SYSTEMS

Used sensibly, business graphics save time and provide impact, both as visual aids when you are presenting information verbally and as illustrations in documents.

Power vs. ease of use

The more powerful a graphics system the longer it is likely to take you to learn to use it. With a simple charting facility such as that incorporated in GUI-based word processors you may be able to produce a graph or pie chart within minutes of first loading the program.

More powerful drawing packages have many more functions, use of which may not always be intuitively obvious. The more flexible the program, the more functions you will have to learn; so the secret is to choose a software package which copes with the work you do frequently. Accept that you will have to seek help for the occasional more complex task, such as producing colour separations from pictures scanned in to your computer.

Simple charting programs

Numerical data are entered either via the keyboard or from a data file, and by means of simple commands it can be displayed in a preset range of formats. Gantt, bar, graph and pie chart styles are usually available, and you can select from a range of line and fill patterns. Usually there is at least a limited caption and axis labelling facility. Output drivers are generally provided for popular models of printers and pen plotters, and the graphs can be saved in a form suitable for inclusion in reports.

Mathematical graph packages

These are more powerful charting programs capable of interpreting complex mathematical relationships between data, including multivariate statistical information.

Computer-aided design (CAD) suites

These are software systems, sometimes running on dedicated computers, but more often on workstations networked to a minicomputer. The software may include draughting and design programs and three-dimensional modelling. The output may take the form of large engineering drawings produced by a pen plotter. Often it is possible to provide machining, assembly and testing information directly from the CAD system; these data may be used to control machines in the manufacturing facility directly.

Illustration and artistic design software

When you want a picture of something which doesn't yet exist, a drawing package with high-resolution colour or many grey scales can help you produce a convincing illustration.

A valuable feature is the ability to convert bitmaps into vectors—curves, rather than pixels. Bitmap graphics develop jagged diagonals as their scale is enlarged, whereas vector drawings retain their shapes irrespective of the scale to which they are drawn.

Fig 9.7

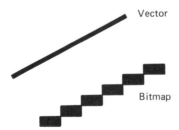

Vector

Bitmap

EXAMPLE

When FICO analysed their costs they discovered that 5 per cent of their revenue was being spent on printing and publishing. Not only that, but graphic design was often a critical path activity in the launch of new products: if they could speed up the publishing process they could get new products to market sooner. They decided to set up their own publications facility to produce brochures, handbooks, proposals and publicity material.

Graphic design is a key element of brochure preparation. For this work, FICO's graphics designer specified his requirements for a *Windows*-based PC application as follows:

1 **Compatibility with their CAD system, AutoCAD.** The system should import, modify and export back to the CAD system drawings produced on *AutoCAD*.
2 **Clip art library**. There should be a range of clip art pictures which can be combined easily to produce handbook illustrations. So, even people with no design background can use the system.
3 **Scanner compatibility.** Not only must the system import bitmap images in various formats, but ideally it should be possible automatically to convert them to vector form so that they can be edited if required.
4 **Compatibility with other hardware and software**. Although FICO use PCs, they need to exchange information with clients, some of which use Apple Macintosh computers. The system should be capable of importing files in *Adobe Illustrator* format, so files can be transported easily between PC and Macintosh computers.
5 **Colour illustrations**. The system should be able to drive a colour inkjet printer for producing up to 50 copies of a colour page. But more important, it must have the ability to produce four-colour film separations on a PostScript imagesetter.

FICO chose *Corel Draw!* as their standard *Windows*-based drawing package, as it meets all the above requirements. Here is a screen illustration of *Corel Draw!* in action:

Fig 9.8

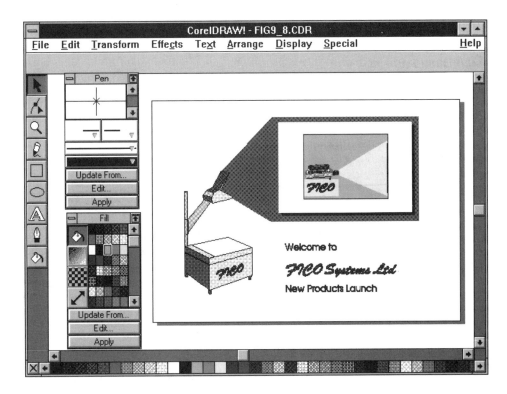

159

9.5

SPREADSHEETS AND DATABASES

Two important software tools for handling large amounts of alphanumeric data and the relationships between the data are spreadsheets and databases. There may be parts of your job where one or other of these tools could help you save time and money.

Spreadsheets

A spreadsheet is a movable computer window looking onto a portion of a rectangular grid. Each cell in the grid can contain text, a number or a formula from which a value can be calculated. The cells are identified by their row and column labels, so formulas can refer to the contents of cells as b8, d4 and so on.

	a	b	c	d
1	a1	b1	c1	d1
2	a2	b2		
3	a3			
4	a4			**d4**
5				
6				
7				
8		**b8**		

The whole grid can be hundreds of columns wide and may contain several thousand rows. Any spreadsheet you are likely to need will use a small part of this range, and your monitor will only be able to display a few tens of rows with characters large enough for you to read. That is why the window has to be movable.

Once you have programmed formulas into your spreadsheet—for example to calculate the price discount you could allow a client for different order quantities and payment terms—the answers will be recalculated whenever you feed in new data. Modern spreadsheets offer graphics facilities, so your results can be printed out as charts.

Databases

At the heart of most major management information systems is a database. This is a set of records which can be stored and searched. What is special about computerized databases, as opposed to say filing cabinets or boxes of index cards, is the database management system (DBMS) which controls the access to the data. A high-level query language using plain English instructions makes it relatively straightforward to extract information from a modern database system. For example, you might interrogate your personnel database asking for a list of persons fitting the requirement:

> *Age between 25 and 35; able to speak German; at least two years' experience in sales or marketing.*

Access to data has to be controlled. Some people may only be permitted to interrogate the database, while others have authority to enter new data. A database administrator controls the creation of the database and its security in use, issuing passwords and personal identification devices to help protect the integrity of the system.

There are also simple database systems which might help you in your day-to-day work. Many of these are simple electronic filing systems in which, for example, you could keep abstracts of useful technical articles: the author, title, date and the name of the journal in which they were published. There are, however, constraints on the storage of personal information in databases. Data protection legislation is designed to protect the privacy of the individual. If you intend storing personal data you must first register stating what you intend storing and how the data will be used.

EXAMPLE: A PERSONAL ORGANIZER

FICO staff make good use of not only the company's mainframe MIS but also standalone PC systems where the information is only needed by one person or a small group of people. Many of the PC application programs can communicate with the mainframe computer via a local area network. But some low-cost standalone productivity tools also prove valuable.

A simple filing system

Janet Masters uses her *Lotus Organizer* running in Microsoft *Windows*. In it she has created a customized 'References' section for published papers and books she might want to refer back to.

Fig 9.9

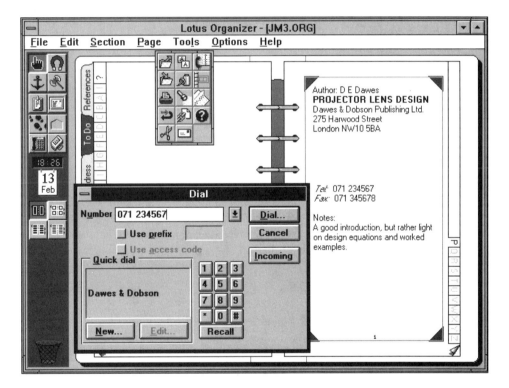

This screen shot shows the structure of the records Janet has set up. It is simple, but does allow her to search for a particular author, and to enter brief notes so that she can check on the contents of any book or article in future. And if she wants to pass on a technical reference to a colleague, *Lotus Organizer* has facilities for printing either single pages or a selection.

Janet can add or delete references at any time, and, if she wishes, she can create separate sections for technical references, customer contacts, component suppliers and so on.

DESKTOP PUBLISHING

Everything you need to produce your own high quality publications: that, supposedly, is what desktop publishing (DTP) systems provide. They don't! Neither do a set of wrenches, a gas torch and a reel of solder wire make a master plumber. Plumbing needs specialist knowledge and skills; so does publishing. DTP has the power and flexbility to produce quite appalling designs if it is misused. But DTP *can* provide a cost-effective route to improved presentation of written and graphic information. The secret is largely in the page design, many features of which can be standardized by using pre-defined style sheets. These are best prepared by someone who understands page design and can tailor the layout to suit their purpose and intended readership.

DTP features

The most sophisticated word processors now provide page design facilities rivalling basic DTP systems. However, for multi-chapter reports and proposals, or for quality brochures and mailshots, you will probably need the capability of a powerful DTP system.

DTP input

Text is usually created in a word processor with outlining, spelling check and sophisticated editing facilities. The text file is then imported via a filter—a process within the DTP software which detects and translates the special format codes for paragraph and page breaks, underline, etc. DTP programs include filters to suit most popular word processors, as well as a standard character code called ASCII which every serious word processor can provide. Beware, however: if you use ASCII code your word processor will loose all of its format codes, so you will have to re-enter them in your DTP software.

DTP programs contain simple drawing facilities for lines, rectangles and ellipses. If you need more complex illustrations you can import pre-designed clip art pictures or create your own using a business graphics program or a CAD system. There are conversion routines within the DTP system for popular graphics file formats such as TIFF, GEM, *PC Paintbrush* and *Mac Paint*, so it's important to choose graphics and DTP programs which are format-compatible.

Typefaces, styles and fonts

A typeface is a set of numbers, letters and other characters which have the same general appearance. Some typefaces have serifs, small strokes at the ends of each letter, giving the characters a traditional look. 'Sans serif' typefaces do not have these extra strokes.

For each typeface you can vary the style—upright or *italic*, standard or **bold**; and you can change character size. Size is expressed either in points (a point is 1/72 inch) or in picas (a pica is 1/6 inch). The smallest readable font is about 6 point, whereas newspaper headlines are commonly up to 72 point, sometimes larger.

DTP output

Most laser printers work at 300 dots per inch. This gives clear enough character outlines for many purposes. However, to project an image of quality via your brochures you should consider having them typeset. Modern typesetting systems can accept disk files from your DTP system and re-set them to 1200 or 2400 dots per inch resolution.

CHOOSING A DTP SYSTEM

FICO use a DTP system and laser printer to produce their proposals, reports and mailshots. They also design their own colour brochures, producing the page layout, diagrams and text, and leaving space for colour photographs. Their printing contractor then uses 35 mm colour transparencies to produce colour separations—individual print masters for the colours cyan, magenta and yellow and a further master for black.

When choosing a DTP system, FICO defined their essential requirements, eliminating any systems which could not provide them, and scoring on performance and ease of use those which offered what was needed. They chose *Ventura Publisher*, which is well suited to their most important need: producing between 30 and 50 illustrated proposals and reports each year.

Ventura features economy of computer storage space. Instead of copying text and picture information into a new format, as many programs do, it simply logs where each file is stored, converting file formats and loading them into computer memory as they are needed. FICO reports and brochures contain:

- Text created by a word processor.
- Text generated automatically by *Ventura*.
- Data files imported from a spreadsheet.
- Line art (vector) graphics created on a CAD system.
- Simple graphics created using *Ventura's* drawing facility.
- Bitmap images imported from a paint program.
- Diagrams captured by an optical scanner.

Fig 9.10

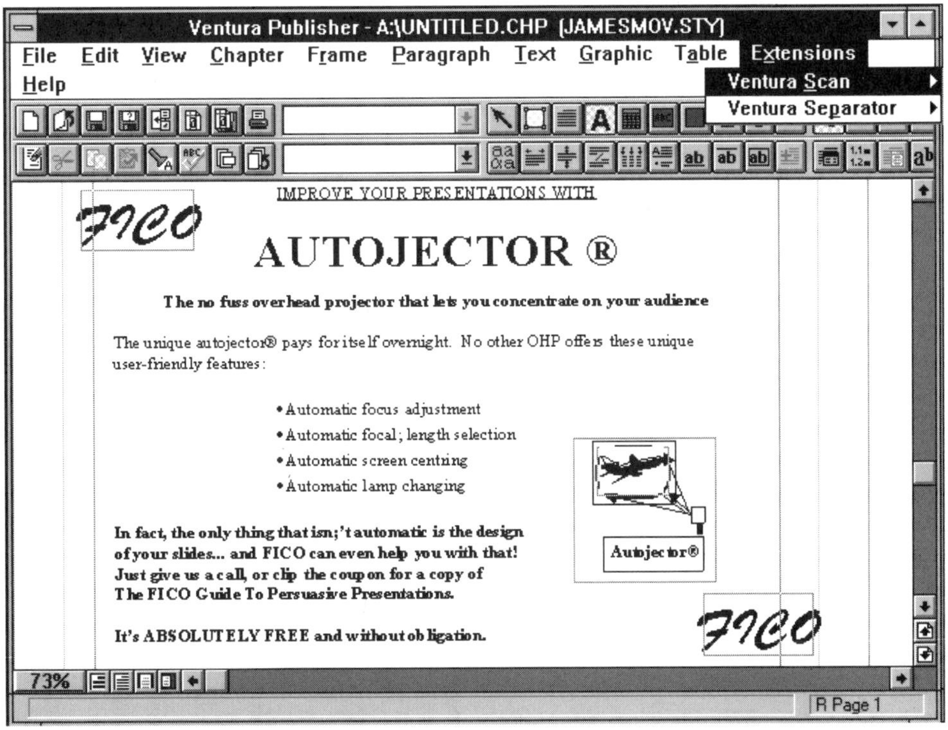

163

9.7 NOTEBOOK PCS AND PERSONAL INFORMATION MANAGERS

The advent of notebook personal computers has altered the working practices of many itinerant managers. No longer need they spend valuable time jotting down manuscript notes only to re-type them when back at base. Instead, they keep a miniature computer in their briefcase. Taking up little more space than an A4 folder, a notebook computer can provide mobile word processing, spreadsheet and graphics capability. A miniature bubble-jet printer can tuck into the same briefcase to provide high-quality hard copy. Data can be sent, via a modem, over the telephone system back to base at the end of each day. Alternatively, once back at base, the notebook can be connected to a desktop computer to transfer data files.

Notebook performance

At the time of writing a typical notebook computer with 60 Mbyte hard disk and a 1.44 Mbyte floppy drive weighs less than 6 lb (2.75kg). With 4 Mbyte of RAM and a battery life of 6 to 8 hours, such a device is easily carried, unlike some of the early laptop computers which weighed up to 15 lb (7.8kg). The microprocessor is an Intel 80386, capable of running graphics-based *Windows* software and giving rapid response on a back-lit liquid crystal display screen. And, when back at the office, you can always connect your notebook to a conventional colour screen if you want to display your graphics with maximum impact. (Colour LCD screens are available for portable computers, but at the time of writing they double the cost of the machine and degrade battery life.)

Personal organization software

Perhaps the most useful software for people on the move is a personal organizer. With such a program in your notebook computer you can keep track of appointments, record your daily expenses, keep To Do lists, names and addresses and telephone numbers, and much more. And of course searching for the information you want is much easier than with a paper copy.

If you need hard copy, this is no problem. Just transfer a disk to your client's desktop computer (or carry a portable printer with you). Your personal organizer software will drive a range of printers.

But computer-based personal organizers are not solely for the itinerant manager. In fact the best systems offer extra benefits to those people who work in groups at fixed locations, for they can use the networking facilities. When installed on a local area network (LAN), organizer software can allow each member of a group access to information belonging to the others—for example, diary entries or names and addresses.

It is important, when choosing such 'groupware', to check out the security facilities. If you keep all your personal information in network-accessible form you may want to mark some of it—family anniversaries, for example—as confidential, and prevent others from reading or altering it.

Pen *Windows*

Personal organizers are an even greater boon if they can work on pen-based notebook computers. A pen *Windows* system accepts input in handwriting (with a special pen) instead of from a keyboard. Optical character recognition software in the operating system converts your manuscript into type and positions it correctly on the screen.

The Sales Support Group at FICO UK spend typically 25 per cent of their time away from the office. All group members have notebook computers as well as their desktop machines. The desktop PCs are networked and share resources such as laser printer and plotter.

Lotus Organizer

In place of conventional ring binder personal organizers, the Sales Support Group decided to look for a *Windows*-based personal organizer so they could more easily check one another's availability for customer or internal appointments. The facilities they needed were:

1 Diary, Address Book, To Do list, Work Planner and Notebook sections, similar to those provided by the ring binders they had been used to.
2 Prioritizing of To Do list tasks.
3 To Do list items automatically showing through into the Diary section.
4 Overdue tasks automatically highlighted.
5 Automatic telephone dialling when the computer is connected to a telephone network.
6 Networking via a LAN so group members can check their own *and other people's* availability for appointments while actually on the phone to a customer.

The program they chose was *Lotus Organizer*. On the screen it looks exactly like the book it replaces—a help when learning to use the computer version. It even operates in the same way: you click labelled tabs to turn to the various sections, and on corners of pages to turn forward or back. The planner sheets fold out, just like a book, to give extra space.

Fig 9.11

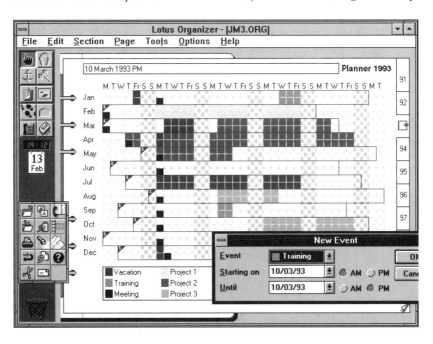

In fact, this electronic personal organizer is more flexible than the manual version it replaces. For example, group members can cross-link one data element with another by selecting an anchor icon and clicking the mouse pointer on the two data elements. So, a client meeting in the diary section can be linked with the client's name and address. If the date have to be changed the client's name and addresss are available at a mouse click, and a letter confirming the change is quickly on its way.

9.8 DEVELOPING YOUR IT SKILLS

Skills development requires planning and managing, and this philosophy applies as much to IT skills as it does to your other management skills. So in your personal development plan there could be an IT skills development plan. This would set goals for achieving competence, with priorities related to pay-offs. And of course, the benefits would have to be weighed against the costs.

Your investment in training and learning

With software systems, the initial acquisition cost is a small part of the investment; training and learning time often dominate. So, you will need to include in your plan the costs of software licenses, a budget for software upgrades (an annual cost of around 20 per cent of initial purchase cost is a guide), and the cost of initial training—trainer's fees plus your time—and learning time while you develop competence. Even after initial training, you may take longer to do a job on the computer than you would have using your old manual approach. Provided you use software tools sufficiently frequently, however, you will in time recoup this investment.

Fig 9.12

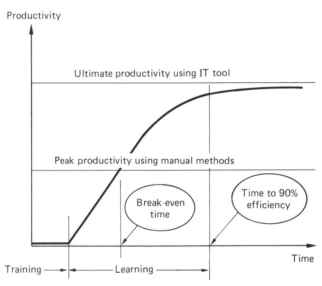

Training and learning times

How can you plan your IT skills development if you don't know how long it will take to learn to use a piece of software? (Unfortunately, learning time isn't quoted in the sales literature, is it?) Someone has to give an estimate, but, like all estimates to do with software, they are unlikely to be accurate.

Why not? Well, for one thing learning times vary from person to person. You might quickly master graphics-based systems, but take longer than average to become a proficient spreadsheet user. A lot depends, also, on the user interface and, in particular, how much commonality there is between programs. In this book all the examples of IT systems run under the Microsoft *Windows* environment, so the screen layouts, icons and menus have much in common. Learning to use a new software tool then reduces to learning to use the functions and commands unique to that tool.

And then again, all the software you need may not be available on one platform (type of computer), so you may have to get used to more than one operating system and more than one user interface. These factors all affect how long it will take you to become a proficient user of a new piece of software.

166

TYPICAL LEARNING TIMES FOR IT TOOLS

Recognizing that you will need an estimate of how long it will take you to learn to use IT systems, in the table below I suggest typical training and learning times based upon my experience in training managers in IT skills.

These estimates of training and learning times are for a manager who has achieved basic computer literacy and is familiar with the type of computer (Macintosh, IBM-compatible PC, Unix system, etc.) on which the software is running.

The assumptions

The typical learning times listed below are based on the assumptions:

1   You are using proven, industry-standard software running with a common graphical user interface (GUI) such as Microsoft *Windows*. Text-based tools of similar capability could take up to twice as long to learn.
2   You receive introductory training off the job. This is particularly important for major applications such as DTP and database systems. (This initial training time is included in the estimates of time to break even and time to 90 per cent efficiency.)
3   You have access to expert advice should you get stuck. This could be hot line support from the software supplier with, ideally, an in-house expert you can call on should the problem prove insoluble over the telephone.
4   You are a manager with a full-time job to do, but I assume you will use the software sufficiently frequently to avoid wasting time re-learning what you have forgotten between sessions. (As a rough guide, this means using a software tool for at least four hours per month.)

Type of software	Cumulative training and learning times (hours)		
	Initial training time	Time to break even	Time to 90% efficiency
Windows GUI	8	16	24
Word processor	8	24	32
Business graphics	4	8	16
Drawing program	8	16	80
CAD	24	48	96
Personal organizer	4	8	32
DTP system	16	24	96
Spreadsheet	8	16	24
Database	24	48	96

Moving on

The times listed are for first use of a *type of program*. Once you have mastered one spreadsheet, you should be able to learn an alternative spreadsheet in about a quarter the time listed here.

CHAPTER 10

IMPROVE YOUR FINANCIAL AWARENESS

AND UNDERSTAND THE JARGON OF ACCOUNTING

By all means leave the caterers to run the staff canteen; get the transport manager to make up your vehicle servicing schedule; let the gardener decide what flowers would best brighten up your reception area.

But whatever you do, don't leave your financial decisions to the finance people!

The challenge

Most organizations employ professional accountants to advise on investment appraisal, corporate taxation and financial control. They can't do it without you. Whether you are a manager in industry, commerce or a publicly funded organization, you need to understand the basics of finance. You may not find it an exciting subject; when there's excitement in the finance department it usually means big trouble! But even if your own organization isn't directly dependent on customers for funding, many of your customers and suppliers will be profit-driven businesses. If you want to understand and predict their decisions, you need to appreciate what they are trying to achieve in financial terms.

Managers in local and central government authorities are increasingly being pressed to work within tightly controlled budgets; so, much of what is covered in this chapter is directly applicable to their work, too.

The benefits

We will cover accounting principles in a simplified form, but with sufficient detail for non-financial managers to understand the jargon of finance.

When you have worked through this chapter you should be able with confidence to discuss business performance with accountants, because you will:

- Appreciate how financial accounts and statements are prepared and what they mean.
- Understand how management accounting is used to control the business.
- Know how to assess the viability of alternative projects.

FINANCIAL ACCOUNTING AND MANAGEMENT ACCOUNTING

In your work as a manager you will almost certainly encounter two aspects of accounting. These are financial accounting and management accounting. Both are needed to run a business properly, but financial accounts are also used by people outside the business management team.

Financial accounting

Financial accounts are summaries of what a business has done recently and what position it has reached, both being expressed in financial terms. Financial accounts therefore give a measure of the value of a business now and, to some extent, its potential for generating wealth in the future. We will look at three financial statements: the profit and loss account, the balance sheet, and the source and application of funds summary. These financial accounts are produced to a standard accounting convention—a set of rules to which all published accounts must comply. They have to be interpreted differently, however, by the owners, by managers of the business, and by people deciding whether to loan money to the business.

The people who own a business—the shareholders—want to know what profit has been made during the past year, and whether their stake in the business has increased or decreased in value. For this information they look to the published accounts and statements, and to the share price if the business is listed on the Stock Exchange. Shareholders, then, are interested in a combination of the income they might receive in the form of dividends paid out of the profits of the year's trading, and the growth (or reduction!) in share price.

Banks and other investing bodies loaning money to the business at a fixed rate of interest view the financial accounts from a different position. They look at the value of everything the business owns—its assets—and compare that with the value of borrowings. If the debts exceed the assets then money loaned to the company could be at risk.

Management accounting

For all but the smallest of concerns, the published financial statements aren't sufficiently detailed to allow managers to make decisions on which projects to fund or whether a proposed investment in equipment is likely to be worthwhile. Indeed, if an organization is part of a group of companies, the parent organization usually publishes consolidated financial accounts in which the performance of individual businesses within the group are not shown. But to control a business the managers *need* these details. In particular, they must have financial plans, or *budgets*, as well as month by month results of expenditure and income for each major activity or work area.

The process of preparing these budgets and controlling them through the year is termed management accounting. Management accounts are for internal use, and they are not normally published outside the business.

Accounting practices

The commercial community needs to be able to measure the financial performance of a business year by year, and to compare one business with another. This is possible only if there is a degree of standardization in the way things are valued. Standards set by law, by the accounting profession and, for publicly quoted companies, by the Stock Exchange, Wall Street and other financial centres.

10.1 MEASURING BUSINESS PERFORMANCE — PROFIT AND LOSS

The profit and loss (P & L) account records the operating performance of a business over a period—a quarter, half or full year. (Inside the business the accounts may be updated more frequently, perhaps even monthly if trading conditions are subject to rapid fluctuation.) The trading year for most companies does not coincide with the calendar year. Many companies in the UK account from 6 April one year through to 5 April the next year. If your business is part of an international corporation, however, your financial year might start on 1 November, or some other date.

Income and expenditure are recognized to have occurred when goods or services are sold or bought. By convention, the date of invoicing is the date the funds are recorded as paid or received. The corresponding transfer of funds may not actually occur until several weeks later. However, accountants, being cautious by nature, prefer to over-estimate likely expenses and underestimate expected income so that, in the worst case, the business is able to pay its way. They know that the penalty for running out of funds to settle debts can be bankruptcy, even though over a longer trading period it may be clear that all debts can be paid to leave a healthy profit.

Cost of sales

This title refers to all costs directly attributable to the supply of goods and services delivered during the trading period. In a retail business these would include merchandise, sales staff costs and a *depreciation* allowance for eventual replacement of fixtures and fittings. A manufacturing concern would incur costs as raw materials, machine operators' wages and other manufacturing overheads.

Other expenses

All other operating costs not included in the cost of sales are included under this heading. Staff costs, telephone charges, maintenance of buildings and vehicles, consultancy fees, rents and rates are examples of charges recorded as *other expenses*.

Extraordinary items

The P & L account records the operating income from products (goods or services) sold, and costs incurred in making those sales. Extraordinary items—income and expenditure relating to activities other than the operation of the business—are recorded separately from trading results. For example, the sale of an office block no longer required by the business would count as an extraordinary item.

Taxation

The tax collector has first claim on the funds of a business. In its annual budget, the Government sets the rate of taxation payable on the profits of businesses, and so the rate can change from year to year. That is why, in the P & L account, the pre-tax profit is the most meaningful indicator of how well the business is doing.

Distribution of profit

The P & L account also states how the profit after tax will be distributed. Part of the profit will usually be paid to shareholders as a dividend; the remainder is ploughed back into the business to make it grow. This re-investing of part of the profit creates what are termed reserves. Reserves are put to work in the business, and not simply stored as a buffer fund for emergencies.

EXAMPLE: # THE P & L ACCOUNT OF AUTOJECTOR LTD

In the last full trading year before they were taken over by FICO Industries Inc., Autojector Ltd published the following profit and loss account:

Autojector Ltd Profit and loss account for year ended 5 April 1992	(All values in £k)	
	1992	1991
Sales	7400	6900
Cost of sales	5330	5027
Gross profit	2070	1873
Other expenses	1520	1250
Operating profit before taxation	550	623
Interest payable	96	8
Net profit before taxation	454	615
Less taxation	136	184
Profit after taxation	318	401
Less dividends	156	201
Undistributed profit	156	200

The previous year's results are usually shown alongside those of the current year to highlight trends. This information is used to forecast performance in the year ahead.

Investors' ratios

Published accounts often contain investors' ratios, the most common of which are dividend yield and earnings per share. Shareholders are interested in the dividend paid per share, as this contributes to their income. However, the profit which is put into reserves also belongs to the shareholders; so the total earnings per share, which includes income and growth, is generally of greater interest.

Profit margin

Managers planning the future of the business use profitability ratios to compare one year's performance with previous years and with other businesses operating in the same marketplace. From the P & L account the return on deliveries (ROD) or profit margin is calculated as:

$$ROD = \frac{Pre\text{-}tax\ profit}{Sales}$$

Because the rate of corporate tax can change from year to year, it is wise to compare pre-tax rather than post-tax profit margin with those of prior years.

Other profitability ratios relate profit to the money tied up in various parts of the business; they are calculated using figures from both the P & L account and the balance sheet.

MEASURING THE VALUE OF A BUSINESS—BALANCE SHEET

The balance sheet is a summary statement, at a particular time, of what a business owns—its assets—and what it owes to others—its liabilities.

Assets

The financial resources available to the business are its assets. This means everything which has an economic value. People, often an organization's greatest asset, are excluded from the accounts (although they can affect the value of a business when it is sold). Assets are classified as follows:

- **Fixed assets** are things which will not be converted into goods or services and sold to customers, but which are necessary for the operation of the business. The recorded value of those fixed assets which will require eventual replacement, is depreciated (reduced) annually.
- **Tangible assets** are fixed assets with a physical entity—for example land, machinery and vehicles.
- **Intangible assets** are fixed assets, too, but their value is not in a physical form. Patent rights, research findings, registered designs and brand names are examples of intangible assets.
- **Current assets** are those assets which will be converted to cash as the business completes its trading cycle. They are things which will eventually be contained within the goods or services delivered to customers. Stocks of raw materials, partly finished or finished goods are current assets, as are debtors—goods and services delivered and invoiced but not yet paid for by customers. Short-term investments, balances in the bank and cash in hand are also included under this heading.
- **Liquid assets** are those current assets which will become cash even if the business were to cease trading. So stocks of raw materials, partly finished goods and finished goods are excluded; all other current assets are included.

Long-term investments

Money invested for a few weeks is available to a business should it see the need, and so this type of investment is usually recorded as a current asset. Longer term investments—for example shares in, or long-term loans to, other companies—cannot quickly be converted to cash, and so they are excluded from current assets.

Liabilities

Payments a business is obliged to make in the future are termed its liabilities. They fall into two categories:

- **Current liabilities** are payable within the next trading year. Bank overdrafts, tax bills and creditors who have supplied goods or services would be included here.
- **Long-term liabilities** are those not due for repayment for at least a year—for example, long-term bank or government loans.

Owners' equity

This is the money the owners put into the business—the share capital—plus accumulated profit ploughed back as reserves. (As businesses can make a loss, reserves can go up *or* down.) There is another source of reserves: if fixed assets are sold at a higher price than was originally paid for them, the excess is recorded as a reserve. Assets may be revalued without selling, in which case a revaluation reserve appears in the balance sheet.

EXAMPLE: # THE BALANCE SHEET OF AUTOJECTOR LTD

Here is Autojector's balance sheet produced at the end of financial year 1991/92, immediately before they were acquired by FICO Inc.

Autojector Ltd Balance sheet at 5 April 1992	(Values in £k)	
	1992	**1991**
Fixed assets		
Land and buildings	290	250
Equipment, fixtures and fittings	1250	1190
	1540	1440
Current assets		
Stocks	270	220
Debtors	80	60
Bank balances and cash	40	50
	390	330
Current liabilities		
Creditors: amounts falling due within one year	280	240
Bank overdraft	40	10
	320	250
Net current assets (Current assets – Current liabilities)	70	80
Net assets (Fixed assets + Net current assets)	1610	1520
Creditors: amounts falling due after one year		
Long-term loans	600	600
	1010	920
Capital and reserves		
Ordinary shares	250	250
Reserves	760	670
	1010	920

Liquidity ratios

Trends in short-term liquidity—the ability of a business to pay its way—can be seen from changes in the relative levels of current assets and current liabilities.

$$Current\ ratio = \frac{Current\ assets}{Current\ liabilities}$$

A longer term view of how vulnerable the business might be to economic pressure comes from the gearing ratio, which relates owners' investment to loan capital. A large amount of long-term debt (a high gearing ratio) can make a business particularly vulnerable to a recession.

$$Gearing\ ratio = \frac{Long\text{-}term\ debt}{Net\ assets}$$

10.3 WHAT HAS CHANGED? SOURCE AND APPLICATION OF FUNDS

The third document which businesses must produce is the statement of source and application of funds (SSAF). This report is sometimes called a statement of changes in financial position, or a cash flow statement. (You will also come across the term cash flow later in this chapter, when estimated future income and outgoings are used to decide between alternative courses of action.) The SSAF of a business shows where the funding has come from and how it has been used during the trading period.

Sources of funds

Trading profit is the major source of funds, but this figure must be adjusted to take into account depreciation, which will have affected the calculation of profit in the P & L account. There could also be income from the sale of fixed assets; this, too, would appear as a source of funds. Other sources of funds are long-term borrowing or the issue of additional shares.

Application of funds

Dividends and taxation use up some of the funds, and more may be consumed in acquiring fixed assets such as machinery, motor cars or new premises.

Working capital

The next item on the SSAF is any increase or decrease in working capital. Working capital is the total of funds employed minus the fixed assets, and is used to finance stocks and to pay the day-to-day running expenses of the business. (Working capital is sometimes referred to as *net current assets*, calculated from current assets – current liabilities.)

Stocks of materials and partly finished or finished goods tie up working capital—funds which could otherwise be invested to earn money. Control of stocks is therefore essential to the financial management of the business. Any increase in stocks, shown in the SSAF, should normally be linked to an expected increase in sales in the near future.

The effectiveness of management in controlling credit to customers and obtaining credit from suppliers is shown by changes in *debtors* and *creditors* in the SSAF.

Bank or other loan repayments made during the year will also appear in this section of the financial statement.

The auditors' report

The shareholders of a business appoint independent auditors to examine the accounts and to report on their findings. The auditors must state whether the accounts have been kept properly and whether they give a true picture of the profit or loss and the present financial position of the business.

The auditors examine the records and the procedures for controlling entries into the accounts, and they ensure that the detailed accounts match the summary in the P & L account, balance sheet and SSAF. They should also check that assets listed in the books are in fact still owned by and being used in the business.

EXAMPLE: # SSAF OF AUTOJECTOR LTD

This was the statement of source and application of funds published by Autojector Ltd in its last full year of trading prior to the takeover by FICO Industries Inc.

Autojector Ltd
Source and application of funds for year ending 5 April 1992

	(Values in £k)
Cash and bank balances at beginning of year	50
Sources of funds	
Profit (before tax) from trading	550
Depreciation	120
Sale of fixed assets	<u>10</u>
	680
Application of funds	
Payment of dividends	156
Payment of taxation	136
Purchase of plant and machinery	<u>50</u>
	342
Increase/(decrease) in working capital	
Stocks	50
Debtors	20
Creditors	(40)
Bank overdraft	<u>30</u>
	60
Cash and bank balances at end of year	<u>40</u>

Auditors' report
We have audited the financial statements of Autojector Ltd in accordance with approved auditing procedures.

In our opinion the financial statements give a true and fair view of the state of affairs of the Company at 5 April 1992, and the published accounts have been properly prepared in accordance with the requirements of the Companies Act, 1985.

Birmingham, 21 May 1992

Ernest P. Wilson and Partners
Chartered Accountants

10.4 CASH FLOW FORECASTING

If you work for a small company, you *may* get involved in the detail of balance sheets and P & L accounts; however, whatever the size of your organization, you are likely to have to estimate your income and plan your expenditure month by month. And eventually all transactions end up in a transfer of cash. If you can't pay your way day-by-day you have a cash flow crisis. Avoiding such a crisis calls for cash flow forecasting.

The importance of timing

You need to include in your cash budget an estimate of every item of income and expenditure for the period—usually three, six or twelve months—of the forecast. But unlike in the P & L account, where income and outgoings are deemed to occur on the date of invoicing, in a cash flow forecast you are concerned with when the transfers occur. For example, cash sales and credit sales made on the same day would appear at different times in the cash flow forecast, where they would be separated by the period of credit you allow your non-cash customers.

Opening balance

At the beginning of the period record any cash and bank balances which are readily accessible. Long-term investments which cannot be cashed at short notice should not be included.

Receipts

Estimate, month-by-month, the income you expect from cash sales, grants and other sources of cash. To this you must add payments expected from debtors. To do this you need to find out the average time your credit customers take to settle their accounts; this may well be longer than the agreed settlement period, particularly if you supply to large organizations.

Expenditure

Monthly outgoings will include staff wages, national insurance contributions, stationery and postage costs—expenditure which is closely linked to the level of business activity. But there will also be fixed costs such as heating and lighting, maintenance, insurance and administrative overheads which remain more or less constant regardless of how much work gets done.

Closing balance

Calculate the closing balance for the first month by:

$$Closing\ balance = Opening\ balance + Total\ receipts - Total\ expenditure$$

This figure then becomes the opening balance for the next month. Repeat this calculation throughout the period of the forecast. If you find the closing balance at any stage is negative, you have two choices: negotiate a loan facility to cover the additional needs, or reduce or delay expenditure to obtain a positive balance throughout the period.

Cash is not profit

An increasing cash balance is often an encouraging sign, but it does not necessarily mean the business is making a profit. A cash flow forecast may not take into account the need eventually to repay long-term loans, and it makes no allowance for depreciation. Indeed, it is quite possible to go broke while making a profit, just as you can, over a limited period, remain solvent while trading at a loss.

EXAMPLE: A CASH FLOW ANALYSIS

Stella Hargreaves is FICO's customer training manager. Her job is to prepare and present courses so that FICO's clients get the very best from their conference communications systems. She holds most of these courses in her own on-site training facility, but occasionally she has to put on programmes at other conference centres in Europe. The on-site facility is also used for sales presentations.

Stella's boss, Jack Scarman, leaves her to plan and run the training facility. Each year they agree a timetable for courses, and then Jack works his programme of sales presentations around Stella's training schedule. The training department has to make sufficient profit from courses to fund all of the on-site sales presentations throughout the year: there should be no net cash requirement over the year.

Stella needs to prepare a cash flow forecast, because the levels of training and sales activities vary considerably. The table below shows her forecast for the first six months of 1993.

Training Department cash flow forecast - January to June 1993							
	Jan	Feb	Mar	Apr	May	Jun	Total
Opening balance	£10 000	£6 050	£1 700	£2 800	£5 100	£10 250	
Receipts							
Cash sales	£250	£300	£300	£400	£400	£400	£2 050
Debtors	£2 000	£3 500	£6 000	£8 500	£10 000	£9 500	£39 500
Total receipts	£2 250	£3 800	£6 300	£8 900	£10 400	£9 900	£41 550
Expenditure							
Staff wages	£1 600	£2 200	£3 200	£2 800	£2 800	£3 200	£15 800
Admin overheads	£1 500	£1 500	£1 500	£1 500	£1 500	£1 500	£9 000
Equipment	£2 600	£3 500		£600			£6 700
Stationery		£450			£450		£900
Maintenance	£500	£500	£500	£500	£500	£500	£3 000
Insurance				£1 200			£1 200
Total expenditure	£6 200	£8 150	£5 200	£6 600	£5 250	£5 200	£36 600
Closing balance	£6 050	£1 700	£2 800	£5 100	£10 250	£14 950	

Over 90 per cent of Stella's customers pay on credit accounts, with an average settlement period of six weeks. The result is that the quiet pre-Christmas period appears as unprofitable trading in January and February—just where she needs to pay for over £6000 worth of new equipment. But by the end of June the forecast shows the training department with a healthy cash balance. This should see them comfortably through the summer months when reduced demand for customer training courses coincides with new product launches and increased sales presentation activities.

MANAGEMENT ACCOUNTING— BUDGETING

A budget is a statement of the financial situation of a business over a fixed period, typically a year. The budget consists of estimates of expenditure and income, and usually includes outline plans showing how the money will be raised and how it will be spent.

The budgeting process

At the start of the budgeting cycle, senior management set provisional targets for the financial performance of the organization. Each department prepares its own draft budget, showing what it will contribute to the organization and what it needs to achieve this. When all these draft budgets are combined they may conflict somewhat with the top level objectives, so negotiating begins. Capital or revenue expenditure may have to be brought forward or delayed; tougher sales targets or a staff reduction may be needed. All these adjustments are put into the master budget to check that, if things go reasonably close to plan, the organization will be able to pay its way month-by-month. If the business can neither finance its planned expenditure nor borrow the necessary money from the bank (or from its parent company, in the case of a subsidiary), then irate creditors could start bankruptcy proceedings. If a business cannot pay its way then it could go 'bust'.

Fig 10.1

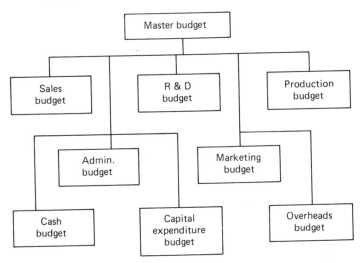

Budgeting trade-offs

All departments with their own budgets must set compatible targets for individual managers, so that the sum of all the management performance targets add up to the overall objectives of the department. And, of course, the department targets must eventually sum to the organization targets. Trade-offs are invariably necessary to eliminate inconsistencies between departmental budgets. For example, the date of release of new product information from design into production should be the same in both the research and development budget and in the production budget.

Budgetary control

Cash flow forecasting is of vital importance in budget preparation. But the budget is more than just a forecast: it is the yardstick against which organization and department performance are measured. Reports on variances between budget and actual income and expenditure help direct management attention towards exceptions from the planned performance: hence the term *exception reporting*.

EXAMPLE: **BREAK-EVEN ANALYSIS**

Every business incurs some fixed costs. These are outgoings which must be paid irrespective of whether goods or services are supplied to customers. Rent, rates and building maintenance are examples of costs which do not usually increase in proportion to the amount of activity in the business. (A small increase or decrease in sales shouldn't require the setting up of another factory or office.) Other costs, such as materials and, to some extent at least, labour, do vary with output. These are termed variable costs.

Adding together these two components—the fixed costs and the variable costs—gives the total cost. Business planning involves calculating how total costs will change as output volume increases or decreases from the budgeted level. Then, when sales and production figures become known month-by-month, the management team can re-estimate the likely profitability by the end of the trading period.

Fig 10.2

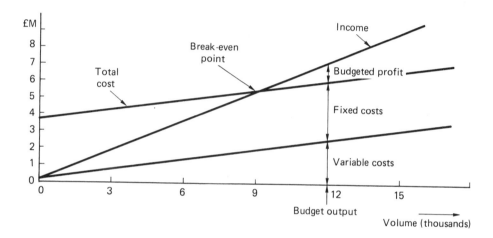

In this example, FICO's Projector Products division plans to deliver 12 000 Autojectors selling at £600 each. The fixed costs are £3.6M, and the variable costs are £200 per projector. So, at the budgeted activity level, the unit cost of each projector would be:

$$Unit\ cost = \frac{£3600}{12} + 200 = £500$$

With a selling price of £600, each projector makes a £100 contribution to profit.

But supposing sales are below target? The graph shows that if sales reach only 9000 units per year then the total sales revenue will just be consumed by the fixed and variable costs. This is the all-important break-even point: if the business operates below this activity level then it cannot make a profit.

So the variable costs *must always* be lower than the selling price for a product to be profitable; but *how much* lower depends on the volume of sales, which affects the ratio of fixed to variable costs.

10.6 COSTING AND WORK IN PROGRESS

The method your organization chooses for calculating the cost of goods or services supplied to its customers will depend on the type of work involved. The way you price your products must also depend on the markets you serve and the sort of price structure your customers are prepared to accept.

Direct costing

In direct or marginal costing, the cost of production is taken as the sum of all variable costs—labour, materials, expenses and those overheads which increase with production volume. These are the marginal costs which would be eliminated if the work in question were cancelled. The cost of sales is found by adding in the production overheads and the other business outgoings, such as R & D, Marketing, Sales, Personnel, Finance and Site Services.

Absorption costing

An alternative approach allocates the full cost of production to specific products or customer orders. Both the fixed and variable elements of production overheads must therefore be attributed to products. In practice this isn't always easy, and some organizations use a system mid-way between direct and absorption costing. Again the cost of sales is found by adding in R & D, general and administration costs, as above.

Production cost estimating

To simplify the task of production estimating, standards are set for the times and costs of each production task. In the estimating system there will be an allowance for scrap and re-work. So, as work proceeds, the actual scrap rates and production efficiencies can be compared with targets. The targets and standards need frequent review, of course, as competition demands ever-increasing quality and efficiency in production.

Work in progress

The stock inventory of raw materials and partly finished goods in a production facility at any time, called the work in progress, is a measure of the amount of working capital tied up. If this capital could be released, the interest on it could be added to profits; or the capital could be invested in a profit-making venture inside the business. So, provided production schedules are not constantly slipping due to shortages of materials, the lower the level of work in progress the better.

Just in time

The just in time philosophy demands progressively reduced stock levels and smaller batch sizes. Each time a bottleneck is revealed management take action to prevent its recurrence. Inventory levels are then lowered further, towards the goal of a batch size of one and a stock holding time equal to the total processing time.

The key to the success of a just in time philosophy is the working relationship between materials suppliers and the manufacturer. A mutual commitment to continuous quality improvement is needed, with the ultimate goal of zero defects.

Pricing policy

A product can be priced either on production cost plus a margin, or on what the market will stand. In the short term, putting a high price on a scarce commodity yields large profits, but it may attract competitors into the market and so ultimately drive down prices.

PRICING DECISIONS

When FICO launched their first Autojector, it offered a substantial technical advantage over other professional projectors available at that time. The relationship between price and demand for high-quality projectors was reasonably elastic—the demand changed steadily with price changes—and FICO knew that at £900 they would sell all the Autojectors they could produce during the first 12 to 18 months. Thereafter they felt they would have to lower the price to the market norm of £600 to match other professional machines, which by then would probably offer similar performance. However, FICO also deal with educational establishments with recurring needs for projection equipment. These customers would be less inclined to pay a 50 per cent surcharge for the extra performance of an Autojector; many would switch to less expensive suppliers.

Should FICO continue supplying their old models, which would limit the rate of production of Autojectors? Or should they risk losing the longer term loyalty of their educational customers in order to exploit short-term rich pickings from conference facilities buyers?

FICO's solution was to launch two versions, rationing the supply of each. The Autojector AJ1P, with a superior finish and special transport case, was priced at £1150. A basic model, the Autojector AJ1E, was priced at £650, with 80 per cent of the first year's production reserved for educational purchasers.

Competitive tendering

When FICO made their bid for refurbishing the National Conference Centre, they were asked to quote a fixed price for the initial installation and the first 12 months warranty. There was a 1 per cent per week bonus for early completion and a 1 per cent per week penalty for late delivery, up to a maximum of 15 per cent. The profitability of the contract was critically dependent on two factors: containing the costs of the work, and delivering a properly working and reliable system by the scheduled date.

Fig 10.3

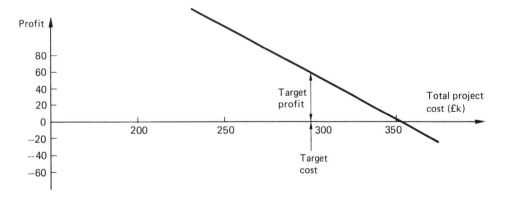

All on-site work by FICO's field service engineers from year two onwards was quoted on the basis of a fixed daily fee plus expenses at cost. This is a common form of contract for consultancy work of this type, where the customer may require occasional enhancements to the original system.

10.7

APPRAISING PROJECT VIABILITY

Faced with the decision whether to go ahead with an investment project, there are five important questions to answer:

1 Do you have the skilled staff and the facilities to complete the project satisfactorily?
2 Could you find the money needed to fund the project through its investment (negative cash flow) phase?
3 Would it be profitable in an acceptable time-scale?
4 Are you prepared to accept the risk of failure? If the project went wrong would it do unacceptable damage to your organization?
5 Is there anything more profitable at the same or a lower level of risk that you could do with your money and other resources?

The first of these questions is to do with technical feasibility; the others are all financial matters. If you could see into the future, you would get precise numerical answers of cash flow, payback period and return on investment. In practice you have to take an educated guess on many of the unknowns. These include:

- How the market will develop or shrink during the life of the project.
- How interest rates will vary with time.
- What actions your competitors will take and how these will affect their costs.
- How much you can improve your own competitiveness during the project.

Time and money values

Often you need to compare alternative projects which span differing time periods. Investments in the early stages of a project are expected to give returns later, when customers pay for the goods or services deriving from your investment. But you can translate all these cash flows into their present-day value by a process known as discounting. You must choose a discount rate for the project; this could be the interest rate charged when you borrow money. More often you would use the rate of return on investment you are currently receiving from your other projects. The latter will usually be a higher figure, justifying the degree of risk you are taking. So with a discount rate of 20 per cent, £100 to be received at the end of year two would have a net present value given by:

$$NPV = \frac{100}{(1.2 \times 1.2)} = £69.44$$

assuming discounting is done at the end of each year.

Down payments and stage payments

The time-varying value of money has little effect on short-term projects unless interest rates are unusually high. In contrast, for projects lasting several years the effects of discounted cash flows (DCF) can be considerable. In particular, projects become extremely sensitive to interest rate fluctuations when there is a large time lapse between investment and return. Not only that, but predicting what will happen to interest rates over several years is extremely risky; so, all other things being equal, short-term projects are safer, financially, than longer term ones. These are all reasons why contracting firms try to obtain from their clients a down payment on signature of contract, and frequent stage payments linked to achievement milestones as the work proceeds.

DISCOUNTED CASH FLOW

In this example FICO Inc.'s Vice President, US Operations, is considering whether to approve the setting up of a facility to produce optical components for a new slide projector to be assembled in Britain. An alternative is to subcontract the development to a camera lens specialist. So, for each option, FICO UK's financial director has estimated the cash flows over the expected life of the product.

Option A— set up a facility at FICO's own factory	Developing a FICO optical facility								Comments
	(all figures in $k)	Annual investment/return							Initial investment assumed all to be in year 0
		Year 0	Year 1	Year 2	Year 3	Year 4	Year 5	Net total	There are no cash flows after year 5
Discount rate = 0%	Cash flow	–300	50	100	150	250	50	300	Net profit = $300k
	Net cash flow	–300	–250	–150	0	250	300		Average return = $60k/yr Ave. rate of return = 20%
Discount rate = 10%	DCF	–300	45.5	82.6	112	171	31	142	Net profit = $142k
	NPV	–300	–254	–172	–60	111	142		Average return = $28k/yr Ave. rate of return = 9.5%
Discount rate = 25%	DCF	–300	40	64	76.8	102	16.4	–0.8	Net profit = -$0.8k
	NPV	–300	–260	–196	–119	–17.2	–0.8		Average loss = $0.16k/yr Ave. rate of return = NIL!

Ignoring the time-varying value of money, option A appears to pay back the initial investment in just three years, and the annual average return on the initial investment is 20 per cent. However, when a more accurate appraisal is carried out using discounted cash flows, the project is seen to be less attractive. At 10 per cent discount rate it takes about $3\frac{1}{2}$ years to recoup the investment, and the average annual rate of return falls to less than 10 per cent. And at 25 per cent discount rate the project never repays the initial investment.

Option B—use the facilities of a specialist camera lens manufacturer	Developing a FICO optical facility								Comments
	(all figures in $k)	Annual investment/return							Initial investment assumed all to be in year 0
		Year 0	Year 1	Year 2	Year 3	Year 4	Year 5	Net total	There are no cash flows after year 5
Discount rate = 0%	Cash flow	–200	100	100	100	25	25	150	Net profit = $150k
	Net cash flow	–200	–100	0	100	125	150		Average return = $30k/yr Ave. rate of return = 15%
Discount rate = 25%	DCF	–200	80	64	51.2	10.2	8.2	13.6	Net profit = $13.6k
	NPV	–200	–120	–562	–4.8	5.4	13.6		Average profit = $2.7k/yr Ave. rate of return = 1.4%

Compare this with option B, where the returns build up more rapidly. Here the project offers a lower profitability when discounting is ignored, but is far less vulnerable to interest rate changes. This option remains marginally profitable even at 25 per cent discount rate.

CHAPTER 11

HOW TO MANAGE PROJECTS
A STEP-BY-STEP GUIDE TO PROJECT DEFINITION, PLANNING AND CONTROL

Projects demand many of the skills required for your other management activities—reports, interviews, meetings and the like. There is, however, one big difference: you do the other things because they *help* you get your job done, whereas the project and your job are often *one and the same thing*. A poor report may be thrown back for correction: embarrassing! A failed project is more serious: you may not get another chance to manage something as important to your organization.

It cuts both ways, of course: a sparkling presentation might be praised and soon forgotten, whereas a major project success can bring longer term recognition.

The challenge

Projects can go wrong for a variety of reasons, including changing market needs or plain bad luck. But many projects overrun their schedules and exceed their budgets due to poor management. This applies as much to projects inside the organization—setting up a new facility, for example—as to contracts managed for external customers. There are even projects with nothing of value at the end. Were they doomed from the start? Or did the situation change without anyone stopping to reappraise the viability of these projects? There may be a tendency to look for scapegoats—a subcontractor let us down, or the original estimates were way out—but in the end the buck stops with the project manager whose company career can be made or broken by just one project.

The benefits

Do new requirements creep in and steal your fast-dwindling budget? Clear statements of work will help you tie down the scope of the job so that you and everyone else involved know what is included and what is not.

Do you have problems dealing with large amounts of planning data? A structured approach will help keep details in the background until you need them.

Do mistakes which should have been spotted earlier mean work has to be done again? Or do people who were supposed to work for you suddenly become unavailable? Then you will certainly benefit from an improved monitoring and control system—one which works *without* creating a depressing mountain of paper.

THE ROUTE TO PROJECT MANAGEMENT SUCCESS

Project success means achieving the technical objective, quality standards and delivery dates while keeping within your materials cost and human resource budgets. This is easy when you do all the work yourself: you know what's happening, whether you are on schedule and how much you have spent. But once your projects are big enough to need other contributors, life becomes more difficult. Planning and controlling the work so that the objectives are met requires special skills: project management skills.

Benefits for all

As you develop your project management skills, your customers, whether inside the organization or outside, will benefit from:

- Valuable help in fully defining the requirements.
- Clear, meaningful and up-to-date progress reports as work proceeds.
- Early warning of any threats to time-scale, quality or cost targets.

And you, as manager of the project, will be better off, too, because:

- You and your team have clear objectives and a viable plan for meeting them.
- Contributors keep you informed with accurate, concise reports.
- Your reputation for achievement spreads through the organization.

Key steps to success

The approach recommended here is straightforward and structured:

Fig 11.1

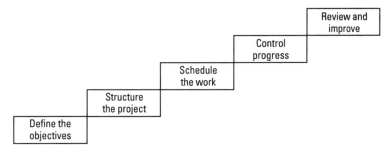

- **Make sure all contributors understand the requirement**
  In the wave of euphoria at the birth of a new idea, it is easy to underestimate the work involved. A major cause of project overrun is extra work, essential to completion, but not considered when the original estimates are made.
- **Structure the work so each task has just one owner**
  Shared responsibilities rarely work out. You need to ensure that all contributors know the extent of their commitment to the project and feel accountable for their performance.
- **Make simple plans that everyone understands**
  Used wisely computers can help you make better plans and so head off problems before they impact on the project. But make the system serve the project; don't become a slave to an over-complex and unwieldy computer-based plan.
- **Monitor only what you need to know**
  Performance monitoring can help you make good decisions, provided you measure the things that matter and then take prompt action to keep things under control.
- **Set improvement targets for next time.**
  Post-mortems on completed projects can help you and other project managers improve the performance of future projects.

DEFINING AIMS AND PRIORITIES

At the beginning of a project, rarely is it clear exactly what has to be done; yet the decisions you make at the outset are usually the most important ones.

The trade-off triangle

There are alternative approaches to most projects, varying in terms of:

- **Quality**: the standards to which work must be done.
- **Cost**: the materials, labour and capital equipment budget.
- **Time**: the dates when the work is to start and finish.

Fig 11.2

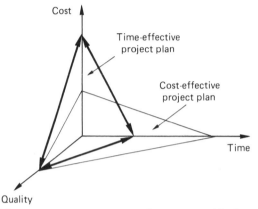

Planning a project is not simply a matter of finding *a way* of doing the work. If there *is* a way of achieving the objective then there are *other ways,* too. Some approaches will take longer, cost more or involve greater quality risks than others.

It's not possible to maximize quality and at the same time minimize cost and time-scale. A rushed project will be more expensive and may not achieve as high a quality as one carried out in less haste. However, management and capital costs increase proportionally to time, so too long a duration also increases the cost. If time and cost are fixed, then the variable must be achievement. If achievement and time are fixed, then you must be prepared to put in more resources if necessary.

Innovation or efficiency?

Completing an innovative project quickly is more important than minimizing its costs. You won't be able to make detailed plans, but project management software can still be useful in helping communicate objectives and record achievements. In contrast, for a competitive 'me too' project, cost control will be your main concern. Then thorough planning and accurate estimating are essential.

Fig 11.3

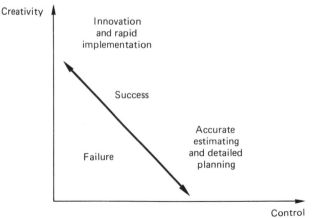

EXAMPLE

The success of the Autojector OHP family prompted FICO to extend its product range, applying the same principle to a 35 mm slide projector. Here is the project launch summary prepared during a feasibility study. It contains a statement of work (SOW) for the development phase of this project.

FICO (UK) Ltd	
Project launch summary	
Project title & Ref. No:	35mm Autojector AJ35B—Development phase
Customer (internal/external):	FICO (UK), marketing director
Project manager:	Vanessa Tippet
Project launch date:	1/3/1994

Aims	
To develop a 35 mm slide projector using the Autojector principle, and to set up manufacturing facilities capable of producing 300 units per week.	

Targets	Priorities
Meet spec. F1/0027/1	2
Production release date 1/11/1994	3
Development cost £200 000 max.	4 (lowest)
System production cost £280 max.	1 (highest)

Inputs	Outputs
Marketing report FM4367/2	1 set of manufacturing drawings and specifications
Operational requirement spec	1 bill of materials
2 Autojector AJ/OHP/1A samples	100 prototypes from pilot production line
	100 copies of user handbook and repair manual

Statement of work	Constraints
Design a 35 mm slide projector based upon the Autojector principle. The system must include the projector, the screen, both mains and control cables, and a carrying case. Pilot manufacture is to be in the FICO (UK) plant.	Operate within existing R&D department staff levels. Access to production test facility is only available after 7 pm and at weekends. Make maximum use of components and modules from the existing Autojector range. Styling to match the existing range, with the Autojector logo on the projector housing, screen and all documentation.

Major tasks	Delegated to
Design projector; produce drawings	J Masters
Develop and make 10 prototypes	J Masters
Set up production line	N Richards
Run pilot production, 100 units	N Richards
Produce 1000 sales brochures	J Scarman
Produce 100 user handbooks	J Scarman
Produce 100 repair manuals	J Scarman

WORK BREAKDOWN STRUCTURE

The first step in making a project plan is to create a work breakdown structure (WBS). This is a list of the phases of the project, and the tasks and sub-tasks (or work packages) which need to be carried out in each phase. Depending on whether you are developing products, supplying new services or improving systems internal to your organization, your project may have some or all of the following phases:

- Feasibility study.
- Project definition and planning.
- Design.
- Development.
- Pilot production or trial operation.
- Maintenance and enhancement.
- Phase-out or decommissioning.

Making the task list

It is often easiest to start at the end of a phase, working back to the beginning, asking:

'What must we have done before we can start this activity?'

The activities you come up with are called immediate prerequisites of the task being considered. This type of dependency is termed a finish-to-start link. There may also be tasks which must be done concurrently, sometimes with a lag between the start of one task and the start of the other. This gives what is termed a start-to-start link. These links determine the order in which work may proceed.

Some tasks have no linking with the rest of a project. For example, you may need to hold quarterly review meetings with a customer irrespective of whether work is ahead of or behind schedule. Then there may be fixed dates, called milestones, which must be met. For example, you might need to use a particular trade show to announce a new product or service. Make a note of these milestone dates, as they will act as constraints when you are deciding how much resource to allocate to the various tasks.

Organization breakdown structure

Every task or work package on a project should have an owner. That person is responsible for completing the work to the required quality standard and on schedule. Problems arise when a task needs people from more than one department, and maybe outside subcontractors, too. It's usually best if you delegate each task to whoever will have the majority of the work under their direct control; that person then must negotiate with others to secure the resources needed to do the work. This means producing estimates for a task, rather than a function, such as a drawing office or machine shop. Then, as the work proceeds, you should record costs for tasks, not departments alone, so you can compare achievements with estimates.

Avoid shared responsibilities. Never have two or more owners of any task or work package. (Of course, there will be instances where individuals will have responsibility for more than one task, maybe on more than one project.)

Your organization breakdown structure (OBS) should mirror one-to-one your work breakdown structure. It's the OBS that defines your project team, regardless of how the organization draws its *family tree*.

A PRODUCT DEVELOPMENT PROJECT

Vanessa Tippet broke down the AJ35B project to produce a 35 mm version of the Autojector into the following phases:

* Feasibility study.
* Development.
* Pilot production.
* Full production.

Here is the development phase, shown as a work breakdown structure in tree form with abbreviated titles:

Fig 11.4

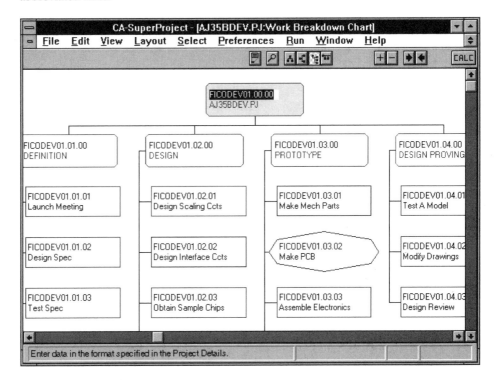

Here, *CA-SuperProject* ® is being used to help plan and monitor the project. It is a simple matter to switch between alternative representations of the project structure.

Vanessa was able to use OHP slides of the WBS, taken from the computer, when presenting the plan at the project launch meeting.

UNCERTAINTY IN ESTIMATING

You can never be certain how long a project will take and how much it will cost, so you must make an intelligent guess—an estimate. These estimates are used to:

- Analyse alternative projects (financial appraisal).
- Create project plans and cash flow forecasts.
- Allocate funds to work package managers and subcontractors.
- Assess the impact of proposed changes as the project proceeds..

If you were to give a task to 100 people and record the finishing times for each, you could plot a probability histogram. This would show a spread around the mean completion date. Here the most commonly occurring completion, the *mode* of the distribution, is Day 6, but because the distribution isn't symmetrical the mean completion date is Day 7.

Fig 11.5

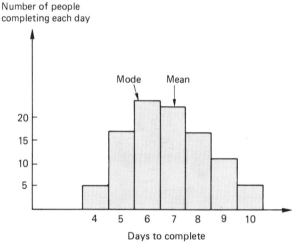

Mean time to complete multiple tasks

When independent tasks are carried out one after another, the mean time to complete all the work is the sum of the means for each task. The spreads do not add directly; but, when you build up an estimate from several parts, the individual uncertainties tend to cancel out.

Fig 11.6

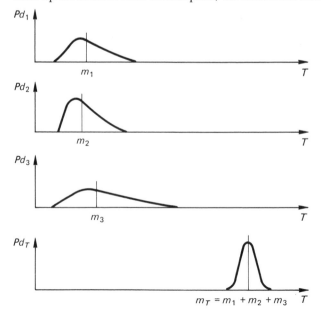

EXAMPLES   Janet Masters is collecting data to prepare a development plan for the new 35 mm Autojector. She talks to Steve Peters in the prototype workshop. It will be Steve's job to produce six sheet metal housings for the development models. What Janet needs is a time-scale estimate, and Steve has all the experience.

> Steve: 'Should take four days each. Assuming I'm not interrupted, of course.'
>
> Janet: 'Right! But what's the basis of your estimate?'.
>
> Steve: 'Experience, that's the basis. I've done nearly all our prototype housings in the last three years. That's at least fifty units.'
>
> Janet: 'Ok. But have you ever managed a prototype in three days?'
>
> Steve: 'As a matter of fact I did. Once! But if you put three days in the estimate don't blame me if...'
>
> Janet: 'Hold on, Steve. I'm not. Now, have you ever needed more than four days?'.
>
> Steve: 'Sure, When things go wrong. The worst disaster was when the router bearing disintegrated. Wrote off the housing, and we had no more in stores. It took nearly two weeks to get that job sorted out. It wasn't funny!'
>
> Janet: 'Right, Steve. Let's go for the four day target, but if you can do better we'll all be delighted.'

Modes and means

What Steve was quoting was the *mode* of the probability distribution, while Janet needs to allow for the *mean*—a rather higher figure because of the asymmetry of the probability distribution.

Fig 11.7

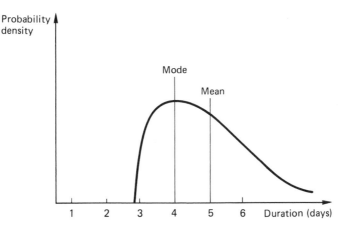

Modes—the most commonly occurring results—are what most people tend to remember, although pessimists may be biased towards a higher estimate than optimists.

Janet decides to build an allowance of five days into the project plan. She also asks Steve to record the *actual* durations, so she will be able to calculate the means when estimating future jobs.

(In the diagrams I have used probability density functions where the total area under each curve is 1.0, corresponding to 100 per cent probability. So the probability of completion occurring between one time and another is the area under the curve between those times.)

11.4 ESTIMATING TECHNIQUES

Project estimates are determined by:

- The scope of the project, as defined in a statement of work (SOW).
- The work breakdown structure (WBS).
- The standards and specifications to be achieved.
- The resource constraints within which the project will be carried out.

Global and synthetic estimates

The basis for estimating new projects is a combination of experience and guesswork. Estimates may be global—a figure for the whole project—or synthesized from a number of sub-elements. Global estimating is useful before the detail of the work is understood; however, synthesized estimates are usually more accurate, and so it is normal practice to build up estimates during the planning phase if they have not been prepared during a feasibility study.

Subjective techniques

Intuitive or subjective estimates—'I reckon this is about a £150 000 job'—rely on the hunches of individuals. You can use these techniques initially to justify the expense of a more scientific approach. They can also prompt searching questions when the results of a more objective assessment differ greatly from what intuition suggests.

Comparative techniques

Comparative estimates are made by referring to stored data from past projects. Sometimes there is only enough time to find figures from your closest equivalent to the new project. More often, however, you can produce synthetic estimates from a collection of comparative estimates at task or work package level.

Parametric techniques

Parametric estimating relies on formal or observed relationships between cost or time and project parameters. For example, a parametric equation could be produced to calculate the cost of delivering a consignment of goods to a customer. The cost would vary in some way according to:

- The weight of the package.
- The volume of the package.
- The distance involved.
- The speed of delivery required.

Parametric estimates (sometimes abbreviated to *metrics*) are often used to predict the cost of developing computer programs. The estimating model requires such information as the number of modules and their average number of lines of code, the programming language, and the amount of experience the programmers have in working with that language. From these data the software model provides a cost and time-scale estimate. Then, as the project proceeds, the actual durations and costs are fed into the model and its parameters are automatically adjusted to improve the accuracy of future estimates.

Whether you use parametric or comparative estimating techniques, keep a record of actual achievements so you can reduce the estimating uncertainty on future projects.

EXAMPLE

Having developed the Autojector Mk I, an overhead projector, Vanessa Tippet was able to refer to the cost estimates which were available at each phase of development, and to compare these with the actual costs at the end of the project. These figures provided a nearest neighbour basis for initial estimates of both development cost and unit production cost of the new 35 mm Autojector.

Confidence growth

At the beginning of the feasibility study, the designers felt they were unlikely to complete the project for less than £100 000, and that it might, at worst, cost nearer four times that amount. As the study progressed uncertainties were resolved and the engineers were able to improve the accuracy of their estimate. So, as confidence increased, the optimistic and pessimistic estimates of the cost of developing the Autojector converged on a single value. The actual development cost became known only when the production line was running smoothly and fault-free products were being shipped to customers.

Fig 11.8

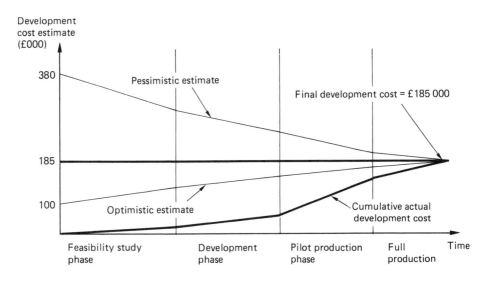

The actual costs at project completion were compared with the baseline estimates prepared at the end of the feasibility study. Studying the variances between actual and forecast costs helped the management team decide in which areas they needed to improve:

- The accuracy of their estimating database.
- The procedures for monitoring and controlling development costs.

Unit cost estimate

The unit production cost also emerged from optimistic and pessimistic estimates, which were refined as the project proceeded. For a high-volume product such as the Autojector, the viability of the project was mainly determined by the unit production cost; so the project manager required frequent updates of the forecast unit cost. Whenever there was a risk of the target unit cost being exceeded, the designers and manufacturing engineers met to review what options were available for value engineering or specification changes.

11.5   SCHEDULING WITH GANTT CHARTS

Scheduling converts estimates of people-hours into calendar dates. To make a project plan, you use the estimates of how long each task will take, scheduling the tasks so that each one starts soon enough to avoid unnecessarily delaying others. If you find this gives an unacceptably long duration then you must either carry out more tasks in parallel or apply more resources to shorten the duration of individual tasks.

Henry Gantt devised a method of representing activities as horizontal time bars. These bars can be marked with intermediate measuring points corresponding to completion of a defined percentage of the total task.

Fig 11.9

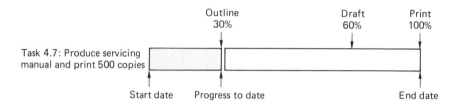

A project can be represented as a set of such bars—a Gantt chart. The work packages which make up a task can also be shown as Gantt charts.

Fig 11.10

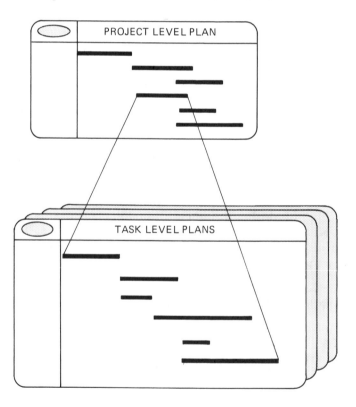

194

A WORK PACKAGE SCHEDULE

The project manager, Vanessa Tippet, needs to see an overview of the whole project, without unnecessary detail. By switching on only the major tasks and leaving off the lower level work packages, a simple and uncluttered Gantt chart for the development phase can be displayed.

This is not enough detail for Janet Masters, the chief engineer responsible for design and development of the new Autojector. She needs to view the individual work packages within each task. She can call up a screen which shows not only the work packages but also the logical links between them.

Fig 11.11

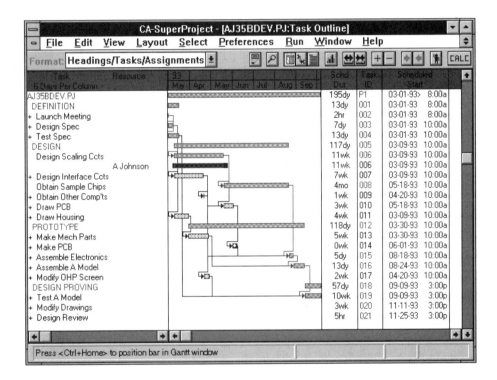

When using *CA-SuperProject* to plan the development work, Janet is able to define the logical links between activities by pointing at one work package with the mouse, holding the button down and pointing to the successor work package to denote a dependency.

PROJECT PLANNING—NETWORKS

The dependence of one activity upon others is not readily visible from the Gantt chart. Networks, commonly referred to as PERT (project evaluation and review technique) charts, overcome this limitation, and are commonly used in planning large projects.

Activity on arrows or at nodes?

Networks can be drawn to represent activities as arrows, and events—usually the starts and finishes of activities—as nodes. Each activity arrow, which need not be drawn to scale, joins all other arrows which immediately precede or follow it in time sequence.

Fig 11.12

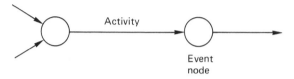

An alternative representation, the precedence diagram, puts activities at nodes. Links then show the dependencies. This style of network is now used in many computer-aided project management systems.

Fig 11.13

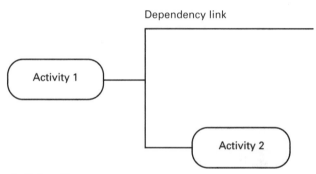

How many activities?

Keep your plans simple. Experience shows that few people can understand networks containing more than thirty activities. So, if a project has several hundred activities, create a hierarchy: project → task → work package, and produce simple networks at project and task level.

The critical path

In any project where several tasks are going on at once, there will be more than one path through the network. One path will have a longer duration than all others, and this is called the critical path. Any delay on the critical path will extend the whole project. By thickening the activity lines on the critical path, it is at once obvious where most management attention should be focused.

Once you know the critical path duration, you can calculate the amount of slack time, or *float*, available on each of the other paths through the network. Activities on non-critical paths need not start as soon as their prerequisites are completed; they can be delayed, if necessary, to reduce the pressure on facilities or to smooth the demands on people's time.

Non-critical activities therefore have two start dates: a *can start on* and a *must start by*. These are often referred to as *earliest start* and *latest start* dates, and they result in two end dates: the *earliest finish* and *latest finish*.

EXAMPLE: A PERT NETWORK

When task and resource information are included with each activity, only a small part of the PERT network of the development phase can be viewed on the computer screen. A printout can be produced in several pages which then need gluing together. Alternatively, a large format plotter provides a single sheet hard copy.

Fig 11.14

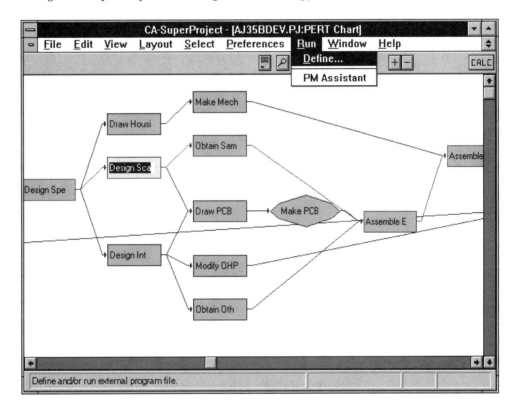

CA-SuperProject allows a choice of PERT views. Here the information on each activity has been reduced to identification code only, and the whole network easily fits on a single A4 sheet.

Recording the baseline

Once the initial plan had been agreed, Vanessa saved it as the *Project Baseline*.

The baseline plan (together with the corresponding cost and schedule estimates which are discussed in the next topic) is compared with actual results as the project proceeds. Only if the business goals for the project alter will this baseline plan be updated.

PROJECT PLANNING—RISKS

Suppose the critical path of a project contains three major tasks, two of which can be estimated accurately. The third task contains a 50 per cent risk of cost and time increase because the work will have to be repeated if a particular event occurs. The probability density functions for the duration of the activities are as shown below:

Fig 11.15

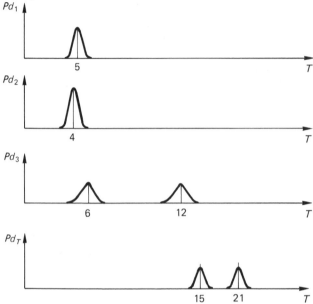

Although the mean completion time is around 18 weeks, the most likely completion times are close to 15 weeks or to 21 weeks.

Risk management strategy

Some approaches to a project are inherently more risky than others. Weigh the benefits of taking a risky route against the costs if things go wrong.

- List all project tasks, recording the nature of any risks and the cost and/or time-scale penalty incurred should the risk become reality.
- Be sure to account for the true costs of extending any task which occurs on the critical path (or which becomes critical if the risk becomes reality). This means allowing for the cost of delaying other non-critical tasks active at that time.
- Multiply each risk by your assessment of its probability of occurrence. This will give you a *management reserve*.
- Allocate only baseline budgets. Retain the management reserve for use in those risk areas where extra work becomes necessary.

Small investigations, mock-ups and studies can help you avoid or minimize some risks and remove others from the critical path. A project in which all major risks occur on the critical path is usually more difficult to manage than one in which many of the risks are resolved without threatening the target completion date.

The perversity of risks

The things which go wrong on projects are not always the risks you foresaw at the planning stage. Sometimes tasks which you thought were straightforward prove to be nothing of the sort. So why bother with risk management? Because experience shows that a plan which can cope reasonably well with the risks you can foresee stands a better chance of being manageable when unforeseen problems arise.

EXAMPLE

The development of the original Autojector was an innovative project. The plan wasn't a forecast of what would happen; it was at best a guess as to how the project might go. But the project manager, Vanessa Tippet, knew that all would not go well. She also knew that the risks in the project would need managing, regardless of how detailed the plan. She was not looking for a plan which would allow the project to be completed on schedule and within budget if all went well. She needed a plan which was least susceptible to the effects of risk, the biggest of which was the possibility that a custom silicon chip might not work properly first time. If this was the case, it would have to be redesigned and a new batch of prototypes made. This would almost double the chip development time.

The custom chip contained the special image-scaling logic as well as the control circuits which connect with the operator controls. The scaling logic was the main source of technical risk, as nothing like it had been done before. The control circuits were straightforward, but could not be finalized until the control panel had been designed.

Turning risk into certainty

The most obvious approach was first to design the scaling and focusing circuits while the control panel details were being sorted out, and then to design the interface circuits before ordering prototype chips. This approach, however, would put chip manufacture on the critical path. The prototyping would take at least 24 weeks, with a 50 per cent risk of an extension to 36 weeks. For this task the best estimate was thus:

$$T_e = (24 + 0.5 \times 12) = 30 \ weeks$$

Instead, Vanessa decided to make a prototype chip containing just the scaling circuits. If this worked first time then it would be a simple matter to modify the design to include the control circuits, and to manufacture new chip samples. And if the scaling logic needed modifications they could be incorporated when the control circuits were added.

The baseline estimate now becomes 30 weeks, with no need for a risk reserve. The increased estimate was acceptable because it ensured the Autojector would meet its crucial launch date target. This is an example of a trade-off between *time* and *cost*.

The table below shows the cost risk reserves (risk cost x probability) planned in to the development phase of this project.

Task	Base cost (£k)	Risk cost (£k)	Probability (%)	Reserve (£k)
Design chip	38	20	50	10
Design castings	26	8	20	1.6
Build prototypes	35	5	50	2.5
Publications	20	0	—	—

A similar table was prepared for the estimated durations of tasks on the critical path.

It was important for the team to realize that risk estimates—of time as well as cost—belong to the project, not to individual tasks or work packages. Indeed, when a risk becomes reality, money from other reserves is called upon, as the actual cost exceeds the factored risk reserve. Task and work package managers are therefore measured against the *baseline* estimates of both time and cost.

11.8 RESOURCE PLANNING

Now it is time to see whether the draft plan is viable. Does it take you where you want to go as quickly as you need, and can you provide the resources—the skilled people and special facilities—to carry out the plan?

Plans which don't take account of resource limitations are unlikely to be achievable. Similarly, project plans which demand top priority from all support services are most vulnerable to disruption when other business pressures alter priorities. It is essential to check the availability of people, facilities and materials when planning a project. In particular, you are more likely to be able to get the resources you need if your demand for the time of people and facilities does not fluctuate unduly from day to day. This means you must plan the total demand on each resource.

Each task may require several different resources, some throughout the task duration, others for shorter periods. People's time needs careful planning: you may need to bar allocations during holidays and weekends, for example.

Resource assessment

Once you have assigned resources to each task, assess how the load on each resource type (specialist people skills or facilities) varies with time. Initially, assume each activity will start at its earliest start date. This approach maximizes the amount of slack or float on all non-critical paths. It does, however, mean money is spent earlier than necessary, and you will probably find also that the resource demands are unacceptable.

Smoothing and levelling

You now need to reduce the peaks and fill in some of the troughs in resource demand. Do this by delaying some of the non-critical tasks (by an amount not exceeding the available slack or float!). If you prioritize tasks according to their degree of risk, you can avoid unnecessarily delaying the start of high-risk tasks, retaining all their slack to cope with risks should they become reality.

Most computer-based project management systems have automatic resource smoothing facilities; their effectiveness is variable. If you decide to use this facility, make sure that task priority and the amount of float are used to decide how much, if at all, a start date can be slipped. (The float in a task is the amount of time it can be delayed before it becomes critical—extending the project duration.) Of more importance in smoothing is the amount of *free float*. This is the amount of start delay possible without delaying the start of any other task. (As other tasks may contain free float, the finish might not be delayed, but the provision for coping with risks could be greatly reduced.)

Even after smoothing, you may still have some over-scheduled resources. If overtime working or extra resources are not available, you may have to extend the project. A *resource levelling* facility will schedule resources until all conflict between demand and availability is removed. To achieve this it might have to delay tasks on the critical path.

The hidden cost of smoothing

Avoid unnecessary resource smoothing. In particular, starting too many high-risk tasks at or near their *must start* dates will make several paths of the project become critical. The hidden cost is reduced controllability: you will have less scope for switching resources to prevent schedule slip when things go wrong.

MANAGING RESOURCES

In the initial plan for the development phase of the Autojector AJ35B, there were resource overloads in the circuit design and model assembly areas:

Fig 11.16

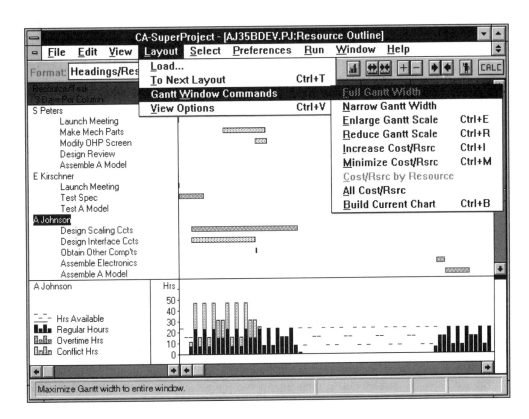

Automatic smoothing

Using the automatic resource smoothing facility of *CA-SuperProject* it was possible to resolve these conflicts without extending the development time-scale.

CONTROLLING PROGRESS

The WBS not only provides a structure for communicating targets and making plans, but also for monitoring achievement. Each task and work package has:

- An owner (defined via the organization breakdown structure).
- A statement of work, defining the targets, deliverable items and standards.
- Planned start and end dates.
- A resource assignment.
- Cost estimate.

Now you can allocate account codes to each task and work package. For a labour-intensive project (software development is an example) you might decide on a single cost code for each account. Other projects may require codes for collecting costs on labour, materials and other costs. (Other costs could include travelling and subsistence expenses for off-site work.) In larger organizations, where tasks are split up on a functional basis—design, marketing, manufacture and so forth—a department prefix is often built in to the work breakdown coding system.

Controlling the baseline plan

It is essential to save the baseline plan and use it as the yardstick for measuring performance. If, as the project proceeds, things go wrong, actual start and end dates for tasks and work packages will differ from those planned. You still need to compare durations with the plan. Indeed, only if the agreed baseline is changed—for example if a revised specification is agreed—should the baseline plan be updated.

Project communications: setting up the internal contract

To manage a project you must communicate the project aims, and motivate all contributors to control their work and let you know in good time if they need help. Where possible, involve them in the planning and estimating; this will help you build a team strongly committed to the success of the project. (See also Chapter 12—Motivating and leading teams.) It is vital that each contributor views his or her commitment to the project as an *internal contract* between supplier and customer.

Reporting progress

Be wary of accepting subjective estimates of what fraction of a task is complete and shading in that fraction of the bar. Some people quickly reach 90 per cent, but seem unable to maintain momentum: the last 10 per cent can take just as long again. If you decide to accept partial completion of work packages, it is wise to limit progress claims to defined measuring points, to help avoid the 90 per cent complete syndrome.

Re-working the plan

Regular re-planning will be necessary on all but the most trivial of projects. People fall ill, machines break down, supplies fail to arrive on time, and resources have to be moved from one work package to another to deal with whatever is most important at the time.

When a task manager hasn't the resources to correct a deviation from the task-level plan, you need to be informed; but do avoid *murdering the messenger whenever you don't like the message*. If you cannot absorb the slip, you will have to divert resources from other, less critical tasks, covering the extra cost from your management reserve. Put most management effort into those areas which are time-critical or contain significant cost or schedule risks.

EXAMPLE

So that all contributors could get to know one another and have a chance to ask questions about the project plan, Vanessa called a project launch meeting. This was also an opportunity to test the level of commitment of those contributors over whose work she did not have direct control.

Before the meeting, each person received a copy of the project calendar, showing planned start and end dates, scheduled hours for each resource, and which activities were on the critical path. The calendar, part of which is shown here, also highlights tasks involving 'conflict hours', where the scheduled working hours for any resource exceed the normal working hours.

Fig 11.17

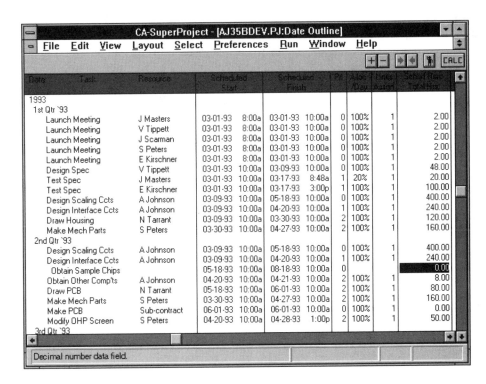

```
┌──────────────────────────────────────────────────────────────────────────┐
│  CA-SuperProject - [AJ35BDEV.PJ:Date Outline]                        ▼ ▲  │
│  File  Edit  View  Layout  Select  Preferences  Run  Window  Help      ♦  │
│                                                          + - │ ♦ ◄ │ ⅋ │CALC│
│                                                                            │
│ Date      Task        Resource      Scheduled     Scheduled    Pri Alloc  Units  Sched Res ▲│
│                                     Start         Finish          /Day   Assgn  Total Hrs  │
│ 1993                                                                       │
│ 1st Qtr '93                                                                │
│   Launch Meeting   J Masters    03-01-93  8:00a  03-01-93 10:00a  0 100%   1      2.00     │
│   Launch Meeting   V Tippett    03-01-93  8:00a  03-01-93 10:00a  0 100%   1      2.00     │
│   Launch Meeting   J Scarman    03-01-93  8:00a  03-01-93 10:00a  0 100%   1      2.00     │
│   Launch Meeting   S Peters     03-01-93  8:00a  03-01-93 10:00a  0 100%   1      2.00     │
│   Launch Meeting   E Kirschner  03-01-93  8:00a  03-01-93 10:00a  0 100%   1      2.00     │
│   Design Spec      V Tippett    03-01-93 10:00a  03-09-93 10:00a  0 100%   1     48.00     │
│   Test Spec        J Masters    03-01-93 10:00a  03-17-93  8:48a  1  20%   1     20.00     │
│   Test Spec        E Kirschner  03-01-93 10:00a  03-17-93  3:00p  1 100%   1    100.00     │
│   Design Scaling Ccts  A Johnson 03-09-93 10:00a 05-18-93 10:00a  0 100%   1    400.00     │
│   Design Interface Ccts A Johnson 03-09-93 10:00a 04-20-93 10:00a 1 100%   1    240.00     │
│   Draw Housing     N Tarrant    03-09-93 10:00a  03-30-93 10:00a  2 100%   1    120.00     │
│   Make Mech Parts  S Peters     03-30-93 10:00a  04-27-93 10:00a  2 100%   1    160.00     │
│ 2nd Qtr '93                                                                │
│   Design Scaling Ccts  A Johnson 03-09-93 10:00a 05-18-93 10:00a  0 100%   1    400.00     │
│   Design Interface Ccts A Johnson 03-09-93 10:00a 04-20-93 10:00a 1 100%   1    240.00     │
│     Obtain Sample Chips          05-18-93 10:00a  08-18-93 10:00a 0                0.00    │
│   Obtain Other Comp'ts A Johnson 04-20-93 10:00a 04-21-93 10:00a  2 100%   1      8.00     │
│   Draw PCB         N Tarrant    05-18-93 10:00a  06-01-93 10:00a  2 100%   1     80.00     │
│   Make Mech Parts  S Peters     03-30-93 10:00a  04-27-93 10:00a  2 100%   1    160.00     │
│   Make PCB         Sub-contract 06-01-93 10:00a  06-01-93 10:00a  0 100%   1      0.00     │
│   Modify OHP Screen  S Peters   04-20-93 10:00a  04-28-93  1:00p  2 100%   1     50.00     │
│ 3rd Qtr '93                                                                │
│ ◄                                                                        ♦ ▼│
│ Decimal number data field.                                                 │
└──────────────────────────────────────────────────────────────────────────┘
```

In addition, Vanessa provided each task and work package manager with a copy of the baseline plan, including the following:

- Task list and statements of work.
- Gantt charts for the complete project and each major task.
- PERT charts at task and project level.
- Work breakdown structure.
- Organization breakdown structure.
- Cost account codes to work package level.

Progress reports

As work proceeded, so actual results were fed into the computer. The monthly schedule report consisted of actual vs. planned progress charts, in Gantt form. Hours, materials and other costs were logged each month so that planned and actual costs could be compared. Again, the report comes directly from the computer system.

11.10   MEASURING PERFORMANCE

Traditional project monitoring systems compare the actual cost of work performed (ACWP) with the budgeted cost of work scheduled (BCWS), relying on narrative reports to interpret the figures and make predictions of time and cost to completion. Optimists may underestimate what remains to be done.

> 'We've not been lucky to date, but if all goes well we can avoid slipping further behind.'

It has been known for the original estimates of tasks remaining to be reduced progressively so that, despite program slip, the forecast completion cost and date remain unaltered. True performance measurements will help you avoid this mistake.

Earned value measurement

With earned value monitoring you measure both cost and time performance against the baseline estimates in the project budget (the estimates before allowance for risks). You still record actual costs, but you also measure the *value* obtained from the money spent: the budgeted cost of work performed (BCWP). Do this by awarding value for each task or work package completed. The maximum value which can be earned is the estimated cost *in the baseline plan*. This value is only earned when the task or work package has been completed, or when a milestone representing a previously agreed percentage of the work has been reached. Any additional work not included in the baseline plan—for example approval testing for which no allowance was made in the original estimate—adds *nothing* to the earned value.

When someone beats their cost target, they earn full value for a task while actually spending less than the allowance in the baseline plan. But if they make mistakes, work more slowly than planned or have to do more work than originally estimated, they incur extra costs above the baseline estimate. In every case they can earn only the baseline plan value.

As work proceeds, reports are prepared, typically once per month, for each task and work package. Work package managers study their own performance and decide if any changes in plan at the working level are needed to ensure milestone dates are met; task managers receive reports from each active work package contributing to their task; and, as project manager, you will normally want to see only the task-level reports.

Using the reports

If performance falls below target, threatening the project completion date and cost budget, then you and your task managers must decide on actions to limit the damage and get back on schedule. You may occasionally need to look at one or two work package level reports, but you should never be over-burdened with heaps of reports. The system is simple and structured so that exceptions from planned performance can be investigated easily. The reports direct attention to where the pay-off is greatest.

Although this is a performance measurement system, it is important to realize that some tasks may be more complicated than originally anticipated; so it is dangerous to assess people by the figures alone. Technical difficulty, risk and luck still have their influence, but a good monitoring system can improve your luck substantially!

EXAMPLE

In the development phase of FICO's Autojector AJ35B, work was planned to start on 1 February and finish on 31 October. The budget at completion (BAC) was £60 000 The chart below shows progress to month 6.

Fig 11.18

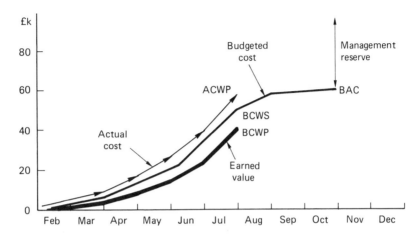

Tracking the progress

The budget line is obtained by scheduling the planned expenditure on all tasks throughout the project. The actual cost line is a cumulative record of labour, materials and other expense costs, updated monthly. The earned value line is also updated monthly from the work package and milestone achievement reports.

There is also a brief summary of progress and a statement of what is being done to solve remaining problems.

Interpreting the chart

By 1 August the development team had earned a value of £40 600, an amount they budgeted to have earned by 10 July. So it appears the project had slipped three weeks in the first 26 weeks.

Another way of measuring time performance is by the *schedule performance index:*

$$SPI = \frac{BCWP}{BCWS} \times 100 = \frac{40\,600}{50\,000} = 81\%$$

The cost performance is also easily calculated. The team has spent £57 200 in achieving £40 600 worth of earned value, giving a *cost performance index* of:

$$CPI = \frac{BCWP}{ACWP} \times 100 = \frac{40\,600}{57\,200} = 71\%$$

Unless the rest of the project is quite different from the type of work involved to date, the best forecast is that the development phase will continue at 19 per cent slip rate, and will therefore take an extra nine weeks to complete. The CPI is likely to remain around 71 per cent, giving a revised *estimate at completion* (EAC) of:

$$EAC = BAC \times \frac{ACWP}{BCWP} = £60\,000 \times \frac{57\,200}{40\,600} = £84\,532$$

Of course, it may yet be possible to strengthen the team and so raise their performance above the present levels; but if nothing can be done it should be no surprise if most of the management reserve has gone by the time the project is finished.

11.11 THE PEOPLE SIDE OF PROJECTS

You could be forgiven for getting the impression that project success depended mainly on defining objectives, planning the work and monitoring actual performance. Far from it! You need to get these things right or you've no chance, but most projects, large or small, will founder if the people involved don't work as an effective team.

Conflicts of authority

On large projects, and particularly in multi-project environments where resource managers provide skilled labour on a temporary and often part-time basis, department heads often come into conflict with project managers.

A simplistic view is that responsibilities should be allocated as follows:

- **Project manager**: what, when and where.
- **Resource manager**: how and who.

However, project managers often hold strong views as to which people they want contributing to their projects. This may be because they know what sort of person will best fit in with the team—a subject covered in more depth in Chapter 12—or, more often, because they have been let down by particular individuals in the past and don't want a repeat performance.

Resource managers, on the other hand, need to keep a reasonably level workload on each of their staff. In particular they are anxious to avoid under-using the talents of their most able people for fear they will look elsewhere for more interesting work. They also need to develop their less experienced people so they will be able to take on more demanding work in the future.

Growing the project team

For a business to thrive and grow it must develop its people. This means developing:

- Technical specialists.
- Resource managers.
- Project managers.

Technical specialists join the appropriate department, where their resource manager or department head should plan their acquisition of the skills and experience necessary to cope successfully with their technical work.

Resource managers are also well positioned to develop their successors. In large departments there may be a need for group or section leaders, the most able of whom can be groomed for larger responsibility.

Project managers have a vested interest in developing the project skills of those who manage tasks within the project.

So who should take the lead in staff development? I suggest it should normally be the resource manager, who could call in project managers to advise on the career development of their task managers.

**EXAMPLE**   FICO recognize the importance of investing in people and they plan the people side of their projects as carefully as they plan the work itself.

Succession planning

Nobody likes to have all their eggs in one basket, especially where the success of an important fixed-price contract is concerned. So, once the organization breakdown structure has been drafted, each key player is allocated a deputy. If that person is absent for health or any other reason, the deputy is expected to be sufficiently up to date to cope with the commitments of the principal player until they return or a permanent replacement is appointed and trained.

The cost of this system is obvious: people have to spend some time updating their deputies. The benefits, as FICO discovered, are greater than mere succession. In briefing their deputies, project, task and resource managers as well as technical specialists improve the documentation of their decisions. Deputies are audited periodically, and they have to answer questions of the type:

> *'Why didn't Tim use standard type M42 lampholders?'*
> *'What was the basis of our decision to subcontract the servicing on the Peterstone project?'*

Develop people or use people?

To decide what new technical skills will be needed in the future, FICO look at trends in the market places they serve. They also consider what technical initiatives they could take and how their resources match up to the skills required for the work. This analysis results in a skills development strategy; project resourcing plans must match this strategy.

FICO use the work breakdown structure to record where they intend using their most able staff and where they can, at some cost, develop others. The decision factors are:

- How important is it to develop improved capability in this type of work?
- How risky is the task in terms of technical achievement or quality failure?
- How easy will it be to detect and put right failures?
- How much slack is there in the schedule?

Under-using people

Peter arrives in the marketing department one morning to find the cleaner stretched out on the floor in agony, having tripped on the steps and broken a leg. He rings for an ambulance. Then, as there is an important customer meeting that morning in the conference room, he sweeps through, cleans the tables and checks the washrooms, too. He did this work without giving a second thought to whether he was the right person to do it. But it would be quite unreasonable for the marketing director to expect Peter to do the cleaning for the next three months.

On the most critical tasks it is sometimes necessary to use a highly skilled person on work well below their capability. This is fine if it is for a brief period, but it shouldn't become a habit. People soon lose motivation if they aren't stretched.

11.12 PROJECT POST-MORTEMS—LEARNING FROM EXPERIENCE

Towards the end of a project team members will transfer to other work. Even so, it's well worth recalling the team for an hour to consider and summarize what they have learned during the project. In particular, what can you do to improve performance on future projects?

Who should attend?

The review meeting needs inputs from the project manager and from the task managers in various departments. You may feel able to involve your customer if the project was sponsored by an outside organization other than your own. And maybe there are some key subcontractors you will want to use again; should they be present for at least part of the meeting?

What should you review?

Start with the project aims and priorities. If the targets had to change, look back and consider why. Were the changes essential, and could they not have been foreseen? What can you do in future to avoid unnecessary changes in requirements?

Next look at the baseline plan. With hindsight, was it a viable plan: resourceable and controllable? This is a good time to review your use of computer-aided project management tools. These types of system are still evolving. They are gradually overcoming their greatest drawback: their long learning time. Project management software has benefited more than most other applications from the introduction of graphical user interfaces. If you are still using a text-based system, check to see if a version with a graphical user interface (GUI) is available. Editing a Gantt chart or a PERT network is much easier than editing a text description of the logic of your plan.

You will also be able to review how well you communicated and controlled the work. Were problems caused by:

- Misinterpretations of initial requirements?
- Essential work which was omitted from the baseline plan?
- Inaccuracies in the original estimates?
- Poor quality work which had to be re-done?
- Mistakes in one area which made extra work for someone else?

Project management success also depends on *people skills*. See Chapter 12 for ideas on how to review the effectiveness of your teamwork.

The action plan

Discussion and agreement are two key steps towards the success of your review meeting; the final step is making and carrying out an action plan. An obvious action is to correct any errors you find in the estimating database. Other actions could be aimed at improving the processes by which plans are made, control actions decided or project information communicated.

It's good to share experience across the whole project team. But it need not stop there: why not summarize the key points in a brief presentation to other project teams within your organization? It takes courage to discuss openly both successes and failures, but the benefits will be multiplied as the learning extends throughout your organization.

CHECK-LIST: PROJECT POST-MORTEMS

Use this check-list to review the way the project work was defined, planned and controlled. (The check-list at the end of Chapter 12 will help you review the teamwork aspects.)

Project title: Ref. No. Date:				
Please mark your assessment here using 4 = Excellent: continue doing it well 3 = Good: scope for minor improvements 2 = Fair: considerable improvement possible 1 = Weak: major improvement essential	4	3	2	1
Definition of objectives				
How clear were the initial aims and priorities?				
How complete was the work breakdown structure?				
Did statements of work define inputs, outputs and quality standards?				
How effective was the project launch meeting?				
Planning				
Did plans contain the right level of detail for communication/control?				
Were the estimates tough but realistic?				
How thoroughly were the risks considered during the planning phase?				
How clearly were responsibilities defined to task/work package level?				
Monitoring				
To what extent were the plans useful for decision-making?				
To what extent were problems spotted early, before they could seriously threaten project targets?				
How closely did reports reflect the true status of progress?				
How realistic were the forecasts of cost and time to complete?				
Control				
How well was integrity of cost accounts preserved so that future projects can safely extract estimating data from the records of this project?				
To what extent were review meetings purposeful and open?				
How effective were quality, cost and schedule control decisions?				
How well were decisions communicated to project contributors?				
Overall achievement				
To what extent were technical targets achieved?				
To what extent were quality targets achieved?				
To what extent were schedule targets achieved?				
To what extent were cost targets achieved?				
How much did the team enjoy working together on this project?				

Improvement targets for future projects:	

EFFECTIVE TEAMWORK AND LEADERSHIP
THE LINK BETWEEN PERSONAL COMPETENCE AND GROUP EFFECTIVENESS

How much does *your* success depend on teamwork? If you can only do your job with the cooperation of others you will be well aware of the importance of effective teamwork. There are other jobs, however, where success depends on motivated, competent people working on their own. Occasionally they need to get together to exchange information, make decisions and agree targets. It is in this second category that the good work of individuals is often wasted by ineffective teamwork.

The challenge

Building a successful team requires more than simply matching the people to the demands of the job. It involves learning to work with 'difficult' people—those with personalities markedly different from your own. The irony is, you so rarely need people exactly like yourself. More often you need those with different insights, skills, values and beliefs—the very people you can have most difficulty understanding and getting on with.

How often do you get the chance to build a team from scratch? You are more likely to inherit or join a group of people either on a part-time basis or as a longer term member, maybe as the team leader. This is where mobilizing the existing capabilities of team members becomes crucial to success. The team make-up may not be ideal but, with effective team processes, members can cover for one another's deficiencies.

The benefits

You don't have to be a charismatic leader to get results. If you draw upon the talents of the others you work with you can still head a winning team.

When the going gets tough, managing a team becomes difficult. You will need to know how to anticipate conflicts and to defuse them before they divert valuable energy away from your goals.

As you take on a more senior role you will join many more teams—technical, marketing, personnel and sales, for example—spending little time working in each. You will need to be able to size up people quickly, deciding how you can contribute from your strengths while getting them to support you in your areas of weakness.

SUPER TEAMS FROM ORDINARY PEOPLE

In many working groups there is competition between individuals. Cliques develop, leading to secrecy and poor communication. Group goals become secondary; individual ambitions dominate. Problems are seen as threats to be avoided; people seek easy targets and try to avoid risks.

Contrast that with the way an effective team works. Communication is frequent and open. Team goals come first, and competitive effort is directed against outside opposition rather than being dissipated in internal conflict. The team welcomes new challenges because members know they can rely on one another for support if the going gets tough.

Successful teams change the way they work according to the nature of the task. At times the nominal leader may give instructions, telling others what to do. On other occasions the expertise of the whole team may be pooled to make a decision. There will even be instances where the most senior person in the team must act upon directions from others in the team. This flexible method of directing the efforts of a team is called *situational* leadership.

Communication: the cost of teamwork

Good teamwork requires good communication, and this takes time. In a large team a large communication overhead will be necessary. But what is the ideal situation? Well, if the costs of more communication exceed any benefits, then maybe too much time is being wasted in meetings, briefing sessions and the like.

How do winning teams work?

It's great to belong to a successful team. You feel involved and you want to commit yourself to the team goals. You know you are working well together when all team members:

- Share information among the team.
- Anticipate the reactions of one another.
- Value the contributions of all members.
- Assess the effectiveness of team processes.

Fig 12.1

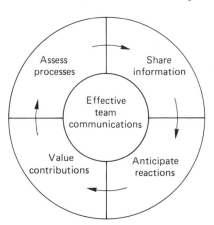

Learning to value others

It's usually easy to see why enthusiastic workers, charismatic leaders, extrovert communicators and creative thinkers are respected by their colleagues. But the quieter members of a team also have essential roles to play. For example, how much use is an optimistic security manager? Provided people are matched to roles which suit their personalities and ambitions, as well as their technical skills, they can all make valuable contributions.

12.1 TEAM SIZE AND DEVELOPMENT

It is important to match the structure of a team to the work to be done. Two factors are the number and the types of people who make up the team. First let's discuss team size.

How many is optimum?

Jobs such as repairing a telephone aren't speeded up by putting more people on them. Many more tasks *need* large teams. (One person would have made no progress at all in building the Egyptian pyramids.) Intellectual work is usually best performed by individuals or small teams. In contrast, for manual work, like laying road surfaces, larger teams can be used; then, the more experienced the people, the larger the team can be.

As you increase the size of a team you reach a point when productive output no longer rises. This law of diminishing returns applies to all sorts of work, but especially where success depends on creativity and initiative. The effect is often most noticeable in teams developing new products or setting up new facilities.

Developing and using team members

So should you always give jobs to the people who can do them best? You need to compare the costs of under-performing in the short term with the longer term advantages of developing the skills of other team members. Consider which are the critical tasks—critical because technical excellence or innovation are vital for success, or critical due to time or cost constraints. Have the staff attained the skills needed to achieve the required standards? If not, can you call upon outside help, or should you arrange training before starting the task?

And what about the non-critical tasks? Some of these—usually those which are not urgent and carry little technical risk—present opportunities to develop the skills of team members. Realize, of course, that giving a three star task to a one star performer will mean someone else has to spend time as an on-the-job coach. So you will incur a short-term cost penalty (shouldn't we call it an investment?) to obtain the benefit of being able to tackle more demanding jobs in the future.

How vulnerable is your team to staff losses?

Do either your department or your project depend on skills vested in just one person? What if that team member goes sick or resigns? You will need to ensure the work of the team does not come to a grinding halt, and this means allocating deputies to each of the key people. Deputies need not, of course, all be members of the project team, but they should normally be employed within the company. And they must be made aware of, and be committed to, your development plans. Agree what training each deputy requires and make a realistic timetable for achieving a safer staffing situation.

Staff turnover target

Is zero the ideal level of staff turnover? Not in most jobs! New people bring in new ideas. Moving on provides new learning opportunities for team members—including yourself. So it's sensible to have a target for staff turnover, and you may need to help some team members find new opportunities inside your organization. It's tempting to try to hang on to able team members for too long. In the short term you may gain, but in time the organization loses as people look further afield for the opportunities denied to them in their present job.

| EXAMPLE: | # OPTIMIZING THE TEAM SIZE |

In the illustration, team A (average) is working well below maximum efficiency and could, in fact, increase output by *reducing* team size! This is not an uncommon situation. Quite often, when a project team begins falling behind schedule additional members are drafted into the team. Confused communication causes conflict in the group; cliques develop and compete internally. All this is at the expense of performance on the job.

Fig 12.2

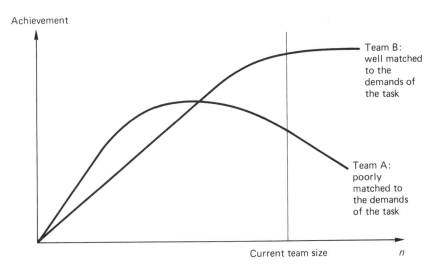

Even though its members are capable of less individual achievement, team B (better than average) is able to out-perform team A.

Building up the team

There would be chaos if salesmen, marketeers, technical experts and authors all arrived for the first day of work on the bid for a new contract. It would make more sense if the bid manager and one person from each department got together to agree a plan of campaign. Then, once the bid strategy had been defined, other contributors could join the team.

The same is true of most projects; it's best to build up the team size progressively, matching both the size and the skills of the team to the demands of the job.

Running down the team

It's just as important to plan the run-down of a project or the phasing out of a facility, and to make provision for cutting back on the size of the team. Some team members will welcome a new challenge: hanging on to creative people once the innovative work is complete can demotivate them. More relationship-orientated people may feel rejected by the team or victimized by the leader, especially if they do not agree with the change.

It is usually best to discuss team run-down plans well in advance. Where people will be moving to another department or project, arrange an early introduction to the people they will be working with, and keep the team informed, as far as you can, about their future roles.

12.2 THE TEAM SKILLS CONCEPT

If you have the job of servicing a racing car, you need a team of mechanics, not musicians. Obvious! Rather less obvious, however, is the need to get the right mix of personalities. If the mechanics fall out over who changes the wheels and who tops up the fuel, the race will be lost not through lack of skill out on the track but by poor teamwork in the pits.

Most jobs involve thought, decisions, communication and, of course, work. We all differ in our abilities in each of these respects. Few of us are all-rounders, capable of handling every aspect of a complex job; most of us have to rely on others for contributions we are ill-equipped to provide. This is the essence of teamwork.

Contributions to teamwork

When people work together in teams someone will usually have to:

1 **Think**. People vary in their effectiveness when faced with a blank sheet of paper and asked to produce a new idea or to plan a complex task.
2 **Lead**. Some people feel comfortable making decisions and then informing their team. Others are natural democrats, preferring to involve their colleagues.
3 **Communicate**. While building close relationships is important to some people, others are happiest when they have a wide circle of casual contacts.
4 **Get things done**. Self-starters respond to the challenge of work to be done, while thorough finishers are most valuable when attention to detail is the key to success.

You may have several of these talents to contribute, but it's unlikely you will have them all in equal measure. Get to know what team skills you have in abundance and where your potential weaknesses lie. Arrange things so that you exploit your strengths and get others to cover in areas where you would be weak.

Belbin's team skills model

Meredith Belbin, working at Henley Management College, devised a team skills model based on styles of thinking, leading, communicating and working. Belbin demonstrated that the performance of teams was related to the behaviour characteristics of various types of team members. He gave people with predominant characteristics the following role titles:

- **Plant**: a creative thinker, or ideas person.
- **Monitor–evaluator**: a sober, unemotional analytical thinker.
- **Coordinator**: a calm, self-confident and involving leader.
- **Shaper**: a dynamic, self-centred, challenging leader.
- **Resource investigator**: an enthusiastic, extrovert communicator.
- **Team worker**: a responsive, caring relationship builder.
- **Implementer**: a trustworthy self-motivating achiever.
- **Completer–finisher**: a quality conscious, thorough contributor.

These team skills relate directly to the four teamwork contributions listed above. The questionnaire and the four topics which follow should give you some insight into your own team skills strengths and weaknesses. Computer-based psychometric tests of team skills can help you match teams to tasks.

CHECK-LIST: A PEER PERCEPTION TEAM SKILLS INVENTORY

Get your team to complete one questionnaire for each member. Rank the team skills from 8 (most evident contribution) to 1 (least evident contribution). It is usually best to record the scores before transferring them to the questionnaire so that members are not influenced by other entries.

Close agreement on a 7 or 8 ranking indicates a teamworking skill strength, while close agreement on a 2 or 1 score suggests either a possible weakness or that the skill concerned is not particularly relevant to the current work of the team. The most versatile team members are likely to find their assessments contain much divergence of opinion. This is not a suggestion of mediocrity, but rather the recognition that the member concerned is a flexible contributor capable of leading or supporting in several styles.

Team member being assessed:		Date:	
Current task of team:	**Names of other team members**		
Teamworking skill being assessed	**Rankings by team members**		
Creative thinker: Coming up with original ideas which help the team achieve the task goals.			
Analytical thinker: Working out the implications of team decisions and getting them to check the viability and practicality.			
Democratic leader: Directing work by involving others and explaining details so the objectives are understood by all members.			
Autocratic leader: Getting others to do things they really don't want to, by pressure if necessary, for the good of the project.			
Extrovert communicator: Seeking outside advice and resources to get things moving more quickly, especially on new tasks.			
Relationship builder: Working to maintain team spirit whenever objectives are not clear or things are going wrong.			
Self-starter: Making a large and valued contribution once the requirements are clear and responsibilities have been agreed.			
Thorough finisher: Making sure the team doesn't get caught out by incomplete plans or lack of attention to detail.			

12.3 INTELLECTUAL STYLES

Increasingly, people at work are expected to contribute intellectual rather than just physical effort. Some team members may show great imagination, while others are better at solving problems by rule-based deduction. At various stages in the work, a task may require different combinations of these thinking styles, so it is important to be able to mobilize the skills of those team members best equipped to contribute at each stage.

Imaginative thinker (Belbin's term: Plant)

Plants are the most imaginative members of teams—those with intuitive rather than purely deductive abilities. These creative people are often difficult to manage, as they tend to resent control. They may behave like spoilt prima donnas if things don't go their way in times of stress. Ideas people sometimes show little regard for the practical implications of their suggestions, and can be impatient of 'red tape'.

Not all jobs need new ideas. (A creative road repairer could be an absolute menace!) However, in work where this skill is needed, as in the early stages of a project where technical difficulties have to be overcome, ideas people are highly valued by the other members of the team. Most people feel they would like to score highly in this category; but too many imaginative people in an organization can be as serious as not enough.

Analytical thinkers (Belbin's term: Monitor–evaluator)

These are the people whose logical reasoning provides sound plans for implementing the innovative concepts dreamed up by creative people. Analytical thinkers usually like to have all the facts before making decisions.

This, we find, is a team role with which few would wish to be labelled. When other team members get carried away in the heat of the moment, it is usually a monitor–evaluator who cools the situation by reminding others that there is a limited budget, or only so much time available. Others tend to see this realism as lack of enthusiasm for change, and consequently monitor–evaluators are not usually good at motivating others.

Competition in meetings

How do people with strengths in one or other of these thinking styles perform in meetings? Much depends on the purpose of the meeting, who else is present and how the meeting is chaired. Creative people usually contribute well to brainstorming sessions *because* they tend to compete with one another. This often results in more innovation and a better pool of ideas for subsequent analysis. Strongly analytical thinkers are often less effective when ideas are being bounced around at high speed. They like to have more time to think through suggestions. As a result they tend to hold back their own ideas rather than to voice them with spontaneity. They also feel inclined to check the practicality of other suggestions, damping down the enthusiasm of others.

In planning meetings where large amounts of data need careful analysis, logical thinkers usually out-perform the more intuitive members of the team. They usually prepare thoroughly and wait for a complete picture to emerge rather than jumping to conclusions. Creative thinkers often find these types of meeting dull, and they may resent the time given to what they may see as trivial issues.

EXAMPLES

Andy McGregor, one of FICO's regional sales managers, is about to chair a brainstorming session with his area sales managers. Andy knows his team *can* think creatively when they are in the mood to do so. He also realizes they are mostly status conscious people who don't want to make fools of themselves. They tend to censor their own thoughts before speaking. He needs to break down these barriers of inhibition at the outset.

> 'Before we begin,' McGregor says, 'I'd like you to hear something George Bernard Shaw wrote. Shaw, who was not short on original ideas, says: "The reasonable man adapts himself to the world as it is; the unreasonable man tries to change the world to what he wants it to be". Shaw concludes that: "Therefore all progress depends on the unreasonable man."'
>
> 'This morning', McGregor continues, 'I want you all to be unreasonable. Don't look for logical connections between ideas. We're looking for something that others haven't tried already, so the connections have yet to be made.'

McGregor then asks each person around the table to say something illogical on any subject they wish. At first people are reluctant, but soon laughter echoes along the corridor of the sales department as everyone begins contributing. And after five minutes of this, when McGregor asks for ideas which might help promote the sales of Autojectors, ideas come pouring in. No doubt most suggestions will prove impractical, but they only need one real gem to put them way ahead of the opposition.

Making connections

Next morning the team meet again. It is time to analyse the ideas. Andy still needs a positive atmosphere, but it will have to be more controlled. For this he needs a structure.

> 'Well, since we last met I've had all our ideas typed up, and I've drafted an agenda for this morning's work. But before we start, could I make a suggestion. Despite all the fun we had yesterday, we'll probably find most of the ideas don't take us anywhere. Anywhere useful, I mean. That's not a failure, and certainly not a reflection on the ability of the people who came up with the suggestions. But if we go down the list looking for reasons for rejecting ideas, we could end up discarding the lot—throwing the baby out with the bath water. Worse still, we might simply end up singing lullabies to nothing more than a load of dirty bath water, if you see what I mean.
>
> 'So, let's begin by looking for logical links between the ideas and our sales objectives. Then maybe some of the other suggestions will link in too. And finally we can try to find one or two themes which we can use in our sales campaign.'

Andy wants to mobilize the monitor–evaluator skills in his team. He needs to do this by encouraging logical thought processes while avoiding an atmosphere of pessimism. And he *must* keep control of the meeting. Each contributor needs to be able to speak without being interrupted, and there must be enough time for people to absorb what is being said and to consider its implications.

To support this analytical process, Andy himself could behave more analytically, speaking more slowly than usual, and leaving longer pauses between sentences than he would normally do. This should encourage others to think carefully before commenting.

12.4 LEADERSHIP STYLES

The ideal leadership style depends on who is involved, the nature of the work, and the situation at the time. No one style is perfect; good leaders vary their style as appropriate—even abdicating leadership if necessary.

Autocracy, democracy or delegation?

Autocratic leadership has one great advantage: decisions are made quickly. If the leader has the ability to choose correctly, and provided the other members of the team willingly carry out the decision, then an autocratic style is the most cost-effective. In contrast, democracy carries an overhead: it takes time to involve others. But it is sometimes necessary to do just that, either because the team leader doesn't have the expertise to reach a good decision, or because the team would not accept an imposed decision.

Democratic leaders (Belbin's term: Coordinator)

This is the type of person who, through a combination of charisma, determination and care for others, is capable of leading a team through long-term tasks where the ability of the team must be developed. This type of leader is able to provide direction while involving others in decisions, and yet manages to keep control of the team, motivating them through the inevitable difficulties which arise on longer term, innovative work.

Strangely, research shows that people with strengths in this area are rarely of outstanding intelligence. Perhaps it is an awareness of their own limitations which gives them the humility to lead by involvement.

Autocratic leader (Belbin's term: Shaper)

Not all jobs involve long-term goals, and not all teams need developing. Fire-fighting leaders can't afford to enter into negotiations as to who should do what when a crisis call comes. Their staff get job satisfaction not from involvement in decisions but from the achievements they make. Given clear direction, a capable, self-motivated team can perform well on short-term tasks. For this kind of situation a self-confident, autocratic leadership style can work well.

People with a particular strength in this area are decisive and they like action. They can be rather self-centred, however, and may have little time for people who are not fully competent in their work.

Delegating the leadership

Good teamwork depends on members trusting one another. Leading by example involves, on occasion, trusting the leadership to another team member who is more competent than you to manage a particular situation. It takes courage to do this, but the alternative is to pose as more knowledgeable and more able than anyone else in your team in all aspects of the work. This is unlikely to be true, and such pretence alienates other able team members who need and deserve the opportunity to develop their management skills, too.

Your comfortable range

In your job, the ideal style of leadership may shift from autocratic to democratic or delegative leader and back again. Managers able to perform well in each of these roles are particularly valuable to an organization; sadly they are far from common. You may not feel comfortable in all these roles, but with practice you can learn to be more flexible, to extend your range of leadership styles.

EXAMPLE: COMFORT RANGES

John Scarman's team in Customer Support have all been with FICO for five or more years. They know their jobs and are confident enough to seek John's help on the rare occasions when they are unsure of priorities. John acts as the focal point for the department, liaising with Sales and Production when new products are being launched, but in the day-to-day running of the department, team members usually make their own work schedules. John plays little or no part in these decisions, merely requiring that he be kept informed of the work plans and progress.

Apart from his strategic role in the organization, John also plans the future of his department. He consults his team of experts when preparing budgets for training and capital equipment. In these decisions he plays a leading role.

Fig 12.3

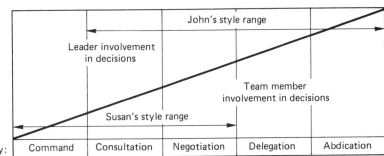

Susan Welburn, a graduate with six years' industrial experience, has been FICO's packing and export department manager for just eight months. Until a month ago Susan was the youngest and newest member of her department, and she relied heavily on the expertise of her team. Then two of her senior staff left with just a week's notice. Now, of her three management team members, two are trainees on short-term secondment from FICO in the USA. The third member, Jack Carson, looks after the export side. Jack has worked his way up from the shop floor. He knows the packing and export side of FICO's business better than anyone. Jack was disappointed at not getting the job of department manager: he is due to retire in two years' time, and the promotion would have meant an increase in his pension.

Susan leaves all export-related decisions to Jack, although she frequently asks him to explain the complexities which are new to her. She also involves him in all other major decisions, especially on budgeting and long-range planning. When they disagree Susan feels she should work *with* Jack to resolve the conflict. Sometimes these negotiations are hard going, but gradually she is winning his respect.

With her other team members Susan usually adopts a more authoritarian style. They are there to learn from her and they respect her decisions. But they respond best when she takes the trouble to explain the reasons behind special instructions or changes in work procedures.

Gaining respect

Extrovert communicators (Belbin's term: Resource investigator)

Asking for help is embarrassing for some people, and what life is all about for others. Pride and shyness are two of the reasons many of us prefer to struggle on alone when there might be others outside our team who could act as a useful resource. Not so the Resource Investigator, a natural communicator, relaxed, gregarious and enthusiastic. Given a new challenge the resource investigator's first reaction is to involve others and seek outside help. This is useful when there is help available, of course, but what contribution does he or she make when there is no external resource to tap? Often the answer is very little.

By bringing in outside help, resource investigators can sometimes avoid their teams 're-inventing the wheel'. However, once the novelty of a project wears off it is often difficult to get resource investigators to contribute wholeheartedly; they want the stimulus of something new to investigate and someone new to meet.

Relationship builders (Belbin's term: Team worker)

When a team takes on a difficult challenge the pressure on individuals can cause stress which dissipates energy and detracts from team performance. This is where team workers (sometimes called team builders) come in useful. These people have the special skill of being able to sense the feelings of others. They watch and listen, and they interpret the emotions behind what is said—or what is not said! These are the people who think of how ideas and decisions will affect others.

Team workers dislike discord. They work to maintain a good team spirit during times of stress. Good listeners, they often take an interest in the private lives of other team members, offering support when it is needed. At work, they aren't usually too concerned about their own roles, as they get a great deal of job satisfaction from team achievements. They will often undertake the less attractive parts of the work themselves for the good of the team.

On the negative side, team workers often become confused and indecisive in moments of crisis. As a consequence they can appear to others as rather meek—even weak willed.

Despite the caring nature of the team worker, few would wish to be classified as such. It is sometimes seen as a non-glamorous role best suited for people with little or no leadership potential. This is a most unfortunate misconception, as caring leaders often make the best delegators; they help the organization grow its people.

Communication needs

Resource investigators are generally respected and valued while the task needs their communication initiatives. But once the team has all the resources needed to do the job, there is less obvious value from the wheeling and dealing of the extrovert communicator. Other team members may come to doubt the loyalty of those who are forever contacting outsiders.

In contrast, most teams continue to need the active involvement of a team worker. Yet this is an undervalued contribution, vital to any team which must remain cohesive under sustained pressure.

EXAMPLE: # OBTAINING TEAM COMMITMENT

FICO UK has now won the contract for refurbishing the National Conference Centre. Vanessa Tippet chairs a meeting to confirm the plan for carrying out the contract. Those attending are:

- Vanessa Tippet, project manager. Vanessa is enthusiastic and likes to get things done quickly. She knows the capability of each contributor to her project, and she is confident they can all do what is needed.
- Janet Masters, chief development engineer, who will be responsible for customizing the projection and display equipment. Janet is always full of new ideas; unfortunately there isn't time on this project to make any substantial modifications to the existing product range.
- Jim Peters, Vanessa's assistant whom she has asked to attend and take minutes. The meeting will be useful experience for Jim, who is a keen observer of people. Jim has been with FICO many years and knows the other members well.
- John Scarman, customer support manager. John will have to manage all the installation work, and it will be another rushed job. John is happier when he can make thorough plans before starting work.
- Susan Welburn, packing and export department manager. Susan will have to get all the equipment onto the site on time and in the right sequence, as storage space at the NCC is severely limited. She has never had to handle such a job before and is worried that she may commit her department to targets they cannot meet.

A plan is quickly agreed, and after the meeting Jim takes Vanessa her copy of the minutes.

> Vanessa: 'How did you think it went?'
> Jim: 'It's a good plan, but I think we've still got work to do to convince the others.'
> Vanessa: 'Really? What makes you think that, Jim.'
> Jim: 'Well, it's just that the team wasn't as united as it should have been.'
> Vanessa: 'But they all agreed the plan. They had their chance to speak.'
> Jim: 'That's just it. Once you had said your piece nobody felt like disagreeing. I mean... Janet suggested a few things, but that's all. It's your plan, not theirs.'
> Vanessa: 'Well, if they don't say anything how am I to know they're not happy?'
> Jim: 'But didn't you notice how fidgety Susan was. She's not usually like that. And John usually has plenty to say, but he didn't today. Didn't you think it odd?'

Vanessa hadn't noticed. And that's the point: Jim, who is sensitive to other people's moods, was able to pick up the non-verbal messages of concern or dissent.

Seeking help

It would be great if Vanessa could improve her sensitivity to the feelings of others, but it's unlikely she will change much in this respect. So she needs to rely more on Jim, encouraging him to speak up at such times and to reflect the concerns of the other team members so that they can be resolved.

WORKING STYLES

If you contribute to several teams, as do most managers, then you will probably spend more time as a team member than as the leader. As well as making your specialist contribution, based on your technical background, it is important to recognize the team roles in which you are most able to contribute.

Purposeful achiever (Belbin's term: Implementer)

This is the type of person with the valuable skill of getting things done. Once a job is clearly defined someone with this skill is self-motivated and doesn't need constant supervision. The term 'implementer' is sometimes used to describe the people whose industry turns the ideas of others into something practical and viable. This can be misleading, as implementers often make good planners and well-organized administrators, and they are usually knowledgeable and respected in their specialist field.

Loyalty to the team and dedication to duty are often looked upon as a sign of weakness, and so some people are disappointed to find that they have a strength in this non-glamour role. It is unusual for people whose dominant team skill is implementer to be exceptionally creative, but without this type of hard-working member a team will rarely succeed.

Conscientious finisher (Belbin's term: Completer–finisher)

In most jobs we don't get paid for doing most of the work, but for providing evidence that the work has been properly *completed*. Completer–finishers have staying power. They like to see a job done properly, and quality of workmanship is a major source of their job satisfaction. This is a role which few non-completer–finishers would choose, although many recognise its importance.

But there are also times when perfectionism is unaffordable. It can be difficult for completer–finishers to let go at the end of a job: they keep finding more work. Provided they are given clear direction on priorities and can apply their high standards of quality and completeness to the high pay-off aspects of the job, completer–finishers are invaluable team members.

Strengths and weaknesses

The descriptions above are for people who have exceptional strengths in one of the eight team skills. Many people are strong in one or two team roles and have weaknesses in others, while a few individuals have the flexibility to perform reasonably well in a wide range of roles. Being aware of your team skills profile helps you more easily find your niche in the many teams you join during your career.

Fig 12.4

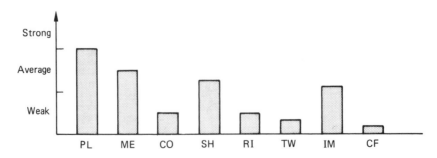

A SKILLS MIX PROBLEM

Susan Welburn, FICO's packing and exports manager, has now replaced all but one of her temporary team members with permanent staff. She is preparing a requirements summary before recruiting an export contracts administrator to replace the person who left recently. She arranges for herself and her existing team members to complete a psychometric test. Together the team study their team skills profiles.

Team member	Team skills scores (W = Weakness, A = Average, S = Strength)							
Susan Welburn Department manager	W	A	S	S	A	W	A	W
Jack Carson Export manager	W	A	S	A	S	A	S	W
Paul Melville-Brown Transport manager	A	W	A	S	W	W	A	W
Belinda Thompson Packing supervisor	W	W	A	A	A	W	S	W
Team skills:	**PL**	**ME**	**CO**	**SH**	**RI**	**TW**	**IM**	**CF**

Team skills key: PL = Plant
ME = Monitor–evaluator
CO = Coordinator
SH = Shaper
RI = Resource investigator
TW = Team worker
IM = Implementer
CF = Completer–finisher

It is apparent at a glance that Susan has made one of the most common recruitment errors of all. She has gathered about her people with personalities similar to her own. As Jack Carson remarked when he first saw the results of the assessments:

'No wonder we have so many flaming rows: all shapers and no team workers! And if we go on like this we're bound to get into a mess. Not one of us scores even average as a completer–finisher.'

Susan had to agree. Together they drew up a profile of the ideal person to fill their remaining vacancy:

Export Contracts Administrator, FICO UK Ltd

Ideally applicants should have experience of export contract preparation and two or more years' experience in a manufacturing organization. Fluency in French and German would also be an advantage, but tuition will be arranged if necessary.

It is essential that applicants should have a proven record of analytic ability. Thoroughness, attention to detail and a concern for others are also important in this post, for which applicants will be asked to undertake a psychometric aptitude test. The results of the test will be kept confidential, but applicants will receive a copy of their own test results.

12.7 MATCHING THE TEAM TO THE TASK

There was a time when people were put into workgroups and expected to see a project through from start to finish: the creative, the analytical, the implementation and the careful checking stages. Few of us cope well with all these challenges, but we should still be able to build and organize *teams* well suited to each stage of the work.

Do you need a team?

The most efficient work unit is one competent, self-motivated person with clear goals and all the facilities to do the work. Recognize that some jobs are best done by loners. But many more tasks are so complex and make such varied demands on technical and personal skills that they can only be done well by teams. And these teams must be matched to the task and organized suitably at each stage of the work.

Suppose you want a group of people to solve a crossword puzzle. Let's consider what team skills are required. Do you need a democratic leader to organize the group?

> 'Now, has anyone had any ideas for one across. Let's check round the group.'

Or would an autocratic approach be better?

> 'Right, Angela! You've got two minutes to sort out three across. Pete, what's the answer to seventeen down. Well?.. hurry up, man, we haven't got all day!'

If all group members are equally inexperienced at solving cryptic crosswords, you would probably get most contribution from the analytical and creative members. But by far the better approach would be to find someone who had experience of solving such puzzles and leave them in peace to get on with it.

Analyse the requirements

Make an outline plan of the task, deciding what should be done by specialists working alone and what needs the combined talents of the team. First agree the allocation of specialist jobs; but make a note of any skills shortage, as this will increase the risk of failure. Next consider each team job, listing the team skills in order of importance.

Match style and process

So, suppose you needed to organize the building of an emergency rope bridge across a rising river. Nobody in your team has built a rope bridge before. The whole project depends on urgency. An autocratic leader would be fine if you had a rope bridge expert to call upon, but imagine the effect of a leader continually screaming 'hurry up' as some rookie bridge designer struggles with mathematical calculations for parts of the structure! A calm, controlled, democratic leader is a safer bet.

Once the calculations are done and checked carefully, to build the bridge you need self-motivated, cooperative workers who do not fuss unnecessarily over fine details. The leadership style can now be switched to a more autocratic one.

BUILDING AND DEVELOPING A PROJECT TEAM

Let's look at how the pressures on a team vary through the life cycle of a typical customer contract. In this example you bid for, negotiate and carry out a design and manufacturing task, providing customer support after delivery.

Fig 12.5

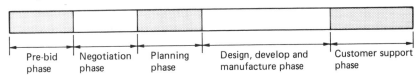

The pre-bid phase

This is when your marketing and sales people try to influence the customer's request for quotation. Extrovert communicators (resource investigators) are needed for this work. Sensitive listeners (team workers) also help foster close relationships with decision makers in the customer organization. Inside the company, the bid team must consult with experts who will work on the contract if you win. They have to negotiate and agree estimates. A democratic (coordinator) leadership style is more likely to obtain commitment to these long-term targets than would an autocratic (shaper) approach.

The contract negotiation phase

Your negotiating team tries to win favourable contract terms. Someone in the team must react quickly to opportunities; this requires intuitive (plant) thinking skills. You must also carefully evaluate customer propositions; logical thinkers (monitor–evaluators) are best at this. Both sides in negotiations are under pressure. Team-building (team worker) communication helps prevent negotiations getting bogged down by personality clashes.

The planning phase

Foresight is needed to create good plans. Creative people (plants) are often good at seeing opportunities; analytical thinkers (monitor–evaluators) are usually better at foreseeing difficulties. A planning team really needs both these skills, and will usually benefit from a democratic (coordinator) style of leadership.

The design, develop and manufacture phase

This is where the bulk of the work gets done. Innovative ideas (plant skills) will be needed most during the feasibility study and initial design activities. Later, people who can turn ideas into reality (implementers) are usually better at getting things to work properly. They convert ideas and outline plans into successful products.

As the project matures the pressure on people often rises too. It is not unusual for this pressure to be increased because of programme slip. The management style may have to move from democratic (coordinator) towards autocratic (shaper). Members with strong team-building skills (team workers) can support their colleagues and prevent friction from dissipating the energy of the team.

The customer support phase

If the support team does a good job you will be in a strong position to win follow-on business. Apart from providing a rapid response to any problems they must build and maintain good relationships with the users. So once again communication skills (resource investigators and team workers) play a dominant role.

MOTIVATION

For people to do well at work they need:

1 A goal, and some idea of how they can achieve it.
2 Enough time to do the work to the required quality standard.
3 The knowledge and skills to do the work correctly.
4 The experience to cope with the pressure of work.
5 Adequate facilities: the tools and a suitable working environment.
6 Teamwork, where the task cannot be completed by one person alone.

But there is a seventh and overriding factor without which people achieve little. They must *want* to do the job well: they need motivation.

Sources of motivation

At different times we may be driven to satisfy the need for:

- **Physical comfort**. When we are cold, wet and hungry we have no other needs but to find physical comfort, a requirement that dominates our thinking.
- **Security**. We may do what is required because we want the security which comes from success and we fear the consequences of failure.
- **Acceptance**. We may do a good job because we value a harmonious environment and we don't want to let the team down or upset our customer.
- **Status**. We may do well because we want to be respected for our ability, and we seek recognition and the increased influence which would come from promotion.
- **Achievement**. We may do our best because we want the satisfaction of developing our potential and doing something worthwhile.

Professor Abraham Maslow observed that the need we feel most strongly determines our behaviour: motivation comes from striving to fill a need. Once satisfied, the need ceases to motivate us and a higher level need takes over.

Hygiene factors

Many factors which relate to working environment—the facilities and the organization policies are examples—can only demotivate people if they are below standard. People won't normally put in extra effort because the roof doesn't leak or they approve of the company's policy on parking place allocations. These are termed hygiene factors, because they can demotivate people if they are below standard. Often the absence of a team worker has this effect on a team working under pressure.

Rewards and celebrations

What one person sees as a reward another may see as punishment; so you have to know your team members as individuals. Tangible needs aren't usually a problem: they will tell you, especially if you ask. But their inner needs are only found by observing behaviour. People rarely voice their psychological needs—*'I want you to like me'*, or *'I'm more worried about who gets the blame than how we can sort out this problem.'*

Most people like praise and thanks for their efforts. Some like being praised publicly; others just need to feel appreciated. Leaders who arrange occasional celebrations of team successes are responding to these needs.

EXAMPLES: PEOPLE ARE INDIVIDUALS

Four members of the accounts department return to work after their summer vacation to be told they have been moved to another department. Here are their first thoughts on hearing the news:

> Peter: *'Why me? I knew I shouldn't have gone away before the reorganization!'*
> Claire: *'But this is a great team! Surely they're not going to split us up?'*
> Danny: *'About time! Now maybe I can get my promotion through.'*
> Sandy: *'I wonder what they want me to do; I'd better go and find out.'*

It is in pressure situations like this that you discover the inner needs of your colleagues. We can all be jolly and nice at the group summer outing... until we discover someone has forgotten to load the packed lunches onto the coach!

Linking rewards to motivators

John Scarman is discussing a proposed change in responsibility for one of his staff, Ken Mullins. Ken is over fifty and feels rather insecure, especially as many of the young people working for him have higher qualifications and are more in touch with modern technology. Ken is also extremely status conscious, and would like his staff to respect him more. John is well aware of that:

> John: *'We're going ahead with the new inspection system, Ken. It's all been approved at board level.'*
> Ken: *'But we still haven't got the present system working properly. Nobody really understands the software, and the new system's even more complex.'*
> John: *'I know, Ken, but we won't make the same mistake this time. I want you to go on the training course first. Check it out thoroughly. Then, when you're happy, I'd like you to brief all your people on how the new system will work and schedule their training in the use of the new system.'*

Here John is not simply giving Ken a pep talk to make him *think* the change will benefit him; he's arranging things so that Ken *will* get the benefits he needs.

Cynicism: destroyer of motivation

In a team of similar individuals there is often competition for supremacy. Members waste time and energy playing psychological games. Here's one you may recognize:

> *'D'you know what they've done now? They've rescheduled the lunch rota so there's nobody in Sales between twelve-thirty and one o'clock.'*
> *'That's nothing! I just heard they've rewritten the expense rules. I can't find anybody who understands how to claim for rail fares.'*
> *'Typical! And another thing...'*

That's the 'Oh gawd ain't it awful game'. And there are lots more, all with two things in common: the outcome is predictable and the value to the organization is nil.

You can often stop games of this sort by pointing out that you know what comes next. Do so in a light-hearted way and others might even appreciate your intervention.

12.9 — TARGET SETTING

On any complex task things will go wrong. What you don't want are people saying:

> *'I can prove it wasn't my fault...'*
> *'There's nothing written down here to say I'm supposed to do that...'*
> *'I knew Jim was going to make a mess of it; but it's no use talking to him, he never listens...'*

...and so on.

What you need is a team committed to the eventual success of the task, and owning not only their defined responsibilities but also the interfaces between contributors. Instead of looking for excuses for their failures they must learn from the experience and try to head off future problems. And when one team member is in trouble the others must do what they can to keep the task on course for success.

Job targets

You won't get that sort of cooperation by imposing job targets. I don't suggest you simply allow people to set their own targets, but rather that you negotiate agreed targets whenever possible. It's likely you will need to set tougher targets this year than those you met last, but there must be realism.

For best results, targets should be:

- Realistic and accepted, rather than arbitrary and imposed.
- Specific and quantified, rather than vague and qualitative.

Skills targets

That's all very well for production targets, launch dates and profit margins. But what about personal performance—report writing or presentation skills, telephone manner and the like? These skills also affect results at work. You can't quantify these kinds of skills—'I want you to improve your telephone manner by 25 per cent this year' is meaningless—but you can assess the effects of an improvement. For example:

> *'Every week we get three or four customer complaints about incourteous responses to their queries. I'd like our internal sales staff to attend our customer care training course and practice professional telephone techniques so that the number of complaints is halved within six months.'*

How tough should the targets be?

The severity of improvement targets must be matched to the person. You may know people who only give of their best when faced with almost impossible odds. Anything less is too easy and they don't feel challenged. Yet others get depressed if they are stressed as much as this. For them, small but frequent improvement targets are required. The ideal is to set targets for each person which secure maximum motivation.

Fig 12.6

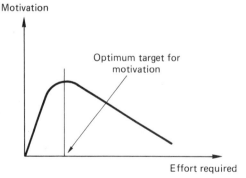

EXAMPLE: REAL TARGETS, REAL BENEFITS

Andy McGregor, FICO's western region sales manager, is discussing next year's sales targets with Steve Gilbert, one of his area sales managers.

> *Andy: 'We need a 10 per cent sales improvement this year, Steve. OK? Let me have a plan by Wednesday showing how you intend achieving it.'*
>
> *Steve: 'Hang on, Andy! Sue Chapman's target's only being increased by 5 per cent. And all the southern region people are having no increase at all. Why are we being pressured like this?'*

Andy should have anticipated this reaction. People look across the organization and compare targets and rewards. There must be a good reason why the western region targets are increasing, and Andy should have explained the basis of the increase at the outset. The new target was based on the best market information available. It cannot be relaxed unless the area managers come up with additional information which was not taken into account in setting the targets.

Once the reason for the new target is clear, Steve agrees to make a plan for meeting it. He decides the best way is to recruit an extra sales assistant and to arrange nationwide TV publicity. He shows his plan to Andy.

> *Andy: 'But this will cost more than twice the increased revenue expected from sales. You can't just throw company money at the problem, Steve. I need a plan based on no more than 10 per cent increase in sales expenses.'*
>
> *Steve: 'Well, why didn't you say so! I'm not a mind reader.'*

When specifying the target, Andy should also have stated the assumptions on which it was based. He should also have made sure the target was fully understood. For example, does the 10 per cent figure refer to revenue received or to numbers of units sold?

Linking targets to benefits

Another reaction, not always voiced but often felt by a person asked to take on a tough target, is 'Why should I?'. 'Because it's your job' is not a good enough answer.

If Andy had prepared more thoroughly before meeting Steve he would have linked the new target to benefits seen from Steve's point of view. Knowing Steve is ambitious for promotion and extremely status conscious, his approach might have been:

> *Andy: '...so that's the basis of the increase, Steve. While other regions are expected to do little more than tread water, we need to increase sales revenue by 10 per cent. And we'll have to do it ourselves: there'll be no extra staff until we prove the region has growth potential. The board feel we can do it. What do you think?'*
>
> *Steve: 'It won't be easy. But what's in it for us, longer term?'*
>
> *Andy: 'I think western is big enough to make two regions, south west and north west. It'd give us more clout: two places in the sales group, Europe.'*
>
> *Steve: 'OK, let's go for it. But I really do need a decent laptop if I'm going to get through more contacts in a week. D'you think the budget will stretch to that?'*
>
> *Andy: 'Could be. Let's make some plans, then we can see...'*

12.10 INVESTING IN PEOPLE

As a manager, you use the skills of other people to achieve job goals. But if this is all you do, your team will not be equipped to handle more demanding work in the future. Advances in knowledge and tougher competition mean your team members need to increase their knowledge and skills, too. This development comes from three main sources:

- **On-the-job coaching**. This is where you spend extra time training your people while they do real work. In the short term it is more costly than using experienced people to do the work, of course, and it requires careful planning so that critical work schedules do not slip.
- **Off-the-job training courses**. These can be run by people inside the organization, or by external consultants. Insiders have the advantage of knowing the business well; however, consultants often bring a fresh viewpoint to problems. In either case you need to define carefully what benefits you want from the training and set up a review system to measure the results. Check the track record of anyone you are thinking of trusting with this important work. Contact people who have attended their courses and ask how beneficial they were.
- **Self-development programmes**. Here the trainees work mainly in their own time, often with the help of distance learning or correspondence courses. You might be able to support them by giving up an hour or two a month to discuss how they are getting on. And perhaps you could get your organization to invest in suitable training videos or workbooks.

Delegation

Delegating part of your job to your staff is an excellent way of improving the capability of your team. They prepare themselves for handling a bigger job in the future, and you get more time to concentrate on longer term planning or to improve the quality of tasks you currently find difficult.

But delegating isn't simply a matter of dumping the least attractive parts of your work on hapless subordinates. Before you can delegate you have to decide:

- Which task?
- To whom, and what long-term benefit will it be to them?
- Can they learn to cope with the task?
- What training, if any, will they need?

Monitoring

Monitor progress frequently at first, relaxing control as people become more proficient. But if someone does get into difficulties, be available to give advice—hands-off, but eyes-on. Never underestimate the value of frequent informal communication: Management by walking the job really does pay. And most important, encourage people to voice any doubts. Make sure they realize help is available if they need it.

Don't take back a delegated task unless you really must: it's terribly demotivating. Accept that in the first instance the speed and quality of work may be lower than you could achieve yourself. Delegating is an investment, and often the most cost-effective way of increasing the capability of your team.

EXAMPLES

Felicity Goodman, personnel development manager at FICO UK, chairs a working party of departmental managers to update the company's training and development plan. She begins with a needs analysis for every member of staff in all departments. From this she produces a summary which shows which courses are most needed.

Training needs key: -2 = serious skills deficiency -1 = minor skills deficiency 0 = close skills match +1 = minor under-use of talent +2 = major under-use of talent	Finance	Personnel	Design & Development	Production	Sales	Marketing	Customer support	Site Services
Specialist skills	0	0	-2	-1	0	0	0	-1
Personal organization	0	-1	-1	0	-1	0	0	0
Interpersonal skills	1	-1	-1	0	-2	0	-2	0
Writing skills	-2	-2	-2	-1	-1	-2	-1	0
Task/project management	0	0	-2	0	0	+2	+1	0
Leadership and team-building	0	0	+1	-1	0	0	0	+1
Financial awareness	0	0	1	+2	-2	-1	0	0
Commercial awareness	0	0	0	-1	-1	-2	0	0
Other special training needs	-1	0	0	0	0	-1	0	0

The needs analysis compares the present and planned workload, and any changes in the nature of work, with the present skill levels of the staff. FICO staff fill in their own assessments before discussing the results with their managers. Because most people are more open about their weaknesses when assessing themselves than when someone else makes the judgement, conflict rarely arises.

Making use of hidden talent

A skills survey of this type often highlights where talent is not being used to the full. This is most likely to happen when people have been recruited from other organizations. Internal job transfers are important in ensuring valuable talent is not wasted for long periods. If not stretched at work many people either sink into apathy and produce poor quality work or they look for a job in an organization offering better prospects.

Training priorities

The training needs analysis helps Felicity set training priorities: serious deficiencies are dealt with before minor ones. The training schedule itself has to take into account both the urgency of the need and the availability of the trainers and trainees. It isn't usually practicable to send a whole department away for two or three days. In any case there are advantages in inter-departmental training courses, where people who need to cooperate at work can get to know one another better.

12.11 PLANNING AND ORGANIZING TEAMS

Professor John Adair has described what leaders must do to get the best results from teams of people. He suggests that they must try to meet the needs of:

- The task.
- The individuals.
- The team.

Planning and organizing the work

Where the aims and objectives of the job are clear, pass them on and check that everyone concerned understands them. A good way of doing this is to get people to explain in their own words what they are required to do and the standards they are aiming to meet.

Unfortunately, not all jobs start with clearly defined objectives. Then it's all the more important to communicate clearly what *is* known and to make sure that everyone understands the risks and how they are to be resolved as work proceeds. That way, when you delegate work, your team members should be able to help you to measure progress and to clarify the objectives in the light of experience gained.

Directing, motivating and developing the individuals

Being fair to all team members doesn't mean treating them all the same; they all have different needs. A good way of finding what people want to get out of their work is to ask them. (It isn't cheating... lots of good managers do it!) They will tell you what they enjoy and what they hate doing; and they are much more likely to put effort into the unpalatable parts of the job if they realize you have organized things so they get a fair crack at doing jobs they enjoy.

Building and supporting the team

The organization of an effective team must be dynamic to adapt to the day-to-day demands of the task. This readjustment of roles happens automatically to some extent as people fall into their natural behaviour patterns as the situation changes. But how much better if you plan the adjustments in good time to take the initiative?

Reviews are essential

In many organizations, managers are required frequently to review how the work is going—perhaps every month. Maybe more often if things are not going well! The individual team members may get an annual appraisal, but even in firms where appraisals are mandatory it's common for 25 per cent or more to slip through the net for one reason or another (such as the manager being too busy?). But how often do we review the effectiveness of our teamwork? Sadly the answer in most cases is not at àll, or we discuss our communication problems as if they were the cause, rather than the symptom, of poor teamwork.

To be really effective you will need to plan and organize the work, to help individuals (including yourself!) organize themselves and develop their skills, and to plan and organize the teamwork. And you won't get it all right all the time, so frequently review task, individual and team needs and check to see if they are being met. If not, prioritize your action plan for achieving improvements in one or more of these areas.

TWELVE STEPS TO EFFECTIVE PLANNING AND ORGANIZATION

Delight your customer (achieve the task)

1 Make sure you understand what the aim is and how the customer (inside or outside your company) will benefit. Be clear about your own responsibilities and the authority delegated to you. Organize your time so that important tasks don't become panics.

2 Work out the best way of achieving the objectives within the constraints you are under. Organize the work and the people to ensure ownership and accountability. Make simple plans which take into account the technical, cost and schedule risks involved, ensuring that you, your customer and your team members understand them.

3 Assess skills and experience against task demands and seek outside help before deadlines are threatened. Set up a progress reporting system which all involved understand, and use objective measurements of performance and progress.

4 Be prepared to rework your plans to optimize performance. Communicate frequently with your customer, not withholding bad news in fear of a bad reaction. Hold post-mortems and make action plans to learn from experience.

Get everyone pulling together (maintain an effective team)

5 Set team objectives as well as individual work targets. Show your own enthusiasm for the task to unite the group and win their support. Communicate the aims, priorities and constraints so that all team members understand them.

6 Compare the technical skills of the team to the demands of the job, and arrange training if required. Use all the intellectual, interpersonal and working skills of members, and match the team size and personality mix to the work they are to do.

7 Try to avoid unfair treatment of individuals which could otherwise destroy team unity. Brief your team frequently on matters likely to affect them. Show pride in your team by seeking their ideas and consulting them on important decisions.

8 Explain the reasons whenever you cannot support proposals you receive from the team. Deal quickly and fairly with complaints which threaten team effectiveness. Celebrate successes and review the causes of setbacks as a team. Review teamworking processes as well as the results of your work.

Support and develop your people (motivate the individuals)

9 Respect and care for those you may not like as well as for those you admire. Take the time to get to know their needs and ambitions. Listen attentively when they express their opinions and needs. Explain their responsibilities, and discuss and agree performance standards.

10 Provide the resources and environment in which people can meet the required performance standards. Create opportunities for them to acquire new knowledge and develop their skills. Provide frequent opportunities for jointly reviewing their performance.

11 Praise them for their achievements, and give them the credit when talking to other managers, including those higher up in the organization. Reprimand wrong behaviour but don't criticize them for their personality or inexperience.

12 Organize work so that each team member can gain a sense of personal achievement. Allow them the authority to make decisions commensurate with their responsibilities. Delegate courageously and foster fearless reporting of both progress and problems.

CHECK-LIST: REVIEWING TEAM EFFECTIVENESS

Get each team member to assess the team using this questionnaire. Use the results as the agenda for a target-setting meeting to help improve team effectiveness.

Team: Reviewer: Date: Performance factors	For each factor listed, how well does achievement level meet the needs of the situation?		
	Level achieved		
	Too little	About right	Too much
How well is the team performing on current tasks? Do we:			
Clearly define technical targets?			
Meet our technical targets?			
Clearly define quality targets?			
Meet our quality targets?			
Clearly define our time-scale targets?			
Meet our important deadlines?			
Agree realistic cost budgets?			
Control costs effectively in line with budgets?			
Are we using our intellectual and interpersonal skills? Do we:			
Mobilize our creative abilities?			
Use effectively our analytical problem-solving skills?			
Support one another when under pressure?			
Share information effectively among team members?			
Listen actively to the views of all team members?			
Seek and obtain outside help when we should?			
How effective is our decision-making? Do we:			
Define objectives and priorities?			
Consider alternative solutions?			
Use appropriate decision making processes?			
Assess risks and benefits of alternatives?			
Record decisions and their basis?			
Review the effectiveness of decisions later?			
How well is our team being led? Does the leader:			
Brief the team and check their understanding?			
Encourage contributions from all team members?			
Treat all members fairly, and avoid favouritism?			
Organize team resources effectively?			
Show concern for task success?			
Show concern for team unity?			
Show concern for the well-being of individual members?			
Show concern for the leader's own personal fulfilment?			

Improvement targets:	

RECOMMENDED READING

Berne, E. (1964). *The Games People Play*. Penguin, Harmondsworth.

Blanchard, K. and Johnson, S. (1983). *The One Minute Manager*. Collins, London.

Fisher, R. and Ury, W. (1983). *Getting To Yes*. Hutchinson, London.

Gowers, E. (1973). *The Complete Plain Words*. Penguin, Harmondsworth.

Handy, C. (1979). *Gods of Management*. Pan, London.

Herzberg, F. (1986). *Work and the Nature of Man*. T.Y. Crowell, New York.

Jung, C. G. (1971). *Psychological Types*. Routledge, London.

Kepner, C. H. and Tregoe, B. B. (1965). *The Relational Manager*. McGraw-Hill, Maidenhead.

Maslow, A. H. (1970). *Motivation and Personality*. Harper & Row, New York.

Nolan, V. (1987). *The Innovator's Handbook*. Sphere, London.

Parker, R. H. (1982). *Understanding Company Financial Statements*. Penguin, Harmondsworth.

Peters, T. J. and Waterman, R. H. Jr (1982). *In Search Of Excellence*. Harper & Row, New York.

Townsend, R. (1983). *Up the Organisation*. Coronet, London.

Walton, D. (1989). *Are You Communicating?* McGraw-Hill, Maidenhead.

INDEX